Frontispiece Graham H. Greenwell

AN INFANT IN ARMS

WAR LETTERS OF A COMPANY OFFICER, 1914–1918

by

GRAHAM H. GREENWELL
M.C.

The Naval & Military Press Ltd

Published by

The Naval & Military Press Ltd
Unit 10 Ridgewood Industrial Park,
Uckfield, East Sussex,
TN22 5QE England

Tel: +44 (0) 1825 749494
Fax: +44 (0) 1825 765701

www.naval-military-press.com
www.military-genealogy.com
www.militarymaproom.com

In reprinting in facsimile from the original, any imperfections are inevitably reproduced and the quality may fall short of modern type and cartographic standards.

TO
MY MOTHER

LIST OF ILLUSTRATIONS

PLATE		FACING PAGE
	GRAHAM H. GREENWELL . . . *Frontispiece*	
I.	HUNTERS AVENUE, PLOEGSTEERT . . .	18
II.	INTERIOR OF THE CHURCH AT HEBUTERNE, 1916 .	44
III.	WORKING PARTY OF BRITISH TROOPS ON MUDDY GROUND, SOMME AREA. NOVEMBER 1916 .	178
IV.	HORSE AND MOTOR TRANSPORT IN DIFFICULTIES. ALELUY-ALBERT ROAD. DECEMBER 1916 .	180
V.	BRITISH SOLDIER CLEANING HIS RIFLE IN THE TRENCHES, WINTER 1916	182
VI.	A MUDDY TRENCH	192
VII.	GERMAN PILL BOX, CHEDDAR VILLA. THIRD BATTLE OF YPRES, 1917	234
VIII.	TRENCHES ON THE MONTELLO OVERLOOKING THE PIAVE RIVER, FEBRUARY 1918 . . .	262
IX.	ASIAGO. NOVEMBER 1918	268
X.	AUSTRIAN PRISONERS HELPING BRITISH COOKS AT A CASUALTY CLEARING STATION. NOVEMBER 1918	296
XI.	BRIDGE OVER THE VAL D'ASSA, 1918 . . .	297
XII.	(*Top*).—SURRENDER OF AUSTRIAN CORPS TO THE 48TH DIVISION, ON THE MOUNTAIN FRONT	
	(*Bottom*).—COLONEL HOWARD, G.S.O. 48TH DIVISION, TAKING THE SURRENDER OF TOWN AND PROVINCE AT THE TOWN HALL, TRENT . .	300
XIII.	GRAHAM H. GREENWELL, 1918	312

TO THE READER

I was eighteen years old in August 1914. I had just left Winchester and was to have gone up to Christ Church in October. Before me lay the agreeable prospect of a more than usually long summer holiday. The outbreak of war shattered these expectations, and within a fortnight I was in the Public Schools Camp at Tidworth, from which I was gazetted to the 4th Battalion of the Oxfordshire and Buckinghamshire Light Infantry. With this unit I remained until demobilisation.

The horrors of the Great War and the miseries of those who were called upon to take part in it have been described by innumerable writers. For my own part I have to confess that I look back on the years 1914–1918 as among the happiest I have ever spent. That they contained moments of boredom and depression, of sorrow for the loss of friends and of alarm for my personal safety is indeed true enough. But to be perfectly fit, to live among pleasant companions, to have responsibility and a clearly defined job—these are great compensations when one is very young.

During the last two years we have heard a good deal of the attitude of the younger generation towards war in general and towards the next war—if it ever comes—in particular. This record, made up of letters written to my mother, does, as it seems to me, faithfully represent the reactions to active service of a normal schoolboy of 1914 who found himself without warning called upon to undertake the responsibilities of a Company officer. As a record of service on two fronts it may have some claim to attention. But for me its main interest lies rather in tracing, which the reader will have little difficulty in doing, the development from the immature subaltern to the veteran of the later years.

GRAHAM H. GREENWELL.

Goring,
  Oxfordshire.

1914

September 4th, 1914.   PUBLIC SCHOOL CAMP,
TIDWORTH PENNINGS,
SALISBURY PLAIN.

I AM having great fun and enjoying it all immensely. I shan't join any unit on the spur of the moment, but I am awfully anxious for a Territorial commission. No one is given any promotion here, as the camp is only a temporary business: we are chock-a-block with men from seventeen to forty-five. But it does not matter, as we are all here to learn—everyone being equally ignorant.

It is a great relief that nobody talks war, though we are in the middle of a camp. It seems so funny to think of you all talking about it hard at home while here we scarcely notice it.

September 6th, 1914.   PUBLIC SCHOOL CAMP,
TIDWORTH PENNINGS,
SALISBURY PLAIN.

Two other men and I started off at ten o'clock to-day after Church Parade and walked six miles over Salisbury Plain to Netheravon—the Flying School. There is a jolly little village there and we had a good round meal at the " Dog and Whistle." Everyone was most respectful to the King's uniform. It is now five o'clock, and we have just arrived back, feeling somewhat footsore, but it was better than sticking in the lines all day.

Yesterday I made application for a commission in

the Oxfordshire and Buckinghamshire Light Infantry. The War Office have written for a list of candidates, who are urgently required for commissions in all the different branches.

This camp is great fun, and I am learning a lot of my officer's job. We had a small squad for giving commands yesterday: I was sandwiched between two of Asquith's sons, and as both of them were sadly deficient in the elements of drill, I had to pull them through.

.   .   .   .

(Through the good offices of Captain (now Sir) Beachcroft Towse, V.C., I obtained at the end of September a commission in the 4th (Territorial) Battalion of the Oxfordshire and Buckinghamshire Light Infantry, then commanded by Lt.-Col. Stockton, and was gazetted Second Lieutenant on October 8th, 1914.)

October 1st, 1914.   4TH BN. OXFORD & BUCKS. LT. INFTY.,
WRITTLE,
CHELMSFORD.

You will be glad to hear that I am settling down all right into this entirely new life and have made one or two friends.

The only thing I do dislike is the physical drill from 7 to 8: it means, among other things, a long run, and the recruits, though all good fellows and very keen, perspire freely!

I am " on the square," as it is called, but I think I shall be taken off after a week, as I am the only officer on at present, and therefore rather a nuisance to the sergeants, who can't curse their men quite so freely in my presence.

The Adjutant came up and made me drill the squad for half an hour yesterday, and I got on remarkably well. My practice at camp helped me a lot. The men all heard my orders and obeyed them pretty smartly for recruits.

Thanks very much for opening an account for me. My expenses besides my Mess bill and £1 1s. a week for my billet are practically nil. But I shall have to give my servant something, and I think I shall have to hire a bicycle, as the Company parade-ground is nearly two miles away from my billet. I gather that Mess bills don't come to more than 3s. a day all told. But when I am gazetted I get my pay from the day I joined and my billet paid.

There are several men here who, like myself, are not gazetted, and three or four have been gazetted from the Oxford O.T.C. I may be gazetted to this battalion, or to the reserve battalion, which last would be rotten. We are several officers over strength, without counting the ones who are at present ungazetted. But no one seems to be taking any notice of the Territorial Army.

There are rumours of our going to India or Aldershot or Havre, but no one knows anything definite.

October 17th, 1914.   4TH BN. OXFORD & BUCKS. LT INFTY.,
                              WRITTLE,
                           CHELMSFORD.

To-day I went for my first long march—18 miles—from 9 o'clock till 2.30: then lunch, then paying the men's billets all the afternoon till 6 o'clock, going into cottage after cottage till I was tired out.

However, the life is splendid, and I feel as hard as a rock.

The King inspected us on Friday, but there is no chance of our being sent abroad yet, because the authorities are in a panic about a German invasion and we are the second line of defence. When the alarm does go, if it ever does, we march straight off to Colchester. General McClintock is in command of my Brigade, and is now in Chelmsford.

Lafayette's have written me their usual card asking for a free sitting and I am pestered with letters from all over England asking me to join clubs, buy clothes, etc. I can't get a sword or revolver for love or money, though Harrods are getting me one. My old one Rosa gave me is no good I'm afraid.

October 25th, 1914.   4TH BN. OXFORD & BUCKS. LT. INFTY.,
WRITTLE,
CHELMSFORD.

There are again persistent rumours in Chelmsford, our headquarters, that the South Midland Brigade are going abroad in the first week of December, which was the original idea. I only hope that we don't stick in Writtle all the winter. And if we have to wait till the spring, Kitchener's Army will be trained by then, as they are being pushed on like wild-fire with crowds of trained instructors, and all the senior officers are regulars.

I am now the possessor of a huge revolver and have got some ammunition for it. I expect it will blow my wrist off when I fire it.

November 4th, 1914.   4TH BN. OXFORD & BUCKS. LT. INFTY.,
WRITTLE,
CHELMSFORD.

I must tell you of the exciting time we had yesterday in consequence of the attempted raid which you doubtless saw reported in this morning's paper.

About 5 o'clock yesterday afternoon a message came to us from McClintock to say that if the " Alarm " sounded that night it would not be a false one and that everyone must be ready with their 35 lbs. of regulation kit. We have heard various rumours of practice alarms: this was to warn us of a real one.

For some reason or other this made everyone very jumpy. Both the Adjutant and the Colonel thought we were off for a certainty that night and most of the officers packed all they could for 35 lbs. All the pack ponies were loaded with ammunition and the men were served out with ball cartridge. We had champagne for dinner to celebrate our departure and there was a tremendous row in the smoking-room afterwards, at which the Colonel was not present.

Hermon Hodge[1] rashly drew his sword, which always means " Drinks all round." We then had a fight with soda-water bottles, in which I got soaked. At any rate we kicked up a hideous din, after which we retired to bed to wait for the alarm.

It never went, but this morning the Colonel told us that he was rung up about 12 and told all about this battle going on off the East Coast. He was ordered to be ready to sound the alarm any minute, so we weren't far off it.

[1] 2nd Lieut. J. P. Hermon-Hodge, killed 28th May, 1915.

November 17th, 1914.   4TH BN. OXFORD & BUCKS. LT. INFTY.,
                            WRITTLE,
                              CHELMSFORD.

I will tell you what I want. A ruck-sack to fasten on the back over the shoulders, like a Tommy's pack. All the officers are getting them, as we shall have to carry what little we *are* allowed on our backs just like an ordinary soldier, and we must get used to the weight, which is rather trying at first on a long march. We put an overcoat, a change of underclothing, shaving materials and etceteras in it.

I am debating whether to get a " British Warm " overcoat, one of those short reefer coats, which most officers have, as they are more convenient than the long heavy ones, but I haven't decided yet.

I am not looking forward to three days on guard duty at the Marconi station at Chelmsford, as it is horribly cold.

I think I shall apply for leave about a week hence, but as I am the only subaltern in my Company (there ought to be two) I don't like to rush off.

December 13th, 1914.   4TH BN. OXFORD & BUCKS. LT. INFTY.,
                            MARCONI STATION,
                              CHELMSFORD.

As you see by the above address, I have been put on duty here. I am under another Captain (Rowell) who didn't want to bring his own subaltern and so borrowed me as I had not been before.

We took over at 10 o'clock yesterday morning. It is a huge building like a large hotel but almost unfurnished. The room we sit in is a large board-room with several polished tables and two sideboards—quite bare, but everything spotlessly clean.

Our main work is at night; the sentries are on all day as well but are doubled at night. It is divided into three watches, one per officer, 9–12 the nicest, then 12 to 3, then 3 till 6. I had 3 till 6 last night. The other officer on duty just before me woke me up at 3 o'clock in the morning and I sallied forth into an absolutely deserted Chelmsford about 3.30 in pouring rain.

First I visited the nine sentries on duty at the main station where we are quartered and had great difficulty in finding them all. Then I went off on a bicycle to another station about a quarter of a mile away at the other end of the town, and inspected the sentries there: from there I went to another station at Broomfield, about a mile away: then home again at about a quarter to five.

I went to sleep again at 5.30, but I kept most of my clothes on and had to sleep on the floor in my Wolseley valise, which had no mattress, rug or anything. Luckily I had my greatcoat, but it was very cold.

The shortage of beds was due to the unexpected arrival of an officer who was to leave for France at 6 o'clock this morning. As we didn't want him to sleep on the floor, he took one officer's bed; the officer whom I relieved took my bed, and as I found when I came back that the visitor had not yet got up I left him in peace.

It isn't such a bad game, and they feed us very well, all free.

They get about 25 to 30 messages from Germany

every day and send them up to the Admiralty. I am told that some of them have had a very important effect on the armies in France.

I have at last secured a servant who suits me. He knows the ropes thoroughly.[1]

[1] Private Goring.

1915

January 3rd, 1915.   4TH BN. OXFORD & BUCKS. LT. INFTY.,
WRITTLE,
CHELMSFORD.

For the last week I have been acting as a Company Commander in Dashwood's absence, much to the amusement of some of the officers, but Dashwood [1] left me in charge and the Colonel and Adjutant more or less recognised it.

At last there seems a definite feeling that we are leaving Writtle either this month or next. General Heath, who commands the Division, told us the other day that he was fully prepared and expected to move soon, and the new rifles have all arrived. I wish they would send us to the Persian Gulf or India; it is so miserably cold here.

March 22nd, 1915.   1/4TH BN. OXFORD & BUCKS. LT. INFTY.,
WRITTLE,
CHELMSFORD.

I feel almost too sick to write anything but a very short letter.

The regiment is off probably on Wednesday or Thursday and I am one of the seven or eight officers left behind at the base: it is too disappointing for words.

The Adjutant announced in the Mess, the night before last, which officers were going—just the bare establishment—and it was found that several of the subalterns who were thought to be quite safe were not

---

[1] Ernest George Dashwood, 3rd son of Sir George Dashwood, of Kirtlington, Oxon.

going—we had got to stay. He was bombarded with questions, but said that the Colonel [1] had made up the list without consulting anyone and that he was sorry he could do nothing.

It is awfully hard when you know the men and have been with them for six months to have to leave them and hand them over to someone else.

Dashwood was very cheery and said I needn't worry as there would be gaps to be filled before three weeks had gone by; already one subaltern has got pleurisy badly and is out of action. So there is some hope.

(At the end of March 1915 the Battalion left for France with the rest of the 48th (South Midland) Territorial Division. Being under nineteen I was left behind and was attached temporarily to the newly-formed 2/4th Battalion.)

April 29th, 1915.   4TH BN. OXFORD & BUCKS. LT. INFTY.,
                                        BROOMFIELD,
                                        CHELMSFORD.

On Monday I am taking charge of the reinforcement or base Company of 100 men and, with the three other base companies of the Brigade, am going to a place called Terling some five or six miles from here to train for a fortnight or three weeks before going out to join our regiments. This is something definite, thank Heaven, at last.

. . . .

(On May 8th I received orders to proceed overseas to rejoin the battalion.)

[1] Lt.-Col. F. W. Schofield.

May 11th, 1915. BASE CAMP 16,
                         HAVRE.

Everything is, so far, splendid.

I had a most easy voyage over and slept on a very comfortable bunk till 8 o'clock this morning. We had breakfast at 9 and arrived at Havre in the most glorious weather at 9.45.

My two friends and I left our equipment in the Hotel Continental and wandered round the town looking at the shops and all the sights of a French town in war-time. We had a gorgeous lunch at the hotel, when I aired my French a bit, and at 2 o'clock we reported to British Headquarters. After waiting an hour, I got a slip of paper telling me to take the Montpellier bus and report to Camp 16—nothing else. However, nowise daunted I hired a taxi with one of my friends. who is still with me, and we arrived at 4 o'clock at a huge English rest camp, or rather series of camps. I found No. 16 and was told to go and seize a canvas hut for myself, which I did. They have wooden bottoms and canvas sides and lids on top which open, no other furniture, no beds or washing-stands. But I have got my beloved valise and have already bagged two army blankets and a bucket, on which I am now sitting. And meanwhile I have enjoyed my day's experience immensely.

May 17th, 1915. CAMP No. 16,
                         HAVRE.

I am in the middle of the first busy day I have had since I have been here. I am Orderly Officer, which means that I have to be present at all the little functions of a camp and incidentally to censor all the letters. It is a weary job, but occasionally amusing, as you may imagine. Most of the men have been wounded or gassed and their efforts to spell the names of the scenes of their accidents are distinctly original. The weather is still grilling hot, but to-day it is again pouring with rain and the camp is very muddy.

I can't tell you how fearfully sorry I am at poor old Dashwood's death.[1] His family will be very much upset. He was such a splendid fellow. I must write to his mother.

May 22nd, 1915. 1/4TH BN. OXFORD & BUCKS. LT. INFTY.,
SOUTH MIDLAND INFANTRY BRIGADE,
2ND ARMY,
BRITISH EXPEDITIONARY FORCE.

I got orders at 2 o'clock yesterday that I was to be ready to go off at 4.30. I was to leave Havre at 7 o'clock and was to draw three days' rations. As the train didn't start till midnight, I had time to go, with two other officers, for a last good dinner at a hotel. Finally, the train started, the men being packed in 50 at a time; we had one carriage between four officers, and as it was very hot I had an uncomfortable night. I am writing this at 5 o'clock in the morning.

We have just reached our first halt, a celebrated French Cathedral town, but oh! such an important military secret—mind you don't guess it. We have just found out that we have to stay here till to-night. My two friends and I had a beautiful wash and shave and some filthy coffee at a little workman's cabin: we intend to go out to breakfast somewhere in a moment, but it is still only 7 o'clock: the men simply camp outside the train, which, of course, is not

[1] Killed by a rifle grenade, Ploegsteert Wood, May 12th, 1915.

drawn up in the regular station: they mayn't leave the place all day. They are running through their iron rations, and bully beef like the devil and I have been seized with the brilliant notion of stopping their cravings with some new bread which I obtained for them last night.

We shall be leaving at about 8 o'clock this evening and I am told that we are going to Boulogne of all places in the world. But I don't think this can be true, as it would be too ridiculous even for the Army. However, you will see by the next letter or post-card where I have got to: it will be an amusing little game for you to follow my track across France.

May 23rd, 1915.   1/4TH BN. OXFORD & BUCKS. LT. INFTY.,
   SOUTH MIDLAND INFANTRY BRIGADE,
   2ND ARMY,
   BRITISH EXPEDITIONARY FORCE.

I must exercise discretion with regard to place names as I am now reaching the last stages of my journey: it is 4.30 p.m. and we have been travelling in this train since 11 o'clock last night, when we eventually left Rouen. As I expected, we did not go to Boulogne, but have passed Amiens and Calais. The train is a very amusing one; the soldiers travel all over it on top and on the footboards. Whenever we want any water to drink or wash with we simply go along the footboard to the engine or wait for a halt, which occurs quite often. The train slows down for a few minutes and everyone gets out and chats; then with a toot it moves sedately off, while we run after it and hop on board before it gets going. All the way along the men are shrieked at by the French peasants for souvenirs, and there is a constant hail of bully beef tins and iron rations.

The weather is divine and I can scarcely believe that we are within a few miles of the line and that this country has lately been fought over.

I shall arrive at my Divisional Headquarters in about an hour's time and shall probably spend the night there.

I tasted my first bully beef to-day and really it is excellent: the ration biscuits are hopeless even for my molars, but the men make excellent birckbats of them.

May 24th, 1915. ROMORIN.

I was really too tired and busy when I did arrive last night to write another letter. We got in to our little station where the railway ends at 5.30. I managed to get rid of my men after walking a few miles. The Quartermasters and Transport Officers of each regiment have their headquarters some two or three miles behind the trenches in a small village, so I handed over the men to their respective quartermasters and then went in search of my own. He and Alan Gibson, the transport officer, are billeted in a little French *estaminet*, where the Quartermaster-sergeant actually fixed me up with a *bed* for the night. The bed rather reminded me of the one in Pepys' *Diary*, but still I was so tired at not having had my clothes off for three days that I didn't mind.

I am enjoying myself tremendously. I cannot believe I am within two miles of this ridiculous war; it sounds just like an Aldershot Field-Day going on steadily the whole time. I am not sure, though, there isn't a battle on just now. We saw an aeroplane or two getting shelled when we arrived, which was a pretty sight: the aeroplane shining quite serenely in the sun with little puffs of white smoke all round it.

I am in Conybeare's [1] Company and I am going up to join him in a minute or two when I have finished this letter.

Don't think of me in *France*—the whole space of *one road* divides me from that country, and when I join the battalion the distance will be greater.

May 24th, 1915.   PLOEGSTEERT WOOD.
10.30 p.m.

I am now at last among all my friends and have seen them all, including dear Hermon: I am supremely happy and have had the most interesting day of my life. I can't believe it is true. At 11 o'clock our *horses* came round and Alan Gibson [2] and I mounted in the most divine sunshine to *ride* up to the trenches! I felt most contented and told him that I could scarcely believe we were so near the war. Our horses shied at all the steam trolleys and motor-vans, but otherwise were good: it was a glorious ride. In a few minutes we came to the village beginning with a P which is just behind our lines, and then I first saw what war meant. It was shelled to pieces and almost every house had a hole in it, although the women and children, poor wretches, were still there! We were riding along gaily enough when we met dear old Hugh Deacon who had come in to buy wine. We pulled up and chatted with him until Gibson laughed

[1] J. J. Conybeare, now M.D., Warden of Guy's Hospital.
[2] Alan K. Gibson, Transport Officer.

and said, " Well, I am not going to stand just here much longer "—we were at a cross-roads, just the place for shells. Ten minutes later, the Germans put their daily quota of five or six big shells into the little village, and Deacon told us later that he was just buying some *vin ordinaire* when a shell burst just outside the shop and the poor woman bolted for her life downstairs and absolutely refused to reappear, even to take his money. Of course we heard the shells going overhead, but the horses didn't mind a bit. We dismounted just behind the wood in which our regiment is, and walked through it along specially raised wooden platforms made by the Engineers which intersect it. They all have names: the main road through to the trenches is called Regent Street. Hyde Park Corner, the Strand and Piccadilly are all official names, so I feel quite at home. I lunched with Hermon and his Company officers—six of them—in a beautiful wooden cabin: we had fresh meat, peas and fried potatoes, then tinned fruits and cheese and coffee. Hermon was very glad to see me again and everyone is very nice.

Conny took me round this afternoon and I went through *all* our trenches with him: they are most weird and quite different from what one expects, not a long continuous line, but all zigzagged anywhere and very bad ones. I looked through all the periscopes and peepholes, and had a quick look at the German trenches round a corner; they are only 40 yards away and it was most interesting and amusing. I kept meeting all my old friends round different corners. We had tea in a little dug-out with six other officers in the trenches, cakes galore and jam: very pleasant. Conny had three or four pot-shots with a rifle through a peephole. Our Company is having its four days' rest in the reserve trenches, so I was free to go round with him; but there are lots of fatigue parties for the men which make life very unpleasant I believe.

At night the reserve companies—two out of four—man their trenches and sleep in them. We may not take off our clothes or boots at all, but I have got a pair of rubber top-boots which are easily slipped on or off and I shall sleep in them. Luckily there is a ruined cottage in the middle of our line which is our Company Headquarters and Mess. I have just had an excellent dinner in it, a beautifully cooked beef-steak pudding and rhubarb tart with cream: your present of a ham arrived to our great joy; also a very distressed letter saying you had not heard for two days, but that is all right now I expect.

I get up at six to-morrow to serve out a *rum* ration to my Platoon, which is the same one that I had before, as the officer who took it was wounded when poor Dashwood was killed. We shall go for a little march behind the line for an hour to-morrow unless there are a lot of shells about and then rest again, but as a matter of fact there is a lot to do, fatigue parties have to be provided for everything.

This is a very quiet part of the line at present, though the guns go on day and night; a few minutes ago there was a large cannonade away to the left, on Armentières, but it has stopped and there is now only intermittent rifle fire. The shells start with a heavy dull bang and then come through the air in the most extraordinary way just like a railway train. The anti-aircraft guns are great fun and very pretty to watch: first a deep plomp like a rocket and then a little cloud of white smoke in the air with an aeroplane gaily circling above it, always quite safe.

I have had a most ripping day: I can't remember ever having had so much pleasure and excitement, seeing so many old friends and experiencing such new sensations. I can see that one must be resigned to keeping one's clothes on all day and night for weeks at a time and to getting sleep always in the open and only for an hour or two on end; but it is all so delightfully fresh after England that the unpleasant side of it does not strike me, though all my friends have been trying to instil into me the gospel of " frightfulness."

I have been made Mess President by Conny and he says that as long as things are packed *very securely* all is well. Good cheeses of the small Dutch variety and chocolates are welcome, but Harrods will make suggestions. In Hermon's Company they have a hamper from Harrods weekly—but I need not tell you what I want because you always know best and anticipate me.

We have great fun inviting people to lunch and other meals and are quite a gay party.

. . . . . .

May 26th, 1915. PLOEGSTEERT WOOD.

I spent the afternoon with Hermon in the wood, where we sat down and had a long chat. He asked very much after you all, and I went back to tea with him. We visited poor old Dashwood's grave, in a little cemetery of which there are numbers in the wood. It is quite close to Headquarters and to us.

Last night I was put on one of the night fatigues

Hunters Avenue, Ploegsteert (*Facing Page* 18)

digging trenches in the open, just 50 yards behind the firing line. Although there was a bright moon, the Germans never took any notice of us and we worked till 12.30 undisturbed except by the usual stray bullets, which make an unpleasant zip, but seldom do much harm. As we were filing out of the trenches I suddenly heard a bullet or two whizz past and heard the man just behind me fall down; I turned to look; my whole party of 75 men had disappeared!! They had got down on the ground as flat as fleas before you could say knife! That is one of the tricks you learn out here at night or day directly a machine gun opens on you. There was I standing up absolutely alone. They all got up roaring with laughter and so did I.

As Mess President I have a lot of extra duty. The first difficulty is to get drink, especially water, which is vile out here and dangerous. We can get chlorine water, but it tastes bad. We get some table water in 3*d*. bottles from Armentières, but it is some way off and out of bounds. So we drink *vin ordinaire*, which is rather filth. A penny ration of beer per man is served out once a day by the Colonel's bounty. Our Mess draws five rations for the five officers, which doesn't go far; but I can't see that I could get anything from England or Paris that would be of any use.

May 27th, 1915.   PLOEGSTEERT WOOD.

I came into the trenches yesterday afternoon. Our Mess is in a dug-out in the support trenches some 50 yards behind in which lunch is just being laid. I am writing on the luncheon table, with old Conny sitting on the other side reading a newspaper: everything is quiet except for occasional rifle shots. I got up at 2.30 this morning, having slept quite comfortably in my little dug-out. 2.30 is " Stand to." Just half an hour before dawn everyone gets up in the trench, stands by and fires a bit to wake up the Germans and I walk round and see that everything is all right. A quarter of an hour after dawn I serve out a tot of rum to each man in my Platoon and they all go back to bed again, except the sentry in each little trench, who stays on guard.

I went back and slept till 9 when my servant woke me. I washed in a bowl of brackish water and at 10.30 or 11 left the trenches and went back to breakfast. Since then I have censored my Platoon's letters: the men sleep and cook and smoke cigarettes; the sun shines and nothing happens. It is really quite peaceful. One letter said: "We have got our Lieutenant back again, Mr. Greenwell—he seems mighty pleased to be out here." They all feel the same about Dashwood, it is very touching. But now I see another brother in the 2nd Oxford and Bucks is missing in that fighting at Ypres—poor Lady Mary!

We go out at night in front of the trenches, exploring the wire; the German working parties are also out, so it is not considered etiquette to fire. The really nasty things are rifle grenades fired from the end of special rifles; they can kill as many as eight or nine men if they do fall into a trench, and the one that killed Dashwood wounded three or four others. But we never use ours unless the Germans get particularly noisy, as on their system of retaliation three for every one of ours come back.

Last night as we were having dinner in our heavily

padded dug-out a machine gun started and we heard the bullets whistling all round it; it was traversing and so it passed away and then swung back again—most amusing: we all stopped discussing to-morrow's breakfast and listened.

My dug-out is called " Hope Cottage " and contains a long box of straw on which I sleep very comfortably in spite of the Huns: the dug-out is padded with sand-bags and looks very funny from the outside—it is just a yard or two behind the fire trenches.

A man has just come in to Conny with measles: it has just broken out and the men pay 2s. 6d. to sleep next to a man who looks like getting it. He has just been sent off to the doctor.

Thanks for the respirator though it hasn't turned up yet. We are being made to take every precaution and get a new pattern of respirator served out nearly every day. Mine is a horrid-looking object in a damp bag.

I am feeling remarkably well and happy, so don't worry about me.

May 28th, 1915.   PLOEGSTEERT WOOD.

You must excuse a mere line to-day.

Poor Hermon was shot through the head at seven o'clock this morning; I had just got out of my dug-out at 10 o'clock when his Captain held out some letters to me wrapped round with one in your writing; he didn't know that I had heard nothing of it.

It was too sad to read your last letter to him and all mine carefully preserved—they must have been on him at the time, as there was some blood on them.

Funny that they couldn't leave even one of my two best friends.

I had a sweet letter from Lady Mary last night: poor woman, her other son has definitely been reported killed now.

Excuse more at present. I shall go and see him buried this afternoon if I can.

May 29th, 1915. PLOEGSTEERT WOOD.

Yesterday was a terrible day for me: it seems so damned hard to lose a friend like Hermon in such a way. I followed him to the little cemetery in the wood, but really the wood is one huge graveyard, because there has been hot fighting here as far back as last September, and on the morning of poor Hermon's death we found the body of an Inniskilling Fusilier, buried only just below the surface in full equipment and with his rifle loaded. Letters were found on him dated August last: it was horrible digging him out again, but it had to be done.

This morning the Regimental Sergeant-Major was frightfully cut about by a bomb accident: one went off in his hand and wounded him all over the body: he may recover, but will be a cripple for life I am afraid. Otherwise everything is very quiet. At the present moment the only thing I can hear is a cuckoo and some birds and a very occasional rifle shot from our trenches. I go out of the trenches to-morrow evening for four days' rest.

May 30th, 1915. PLOEGSTEERT WOOD.

We get daily newspapers with the rations but only the *Chronicle*. If you could send out a paper called the *Weekly Times*, which is, I think, a sort of summary of the news of the week, I should be delighted.

I am writing this in practically dead silence except for the morning twittering of the birds; it is 8 o'clock and a very quiet time for the Bosche. The night is divided into four watches, 9–12, 12–3, 3–6.30, 6.30 till 10 o'clock. I am taking the last at the present moment. During the night working parties go out to build up the front of the parapet and repair the wire till about 12 o'clock when the machine guns get busy. They sweep our wood, and every time you hear them begin you have to duck down flat as a pancake wherever you are and wait for them to stop.

The officers have their meals in a dug-out 50 or 60 yards behind the firing trenches in the support line, and we have to go backwards and forwards through the wood at night to get there: just as you think you are going back to the trenches there is a loud crack and you think you will have a little dessert before you go out again.

It is a beautiful June morning and it is hard to believe that there is a war. All my men are snoring away happily in their dug-outs, except for the sentry on guard in each trench; little fires are burning here and there boiling tea for their breakfasts and the Bosche is doing the same. There is an infernal little game going on opposite—the Germans are building up a tower with sand-bags in the middle of their line for no good purpose. We have blown it down once with guns but the devils are at it again. But old Conny won't let us fire rifle grenades or trench mortars at them because they always send back at least four for every one of ours. He says he prefers a dignified silence unless they begin it. So except for the machine guns we don't get much devilry except the ordinary bullets, which are only really dangerous to the people behind the trenches in the wood. I haven't seen a German yet, I am sorry to say, but have been looking at the shadow of one just now passing and repassing behind a loophole. My field-glasses are splendid and very useful to me in conjunction with periscopes.

May 31st, 1915.   PLOEGSTEERT WOOD.

We came out of the trenches yesterday evening and are now back in reserve for four days. I am not sure that I don't like the trenches much better, as we spend our nights here guarding breastworks all round the wood where there are no dug-outs and you have to sleep out *in the open* on the bare ground.

I was most frightfully cold last night though I had all my clothes on, plus an overcoat (a Canadian one I have picked up out here) and a blanket. To-day I walked into the little village behind our wood. The place has been most hopelessly shelled and the German big guns still shell it every day for half an hour or so when they have nothing better to do; but the villagers still stay on; it is most pathetic; there are one or two shops still open and I got milk, butter, eggs, lettuces, etc., there for the Mess. The church has been gutted but the tower still stands with a yawning gap in its side.

I went with one of our officers who had been billeted there earlier to see his old landlady, who gave us beer and took us all over her little garden, which had escaped " les obus," though there were one or two gaps in her back yard.

They all take the war pretty philosophically. They have had both English and German billeted there since the beginning of the war. I don't think they were too fond of either.

June 2nd, 1915.   PLOEGSTEERT WOOD.

We had great fun at the baths yesterday—they are in a dye works at a small town—Nieppe—about two or three miles from here, and the men go in and have all their khaki well fumigated while they wait; their underclothes are taken away and fresh ones served out, so it is a splendid thing for them.

I went up to the trenches yesterday afternoon with Conny to try my new periscope; it is a very good one indeed, though apt, I think, to catch the sunlight rather conspicuously: however, it wasn't shot at.

It seems very funny to be able to take a stroll up to the firing line when you like even when you are in support, but this wood affords such excellent cover that we can walk about as much as we please, though of course we are technically under fire. In practice there is little firing during the day except sniping, but of course all shots that enter the wood are bound to go fairly high, as they have to come *over* our trenches, which are *built up*, not dug down.

The beastly Bosche began firing rifle grenades yesterday evening when Conny and I had just left; it is very seldom the peaceable Saxons get so offensive: I think Conny must have annoyed them. He had just been firing about 50 shots at one of their loopholes. At any rate two men were wounded. However, we had the courage, I hear, to fire back at them, which is excellent.

This morning they have started with another devilry called a trench mortar, but otherwise nothing is happening. I believe that if there was even the rumour of a truce the enemy would be out of their trenches in two minutes and shaking hands. They all speak excellent English and constantly start conversation at night, but for some ridiculous reason our men are not supposed to answer them back.

It is a curious life, depressing at times, on the whole rather boring but occasionally exhilarating.

If we go where it is rumoured we are going, things will wake up considerably, but the men want a rest first; you see, even back here in reserve they have to wear their boots and equipment all *day* and *night*. No one is supposed to take his boots off, and as the men are up most of the night on fatigues of different sorts they are getting a bit tired.

June 4th, 1915.   PLOEGSTEERT WOOD.

Everything has been extraordinarily quiet since yesterday evening, not even the usual evening " hate," which the Bosche seldom forgoes. They put a few shells into the wood as we came up yesterday afternoon which weren't far off, but that was all.

I believe we shall stay here after all for some time, which will be all right provided the Prussians don't come along. The Saxons hate them much more than they hate us, and when they are relieved by them they call out: " Give it them hot to-morrow, it's the Prussians."

If you could see the opposing trenches and realise the difficulties and dangers of an attack, you would understand how permanently fixed we are. A Division of 20,000 men is needed to make an attack on *500 yards* of frontage, and then what is gained? one mile at the most.

June 6th, 1915.   PLOEGSTEERT WOOD.

We have just been through our nearest approach to a battle since the regiment came out; nothing to make a fuss over, but sufficiently exciting to begin with, though I am glad to say it only lasted an hour.

The Engineers have long been engaged on mining the German trench just in front of us; doubtless you have seen pictures of mines exploding : they will give you an idea of the sort of thing. The wretched infantry never like these mines, and rather naturally, as they are expected to attack after it has exploded and when the wretched Germans are being blown sky-high.

Last night we were told it would probably go off about 7 o'clock in the evening: there would be *no* attack, but every man was to get his face over the parapet and fire his rifle: grenades and every kind of bomb would be thrown and then everyone would rush into the dug-outs and await the German shells. All through the night it kept on being postponed and everyone was rather excited, because the German counter-mine was only *one foot* away under the ground and our Engineer's could hear them working though our mine was still unknown to them. Finally, at 10 o'clock this morning we were warned that it was going off in ten minutes' time and every man was to get into his dug-out. My men were in the reserve trenches 50 or 60 yards behind the front trenches, just the place which the German big guns shell at such times to prevent reinforcements from being sent up to the front trench. As I sat in my dug-out reading *Land and Water* with philosophic calm there was suddenly the most appalling explosion and the earth quaked alarmingly. This was followed by a positive inferno of noise. The mountain gun which had been brought up to the trenches the night before started about five seconds after with *six* shells a minute, then our men opened rapid fire, the big howitzer batteries right behind the wood sent over a succession of the largest high explosives, and rifle grenades and trench mortars brought up the chorus to full strength. Meanwhile I sat and waited for the German reply, wondering whether it would be shrapnel or high explosive, my dug-out being proof against the former but absolutely useless against the latter. Although the Germans must have been taken absolutely by surprise, although over 60 yards of their trench had been blown clean into the air, and although they were being bombarded by every conceivable kind of devilish weapon, they began to reply within two minutes, and my God! the noise was terrific; they opened with machine guns and the bullets fairly whistled outside the door of the dug-out; it seemed as if they must come in, though, of course, they couldn't: at the same time they began shelling the supports and the whole wood with shrapnel; the leaves began to fall and the tops of the trees were badly knocked about. It was the most colossal shindy for about 15 to 20 minutes. Finally, it quieted down and the guns began to stop; at 11.15 Conny came into my dug-out from the front trenches where he had been, and asked how we had got on. They were quite all right in front; the machine guns had made them keep their heads down, but they hadn't been shelled.

It is now one o'clock and things are so quiet again that I expect the letters will be able to go back through the wood after all. We had no casualties in either of the two companies, but of course our time is to come. We really ought to be relieved to-morrow evening, but I expect the Germans will give us a bit of retribution to-morrow in the grey hours of the morning; they will probably give us the devil of a shelling and so prevent anyone coming near us all day. We have got food for two days in anticipation. You see our little boost was quite an unprovoked and unnecessary piece of " hate " and I can't see myself what the use of the whole thing was unless we were going to occupy their trenches, which, thank God, we didn't, although I think we could pretty easily have done so, as they must have been blown to pieces. I must go up in a minute and have a look at the wreckage; the earth could be seen *above* the tops of the trees; you can imagine the force of the explosion. Now that it is over, I feel pretty brave again, but during the entertainment I found it difficult to smoke my pipe with my usual *insouciance* although I was in comparative safety the whole time. The only thing that can harm you in a dug-out is high explosive; if one bursts bang on top you are simply blown to smithereens; but they weren't using it, for shrapnel is much better against troops in the open as they thought we should be.

I hope this gives you an idea of my first real acquaintance with modern warfare as it is played.

I am glad to say that sort of thing, though of daily occurrence at Ypres, is rare down here and I am afraid the mild Saxons will resent it.

June 8th, 1915. NIEPPE.

The Germans after all were thoroughly cowed by the wholesale slaughter and bombardment, and although we spent a somewhat anxious night, nothing happened nor were we shelled yesterday after all.

You will be glad to hear that we were relieved in the afternoon, and instead of just going further back into the wood as we usually do, the whole battalion marched back two or three miles to Nieppe for a four days' rest, which is very pleasant. We are billeted in a large empty château built on the same plan as Uncle Leonard's but a good deal smaller although it has a nice garden. Headquarters are also in the château.

Conny and I have a room to ourselves and make ourselves very comfortable with our valises and straw. We had a beautiful hot bath this morning in the water vats, but the heat for the last two days has been intense and to-day we have been dripping with sweat, and having nothing to drink makes it worse. The beer of the country is muck—very flat, ordinary water isn't allowed and the special stuff supplied stinks of chlorate of lime and is too filthy for words. A drink of clear cold water would be a luxury. However, I hope to get some Perrier from A or B Companies this evening. We have been drinking that a lot with the ordinary *vin ordinaire*, of which we get plenty.

My Platoon made a successful sortie from the

trenches at 4 o'clock yesterday morning behind a convenient mist to an old disused trench some ten yards away in front which they found pretty full of dead Germans; they collected considerable booty, including some smart picklehaubes, three or four German rifles, lots of ammunition and twelve pretty little silver drinking cups. So they didn't do badly. They gave me some ammunition and a rifle and revolver, and I could have bought one of the helmets for 10*s.*, but I wasn't sure whether you would appreciate it.

June 9th, 1915. NIEPPE.

Yesterday night Conny and I went out to dinner with Alan Gibson, the Transport Officer, and the Quartermaster; it was quite like old times; they have got a good billet and the woman cooked us a most *recherché* meal; to-night I am giving a return dinner in my château and have spent fabulous sums on fresh fruit, cauliflowers at one franc each, etc. Conny, Gibson and I had a ripping bath again this morning. Later I went riding with Conny and had quite a jolly if rather dangerous ride, as they gave me a horse which is very shy of motors, especially of big vans, and I rode down the main street pirouetting every time a van came along; it was rather annoying at first.

June 12th, 1915. Trenches, ST. IVES, DOUVE VALLEY.

Here we are, here we are again!!! back in the old trenches, smells, flies, etc., as usual.

We came in at 4 o'clock yesterday afternoon and found that they were the same trenches in which our men had been eight or nine weeks ago, although much improved and in fact most remarkably safe. The German lines are over 300 yards away and quite invisible because of long grass in between; we can be seen or rather overlooked from the small village of Messines on our left, which is now a picturesque ruin, thanks to English and German shells in turn; but it is a long way off; we are on the left of Ploegsteert Wood and just outside it, so the smells are not so bad and it is much fresher: the men are very pleased to be back in their old quarters, and the first thing to which my Platoon introduced me was the "kitten's dug-out," where there were the two sweetest little kittens imaginable playing round with the mother inside, and a notice outside from the last lot that care should be taken of them. The men were delighted, as they were in the trench when they were born about six weeks ago!

We found a photograph of Poulton-Palmer, of the Berkshire Regiment, in my trench stuck up on the parapet at the place where he was killed. He was Conny's oldest friend. He and I are sharing a sleeping dug-out and using another as our private sitting-room. We have also got a little alcove sandbagged on two sides as the Officers' Mess for the Company—that is five officers—with some chairs in it.

Unfortunately we cannot get any water to wash in except from a farm just behind our trench which is only a ruin of bricks with a few walls standing and which it is dangerous to enter by day, as one may be seen; the water from there is supposed to be used only for drinking purposes; it is boiled, of course. We shall be here only fours days and then back in support; it is a great pity, because everything is very quiet and comfortable and I don't think they ever shell this part of the trench.

The day after we left our old trenches the Germans exploded a mine in the middle of the wood. Very luckily it was just between the fire and the support trenches: I believe that only two men were wounded.

June 13th, 1915.   Trenches, St. Ives, Douve Valley.

Best thanks for the ham and the tongue. The beautiful large cake has just appeared on our luncheon table at which I am writing, clean and cool and with only the distant crash of a gun and the very occasional ping of a bullet against the parapet to disturb me. On our table there is some nice nobbly lettuce in a bowl with some very loud onions, some cold beef, a bottle of white *vin ordinaire* and another of table water; a Dutch cheese, some small cheese biscuits, some tinned fruit in a bowl, jam and marmalade, and lastly your cake. On the sideboard there are numerous varieties of potted meats, cigarettes, chocolates, pickles, dates, acid drops, revolvers, field-glasses, the *Bystander*, *Punch* and *Times*, so we might quite well be in rooms at Oxford, mightn't we?

June 24th, 1915.   Huts, near Neuve Église.

Yesterday afternoon Conny and I went out for a walk to Neuve Église, the centre of which has been almost completely wrecked by shell-fire: we are not supposed to go there by day because of the shells, but the Colonel said he didn't mind. It was an extraordinary sight to see this large French village absolutely deserted except for a few military police in the safe end, the grass growing in the streets and ruins everywhere. The market square with a large church on one side of it had been the Germans' chief target and you can't imagine what a sight it was, huge deep shell holes like craters, and the church and all four sides of the square all spattered with holes; the houses were quite gutted, but just outside the square in the main street, which leads down to the next village, which is held by the Germans, there were several houses or wrecks of them with " Inhabited " chalked on them. We saw no one till we came down towards the German lines or rather towards our trenches, which are about a mile or two in front of the village. Then I saw a solitary woman in black standing outside a ruined house. We asked her all about the village; she said that the Germans had been in it for a few days in October and that since then it has been constantly shelled till everyone had left, but that she herself couldn't go as her mother was dead. But it was difficult to understand her as she talked Flemish very fast and seemed, I thought, almost crazy. The whole of the front room of the house was a ruin, one side of it blown down. She apparently lived in the kitchen and some kind of garret upstairs; we went through into a sort of garden behind where there were some large shell holes made by high explosives. She seemed quite resigned to being killed and didn't appear to think it worth while to run away. The churchyard just behind her house, through which we came, was quite wrecked, and large stone monuments were smashed to pieces. Every time we heard a shell she shivered, but she wouldn't budge. Just a little bit higher up the street, about a quarter of a mile away, some old women were making lace outside their cottages as if there wasn't a German near; but they were more or less safe, as only the middle and the end of the village has been destroyed.

Conny is very well and the same as ever; hating the war and working harder than anyone else. Have you seen in the papers how his father has been putting his foot in it at Oxford? There was a leading article in the *Morning Post* headed "TRAITORS IN THE CAMP" and much indignation in the *Oxford Magazine*. He wrote a letter to Kuno Meyer, the German Professor at Oxford, who is now in America, and which he never intended to be published. Meyer is a great friend of Conny's and sends him charming letters from New York which he shows me.

June 27th, 1915.   Billets, GONNEHEM.

Such a week of changes! I have visited so many different places since I left those old huts *en route* as I thought at first for Ypres that I cannot remember them all, and now as I write we find ourselves eleven miles away from the firing line and to-night move on again another three or four miles *back!* I have at least had a safe time lately. We marched from our hut camp to Bailleul, where we slept the night and where we spent the whole of the next day till 9 o'clock; then we marched off again for about five or six miles and reached a village, Vieux Berquin, at midnight, where our whole Company was billeted in a large barn. Conny and I got a bed in a farmhouse; we had a very comfortable day there yesterday in spite of the farmyard smells. Last night we left at 9 o'clock and reached Gonnehem at 2.30 a.m. after marching all night and seeing the dawn come up as we trudged along with that beastly equipment biting into our backs. We did fifteen to seventeen miles, a tremendous trial out here after growing fat and lazy in the trenches and with so much to carry. The men stuck it very well, though as we came in a few fell bang down in a faint. I don't think it was anything worse.

After settling the men down in farms, etc., Conny and I got to bed in our valises at 5 o'clock this morning, but as we were up again at 10, we didn't get much sleep. But I feel quite fresh and well to-day and equal to the four or five miles we have to do this evening. We are in France again now and are moving south.

July 2nd, 1915. ALLOUAGNE.

I spent a most pleasant afternoon yesterday. Alan Gibson and I rode over to pay a call on the Coldstream Guards and to see an Etonian friend. When we got there, we found a lot of the officers playing cricket, and the first two people I saw were friends of mine. We stayed to tea. They were all very nice fellows and smart as paint, though only just out of the trenches for four days' rest. One of the officers I knew—Darwin—was in Little's house: the other—Burn—was Captain of Cricket a year ago and was just going into the Army before the war. We stayed there some time instead of going to Bethune and watched them play cricket. During the game the Prince of Wales came along with a friend: he knows them pretty well. Later on we rode into Béthune and there we met him again. He seems to enjoy himself. Altogether we had a splendid ride, about twelve or fourteen miles, with some good gallops.

Mrs. Ovey sends out a weekly consignment of comforts to the men of the Battalion. Can you get some contributions for her fund? I daresay Father would send her a cheque. It is a great thing for the men and Mrs. Ovey goes to a great deal of trouble over it.

July 8th, 1915.   ALLOUAGNE.

We were inspected by Lord Kitchener this morning. He came down the road in a car followed by two or three other cars containing staff officers, among them the Prince of Wales.

Do you notice that the Kaiser says the war is to be over in three months—by October? But I am convinced that it won't be over by then and have bet a brother officer a sovereign to five against it.

July 12th, 1915.   ALLOUAGNE.

We are off to-night to the trenches again, stopping one night on the way, so it will be two days before we get there. We have had a very jolly little holiday, but it was getting a bit dull and these are rather good trenches I believe, surrounded by coal mines—rather amusing country on the whole.

July 13th, 1915. Near NŒUX-LES-MINES.

We marched off last night and arrived to the tune of the guns at our halting-place for the night—a field. So here we are, having again cast off civilisation. We simply bivouacked where we were, and it was very cold. Luckily I had managed to stick on to my blanket ever since I left Havre, so with two great-coats, Conny and I made ourselves fairly warm, and here we are in our field still, waiting for darkness before going up to the trenches this evening. That at least is the present arrangement.

A bomb accident occurred about an hour before starting yesterday which resulted in wounding twenty men and killing two and possibly three. One officer, a young fellow called Vyner, is very badly wounded in the stomach, and I think legs and hands. Conny saw him and told me that he thinks he will probably die from internal bleeding. This puts everyone still more out of humour with bombs, and Major Ovey, who is in charge of the Brigade bomb-throwers (*i.e.* a party from each battalion) dislikes his new job even more than before. The trouble was caused by a deadly little affair called a lemon bomb because of its size and shape. The bomb has a safety pin which has to be extracted to put it in action: when you have pulled the pin out, you must grasp the thing tightly in your hands, as it is timed to explode five seconds after you have released your grip, which of course you do when you throw it. It goes about 40 or 50 yards before exploding, but even then the bits fly so far that it is advisable to throw it from behind cover. In this case it is thought that a piece of instantaneous fuse was used, thereby causing it to explode when only a foot from Vyner's hand, causing appalling damage, as they are like miniature high explosive shells. However, I daresay the truth will never be known as it is rarely possible to get at it in these cases, which unfortunately occur pretty frequently.

The men are just getting their luncheons from the steaming field cookers and I must do likewise.

July 15th, 1915.   Nr. NŒUX-LES-MINES.

Last night was quite the worst I have ever spent since I joined the Army. We left our field yesterday afternoon for another one, where luckily there was a small cottage of which Deacon and I took possession in the name of the Mess—the two Companies being bivouacked together in the orchard outside. At 6 o'clock a large digging party with seven officers was detailed to dig trenches that night some three or four miles behind the line. At 7 o'clock it had begun to rain and then arose the following problem.

The men had to go out and dig: on the other hand, they had to sleep in the orchard on their return and therefore *must* leave their waterproof sheets to keep a small piece of ground dry for each man. Again it was no good sending the men out with their overcoats, as these would only get wet and leave them nothing dry on returning at midnight. So the whole party paraded without coats or waterproof sheets in the pouring rain. The Colonel ordered the officers to wear mackintoshes, though we were also going out without coats. We marched towards the low-lying waste country which you see so well on that card of Notre Dame de Lorette which I sent Bridge, and at 9 o'clock, after having been soaked through, we began digging; the rain stopped for about half an hour, but then began the most appalling storm I have ever known: the men, of course, had no prospect of a warm billet to return to or even of a change of clothes. Of course, all the newly thrown up earth turned to the deepest mud, into which we constantly stumbled and fell headlong, as it was pitch dark, although the lights from the flares all along the firing line in front occasionally threw a dim light upon the ground.

The wretched Gloucesters were due to relieve us at 11 p.m., but meanwhile there was considerable danger of rifles and equipment being lost in the mud, and it is a marvel to me that the men did not lose their stuff. Luckily the Germans did not shell us, which would have been the limit; the men didn't attempt to dig during the worst parts of the storm and indeed it was practically impossible. I forgot to mention that all these men and the rest of the Battalion who had been left behind had to come out again at 6 o'clock this morning on another digging party, from which luckily Conny and I were exempted.

We returned at 12 o'clock and I never before felt so sorry for the men as when I saw them creep absolutely soaked to the skin and caked in mud into the small " bivvies " made by a waterproof sheet to get a few hours' rest till 6 this morning. The officers had decided to sleep inside the cottage, and so Conny and I had a comfortable bed to get into and of course a change of clothes. To-night we have got to go out again, but it is a fine day with a strong wind, and if my clothes are dry it should be less unpleasant. To-morrow we are moving right back.

July 19th, 1915. TERRAMESNIL.

I am very much afraid you will have missed a letter for a day or two as we had another big move yesterday.

We entrained at 4.30 p.m. and travelled till 9.30—only covering about 30 to 40 miles—into quite different country, beautifully wooded and right in the French area. It was too amusing to see the excitement and enthusiasm of the French people and soldiers along the route who had never seen the English soldiers before. The little red-bottomed Frenchies ran like the deuce to catch a glimpse of " les braves Anglais," who naturally kicked up the devil of a noise in reply.

After waiting till 11 o'clock at the big station for the transport to unload, we marched for two hours and arrived at a village at 1 o'clock where the men were put into billets. Conny and I got beds, and with the exception of the Colonel were the only officers in the Battalion who did!

At 5 o'clock this morning the Colonel went up to the trenches, which are about 10 miles away. I think we move to-night and take over from the French to-morrow. The Colonel says they are the cleanest set of trenches we have seen yet. It will be quite a new experience to be right in the middle of the French line.

Altogether with a renewed spell of fine weather and new surroundings I am very happy.

July 22nd, 1915. HÉBUTERNE Trenches.

Now I have a chance of writing you a long letter again, while English and Germans are enjoying their morning sleep and the buzz of the myriad flies is only interrupted by the regular whirr and bang of shells into the luckless village behind.

All the officers of our Battalion went up to the trenches together from the village some eight or nine miles behind, where we bivouacked on the night before taking over; we inspected the trenches, talked to the French and were shown round so that we should be able to bring our men in the same night, which we did without mishap, though we had to be up all night carrying ammunition.

They are very nice trenches; fairly deep with good dug-outs in which you can easily stand upright; but there are several disadvantages of which the chief is that we are not allowed to do any cooking at all in them. There is a perfect maze of communication trenches, and the Germans are supposed not to know our exact position. Consequently we came off rather badly for food the first day, having no ham nor any of those delicious ham and tongue conserves which you sent before. However, we have now arranged for breakfast at 8.30 a.m., consisting of hot coffee brought up by our servants from the village behind, about ten minutes' walk, and cold bacon (rations).

We divide the night into four parts: 9 to 12; 12 to 3.30; 3.30 to 7; 7 to 9. This morning I was on from 7 to 9 and have just come off duty. During my tour General Fanshawe,[1] commanding the Division, came along with his staff and I had to show him round. At one place where there was a low gap he pulled me down and told me to keep my head down as the German trenches were easily visible about 200 yards

[1] Major-General Sir Robert Fanshawe, K.C.B., who commanded 48th Division from 1915 to 1918.

away. But I explained that the trenches he referred to were part of our own line, which makes a considerable circle at that point and that the Germans were 600 yards away.

They are really extraordinarily safe trenches as long as you are quite quiet and don't do much; as a matter of fact my men haven't fired a shot since we have been in them. The Company on our left had a man killed yesterday evening by a stray shot, which was very bad luck indeed. But we can get no water to wash in; all drinking water has to be sent up from the village.

But you can't think how quiet and glorious it is here at the present moment, now that the guns have stopped firing and everything is absolutely still. The trenches are covered with thick clusters of green on top and large bunches of marguerites; one of them is named "Tranchée Marguerite," and the communication trench behind, in which my dug-out is, is "Le Boyau d'Alsace."

In fact everything seems absolutely permanent and set in for the winter.

August 2nd, 1915.   Hébuterne Trenches.

You would smile if you could only see my little dug-out up here in the new trenches, to which I came up last night.

There is a small bed with French lace curtains above it, three pictures over the bed—two of red coated huntsmen, or rather the French idea of them. At the foot of the bed there is a large and very handsome mirror in a heavy gilt frame; to the right there is a small table and chair, above which there is a bookcase with a few books, including a History of Europe, a book on Geometry and a few other works on miscellaneous subjects. To the right of the table is a funny old French clock let into the dug-out with a painted face and a long pendulum. The floor is tiled and there is a little washing basin on a gaudily coloured sort of stand, and a door. Everything, as you see, is perfect, but there is one great defect; it isn't *shell-proof*. It was the dug-out in which the last officer was so neatly buried and had to be dug out. You see the doorway faces the exact direction from which the shells come, so you may get one exploding right inside. This is really quite the worst bit of trench I have ever been in, especially the advanced position, where my Platoon happens to be. Poor old Deacon, whose Platoon was relieved by me last night, had evidently had enough of his four days in, and said that they had had an awful time of it. Yesterday, for some unknown reason, the Germans had a thorough good hate and must have loosed off over 200 shells, all round the trenches. We got them in the support trenches, and when I went into the villages, blowed if they didn't follow me there. When we got into the trenches last night, thank God they had stopped shelling, but as I was standing with ten men behind the last barricade on the road running through the trenches, we suddenly heard Fizz, Bang! and were flat in the ditch before you could say knife. The shell burst quite 20 yards away on the other side of the barrier, but it sounded as if it was coming straight at us. When shelling of any sort is likely to disturb you, the best thing to do is to get into a deep trench and a narrow one; because they can't come right into

Interior of the Church at Hebuterne, 1916. Courtesy Imperial War Museum.
(*Facing Page* 44)

the trench then and the chances are against them even hitting the sides.

August 3rd, 1915.   HÉBUTERNE Trenches.

You would never believe the state your beloved first-born is in.

Yesterday the Germans left us fairly quiet, and only put over a dozen shells, which hit no one; but at about 4 o'clock we had a terrific thunderstorm; the artillery was silenced by the clamour of the thunder and in two minutes our beautiful little trench was a revolting quagmire. By a most fortunate chance I had borrowed a pair of top-boots from a friend who was not in the trenches. I was on duty last night from eight till midnight, and when the time for me to wake Conny up arrived I was plastered in mud from head to foot and the water had got in over the tops of my boots, which is fatal.

However, I went to bed till 3 o'clock in the morning, when the weather seemed to have cheered up a bit. It was a beastly night and has made a hopeless mess of the dug-outs, though mine is pretty clean and I am now burning "ruban de Bruges" furiously to take away the smell of the mud, which is caked all over my boots and up to my middle. I don't know how we shall clean up, but I am glad to say that we are being relieved very soon and shall not return to the front trenches till the middle of August.

I had a great piece of luck yesterday and saw some Germans quite plainly for the first time since I have been out here. I was using a good telescope and saw a typical German calmly walking along in the open behind their second line of trenches, laying a telephone wire, I think: he was joined by two others in grey uniforms. I watched them for about half an hour, but of course they were far too great a distance away to fire at—nearly three miles I should think.

The French are convinced that the Germans are going to attack here and constantly send us warnings, so we have to keep a careful look-out at night. Last night another subaltern, Rose,[1] and I, with a few men, were going out on a patrol in front of the trenches, but Conny wouldn't allow me to go as only one officer should go at a time. However, I saw Rose at twelve o'clock after he came in and asked him if he had come across any Germans. He hadn't met anyone but had a most singular experience. Having posted his four men in a line quite close together and told them to listen, he went off himself with his cap reversed so that it shouldn't blow off, or for some such reason. Apparently he went along to talk to one of his men called Saunders, and he (Saunders), mistaking him for a German, leapt at him. Rose thought that Saunders had been killed by a German and that his party of four men had been surrounded by a larger one. However, he fought like the deuce, rolling over in the mud; fortunately he couldn't use his revolver. He finally managed to overcome Saunders after nearly strangling him. He asked him to surrender and come back quietly to the trenches with him. Saunders surrendered and they then discovered their mistake. Meanwhile, of course, the three other men had been standing round ready to bayonet Saunders, whom they also didn't recognise, and of course as they had kicked

[1] Captain G. K. Rose, M.C., later Second-in-Command of the 2/4 Battalion (Metropolitan Magistrate, Lambeth, 1934).

up the devil's own row, the Germans started firing at them. They got back home very quietly and that was the end of that patrol. But it really might have been a most tragic affair if the man had stabbed Rose with his bayonet and then been killed by his own pals. It illustrates rather well the extraordinary confusion arising in the dark even with two or three men who all know each other. Otherwise it might have been rather comic.

August 5th, 1915. HÉBUTERNE Trenches.

A mere line to-day to say that mud-larking terminates to-night when we are relieved for eight days' rest.

It has been the worst four days we have had. The mud has been awful and I am caked in it; you can't see my top-boots and it is all up my breeches. We have had no hot water to wash or shave in, and no hot food, so now you can imagine how grateful I was for your sausages and cold chicken and ham.

Conny, another officer and I went out last night just after dark with a patrol about 150 yards in front of our wire towards a sinister-looking tree where we posted the men in the long grass to lay in wait and capture Germans; but although we had them out till two o'clock this morning, no one turned up.

August 9th, 1915. HÉBUTERNE.

If I had kept my yesterday's letter a little longer I might have put in a piece of news for you, because just after I had sent it off the unspeakable Bosche "strafed" this innocent village with no less than a dozen " Little Willies "—high explosive shells. Conny and another officer were just going out for a ride and the groom had just arrived at our door with three horses when the first one whistled over and burst about 200 yards away; however, the horses didn't seem very much alarmed and we brought them into the garden and put them under the wall of the house, with the house between them and the shells. One or two of them came moderately near, but the horses weren't hit. But one shell went clean into a barn where ten of our men were billeted and exploded inside, wounding five but fortunately killing no one: that was the sole damage they did.

It is getting very hot again now and a daily run of an hour is no joke. Major Ovey and Alan Gibson came to dinner last night and we had another very cheery evening; this sort of thing makes the life out here quite tolerable. The Major says it is no good trying to make a disciplined soldier of Conny or me. However, he agreed that he had a jolly good dinner, which is something.

We have lost three machine-gun officers since we have been out here.

Long has been made Brigade Machine Gun Officer, which takes him away from the regiment: his understudy had been Hermon, who would have done very well, but who was killed before Long left: the third was Vyner, who never got the guns, as he also was killed.

August 10th, 1915. HÉBUTERNE.

I am glad you found my description of the French trenches interesting: there is no need to worry about that dug-out, because after all you can always come out of it and have important business with the telephone operators, whose dug-out is exceptionally strong.

This morning Conny and I strolled out and watched the big guns firing at the enemy over a broad stretch of country, with a few single trees dotted here and there over the fields; it all seemed very unreal and unnecessary. It was interesting to see a little puff of black smoke suddenly appear in the air about half a mile away, and then hear the whirr and explosion of the German shell afterwards. The effect of shells bursting some distance away from you is very curious.

Last night I dressed up in the gorgeous uniform of a *Garde Civile* or something of the sort, which I found in the Curé's bedroom. A large cocked hat with tricolour cockade of the Empire period trimmed with tarnished silver braid, a tail coat also silver braided and with gilt epaulettes and great baggy trousers with broad stripes down the sides. I gave Conny quite a shock.

The day after to-morrow we return to the trenches.

August 14th, 1915. HÉBUTERNE Trenches.

When I arrived up in the village last night and found the wretched little ruined cottage 600 yards behind the trenches, where we had got to live for four days before going up, I wasn't sorry to be told that I had to go up to the trenches that evening with another Company Commander, Fortescue, as he had only three officers. One of his, Maurice Edmunds, a Wykhamist, had been badly kicked by a horse yesterday. So at 11.30 p.m. I went up and went on duty till 4 o'clock this morning.

There is little news except that the Germans are very quiet. Yesterday the Berkshires told us they put up a board with " Warsaw gefallen " on it and the reverse side " Gott strafe England," and to-day they tell us that they saw some ladies in white dresses being shown round.

August 15th, 1915. HÉBUTERNE Trenches.

Another day passed in the trenches and again the rain has started after we had cleaned up last week's ravages. It is rather disgusting, but I expect this afternoon I shall go out to the village and come back with Conny's Company in two days' time. Freddie Grisewood, who returned from England last night, brings us the news that an early but unsatisfactory peace is expected in England. I doubt if this is reliable, but most people seem to think that any peace would be satisfactory: I doubt if they would begin this war again if it was once stopped. As usual, the great majority who are fighting don't know what they are fighting for; a great many think they are fighting for something they aren't fighting for at all and a few realise by this time that there will be no final decision, but only a salutary blood-letting to cool the overcharged European atmosphere of the last ten years.

August 17th, 1915. HÉBUTERNE.

We had rather a bad day yesterday, yet such were the circumstances that I didn't know anything about it till the evening. We had five men hit by shells, one of whom was killed; the Berks had, I think, two men killed.

As I write the Germans are shelling the village in

the same quiet unobtrusive way and we hear the shells whistling and bursting not more than 300 yards away. There is nothing really very terrifying about it when you get used to it—though it gives you a slight foretaste of what a real bombardment is like.

Five officers are going on leave within the next few days, the Colonel, two Captains and two Subalterns. Leave only goes on when we are actually out of the trenches and stops for the eight days during which we are in. So cheer up and be prepared for another month or two's waiting before you see me: time goes miraculously quickly out here.

August 19th, 1915. HÉBUTERNE.

Just after I finished my letter to you yesterday we had another very violent rain-storm lasting two or three hours and it has been raining slightly most of the day.

You can't imagine the awful state the trenches have got into; the water is two or three feet deep in the sumpholes and very often nearly a foot in the ordinary trench; poor old Conny went in up to his knees and I was congratulating myself on having gum boots and a good Burberry when I, too, while slushing along through a long cut of water, went clean in up to the top of my thighs, and my boots filled with water, thereby making them useless for the rest of our time in, as they never dry. It was too annoying for words. Later in the day my servant went down to the village and brought me up a new pair of breeches, but every time I go out of the dug-out or go on duty for three or four hours I have to put on my wet pair of socks and the wet gum boots, which was most unpleasant when at 12 o'clock last night I got up to go on duty till 4 o'clock this morning. I had cold feet with a vengeance by the end of the time and was thankful for our new Primus stove which provided us with boiling hot Bovril. It is a wonderful improvement; we now get hot bacon and coffee every morning in the trenches.

And now, after working all yesterday and having reduced the mud and water to some sort of order, a heavy storm again hangs over us for some big gun to bring down on our heads: that will fairly put the lid on it.

Yesterday we took it into our heads to harry the wretched Huns, and Conny rang up the French '75 Battery at about 12 o'clock because we had spotted them bailing out their trench in front. The '75's opened fire at once and there was a long line of huge gouts of black smoke at twenty-yard intervals. They made very good shooting and I watched it over the parapet.

Later on at 2.30 our big five-inch guns practised on their front trenches, making more noise and doing more damage: finally, between six and seven about six machine guns fired into the wood in front of us for about half an hour. The Germans seemed rather cowed and contented themselves with putting two shrapnel shells into my bit of trench, which did no harm, and with shelling the village a bit.

This is all the military news: we are now discussing ways and means for the winter and wondering what it will be like.

August 20th, 1915.   HÉBUTERNE Trenches.

No news to-day except that things are drying up a bit. Last night was beautiful with bright moon, unfortunately behind us. Six Germans were seen, or rather heard, at a tree about 150 yards from our line. We were outside, myself, Rose and about three men, and decided to fire a rifle grenade at them—they are deadly little things which make a noise as loud as a shell. However, some fool sent up a flare light over our heads and then fired some rifle shots at the bottom of the tree, which only served to light us up and make us lie flat while the Germans moved off; so nothing happened.

August 22nd, 1915.   HÉBUTERNE.

Two more officers have just arrived; one of them, Bridges,[1] the son of the Poet Laureate, is with our company.

We are just beginning our eight days' rest—so called: as a matter of fact the whole time is taken up night and day with huge working parties digging, building and cleaning up the village. I am supposed to be in charge of fifty men now from 8 a.m. till 12 noon, but the R.E. officer has split the party up into several small groups, and I am not obliged to stay with any one of them.

August 23rd, 1915.   HÉBUTERNE.

As you say in your letter of the 18th received last night, " What a black week! "

When you wrote, however, the news of the sinking of the *Arabic*, the fall of Kovno and Brest Georgievesk

[1] Edward E. Bridges, afterwards Captain and Adjutant, wounded 1917.

had not arrived. Even the daily communiqués served out to us out here can't disguise the complete failure of the Russians to hold the Germans. It looks as if another month would see the capture of their entire field army.

Leave has been suddenly stopped, so at present our officers who went off four days ago can't return. This is due, we are told, to a submarine in the Channel which is defying capture so that all the leave boats are being kept in harbour.

I suppose you have all heard the extraordinary story of our means of capturing German submarines in the Channel. It sounds much too strange to be true, but the most amazing stories are going the rounds and forty German submarines in Dover Harbour is by no means the strangest. This morning some fool has started the story that the German fleet is in the Bristol Channel and that Liverpool Street Station has been blown up!

Another story which may possibly have some foundation in fact tells of a large French concentration to the north of us. It seems that we must resume the offensive again here if anything is to be done to save the Russians.

August 24th, 1915. HÉBUTERNE.

Yesterday I had the delightful experience of a hot bath in a good old English long bath at the Field Ambulance; while Conny was having his just before me, a whacking big shrapnel shell burst just over the house, spattering the place, but nothing came indoors except bits of the ceiling and no one was the worse.

To-night I have to go out with a party of 150 men

on fatigue with picks and shovels to dig new trenches, make barbed wire entanglements, dug-outs, etc. All very dull.

August 27th, 1915.   HÉBUTERNE.

I am so hot that I can scarcely control my pencil.

I have just been having a tremendous fight against Conny and Freddie Grisewood, armed with long sticks and apples. It is much more fun than real war.

The weather is glorious; I was out again last night under a full moon, putting up barbed wire defences; but there was such a glorious moon that I quite enjoyed it.

August 30th, 1915.   HÉBUTERNE.

No news to-day except that the Battalion returns to the trenches to-morrow for five days. Our Company is in reserve just behind, carrying bricks, etc. They are new trenches this time; further to the right. Conny went up to look at them this morning and pronounces them to be something quite novel. They are old German ones which the French captured in June just before we arrived. There are many gruesome relics lying about—corpses or rather bits of them—in queer places, and there is said to be a dug-out where three German officers are still seated playing at cards—killed instantaneously by turpinite. The last regiment who were there said they saw them, and the Warwicks who are holding the trenches now are having a look for them. Also there is one place where, so Conny tells me, the two lines get as close together as 30 yards and afford excellent opportunities for bombing. Altogether they will be rather interesting I expect, but it will be some time before I shall actually be in them, as after four or five days we shall go back somewhere, but not, it seems, as far back as I thought. However, I daresay I shall go up and visit the other Companies there as there isn't much to do when the men are carrying bricks and meals up to the trenches all day.

August 31st, 1915. HÉBUTERNE.

If only you could realise how quickly and more or less happily the time slips by out here, and how immersed we all are in the petty details of daily routine rather than in the Great War, you wouldn't be so anxious for me. It is so much easier for us out here knowing the dangers, such as they are, and they really are not great.

Conny and I want to arrange to come home on leave together, and as his leave is due almost next he can ask to go later if he wants to, and he doesn't seem to mind very much when he goes home. I hope we can arrange it, but it is still some little time ahead.

September 3rd, 1915. HÉBUTERNE.

Yesterday I went out at dusk over the battle-field and I never saw such a desolate sight; old trenches smashed in and half filled up, the whole ground pitted with enormous shell holes, derelict dug-outs smashed in and every kind of decaying rubbish lying round—clothing, tins, pieces of German equipment, broken parts of rifles. Twice we had to lie flat in the mud as a machine gun from the distance opened fire; it makes you feel awfully foolish, but while we were down, blowed if a Hun bullet didn't strike the ground with a plonk about four or five yards away or less: so we concluded that it wasn't such a delightful spot. An unpleasant sight was a cemetery in rear of the trenches, all knocked to pieces, and two of those large French grave-vaults laid quite bare, the whole of the massive stone-work on top having been smashed to atoms.

Yesterday Conny and I were sitting in the doctor's room reading the papers when the Germans started putting over shrapnel. Three of the Berkshires were hit and one of them was killed I saw another man in the dressing station, which fortunately was just opposite. Beyond having his face covered with blood I don't think he was hurt much—just a flesh wound. After all there's no place like the trenches for safety. It's a rum life.

Your letters and parcels make all the difference here and render life quite tolerable. Whenever I get depressed (which is very rarely, I may say) I keep repeating to myself, " Thank God I didn't go to the Dardanelles," and by the time I have said it two or three times I am usually in the best of spirits.

September 5th, 1915. HÉBUTERNE.

We are again in the midst of packing up all the Mess furniture and etceteras, on the trek back to our rest village, where I hear we shall be for about twelve days. Nobody is sorry to leave these trenches; they have been about the worst we have yet been in. I walked nearly up to the front line yesterday afternoon on business and I was much disgusted at the fearful dilapidation, ruin and general air of decay of the whole communication trench leading to it.

Old German dug-outs hastily filled in, clothing, equipment and rifles everywhere, with crosses of every kind stuck into the side of the trench—the graves of French or German soldiers who had been killed near by and hastily covered. These trenches are full of mud and water, and are more dangerous than the others, as they are often shelled and often, so I am told, fall right in when a shell does hit them. On the whole our Company was very lucky to have had such a comfortable five days back here.

Both Conny and I were overjoyed to see in *Punch* that Alan Herbert [1] was going on splendidly in hospital; as a matter of fact we didn't even know that he had been wounded.

September 6th, 1915. COURCELLES.

Here we are again! Back again among the civilians in quite a pretty little village for at least twelve days. We had to march over here in small sections at a time of about eight or nine men at 200 yards distance, as the enemy's observation balloon was up and could see for about six miles behind our lines. But we got home safely without being shelled. Unfortunately we haven't got much of a billet—an empty house, very dirty, with two rooms—one small one with a filthy stone floor for the six officers to sleep in, and the other—without a stick of furniture—for the Mess. True, I was able to borrow a table and six chairs from a house near by; but the room is very uncomfortable. We are told now that we are permanently here for the winter, taking turn and turn about in the trenches with the other Brigade,

[1] A. P. Herbert of *Punch*.

though I don't suppose that this is any more permanent than any other military arrangement.

The two grouse came last night, so we had them for dinner, after hot jugged hare, which made an excellent meal.

September 7th, 1915.   COURCELLES.

The weather here is glorious, the men are getting a good rest at last, and are now beginning to draw a blanket apiece.

Leave is still very slow, though apparently sure. Two officers go per week; two leave on Friday and there will then be eight more to go before me. Rather a lot, isn't it?

The country round this village is charming, dotted with little villages hidden by their fruitful orchards which completely cover them from view. The peasants continue working in the fields as if nothing much was happening. Yesterday Conny, Alan Gibson and myself helped them to bundle their corn or whatever it was, at which they were mightily amused.

The billet isn't at all bad after all, although our wire bed has collapsed after many dangerous warnings.

September 11th, 1915.   COURCELLES.

The weather is glorious: we have another five days here at least and my leave gets nearer and nearer. It will be five months since I have seen any of you, but unless something extraordinary takes place I should be back about the middle of October. The actual date can never be fixed till about twenty-four hours beforehand. It will be sad having to go through the parting again, but it will be worth it.

Is it really true that those devilish Zepps have been over the Strand? I shall certainly be frightened at the prospect of coming home. What with the Zepps in London and submarines in the Channel, I shall run more risks than I ever did in such a peaceful spot as the firing line, "front" or whatever you like to call it!

September 18th, 1915. HÉBUTERNE Trenches.

I got your long letter of the 14th last night in the trenches. I was dead tired, as I walked up at 11 o'clock that morning from the village three or four miles away in full kit and under a broiling sun and spent the remainder of the day going round the trenches and looking for dug-out accommodation into which to put our Company. As I anticipated, we couldn't go into the front trenches last night as a Company of Kitchener's were in for instruction.

We have gone in this morning, but my Platoon is in a reserve trench behind for three days and I am living in a deep German dug-out, fifteen steps down and with the inside all beautifully boarded. I am sharing it with the Adjutant, Freddie Grisewood.

As I awoke this morning I heard this message being ticked through on the telephone to the Adjutant:—"Please supply the names of three urgent cases for leave at once to the Corps Commander": that is the thin end of the wedge and I think another officer goes on Monday.

September 19th, 1915. HÉBUTERNE, G Sector Trenches.

The weather is keeping us all cheery and the trenches aren't so bad. I think my Platoon will remain just behind the front, which is a great rest for them as they don't have to be up all night. I am taking duty in the trench as usual.

The snipers in front are very busy here, and yesterday followed Conny from traverse to traverse all the way along, shooting at his periscope, which was a beauty belonging to Bridges and telescopic. It was quite like the old Plug Street days. Earlier in the same day he had a very lucky escape from a shell. He was walking along with the Company Commander of the Kitchener Battalion and his sergeant when a shell burst in the trench about fifty yards higher up, so he said: " Oh! I will go on and see if anyone is hit." Just as he had got round the corner of the trench into the next one, another Little Willie burst in the trench he had left and wounded all four men in it! The Captain got slightly light-headed and bunked down the trench dripping blood till he came to his Second-in-Command's dug-out, where he handed over to him, saying that it was rotten luck that after having been hit twice in South Africa he should be hit again in the first fortnight out here.

The Germans this morning displayed a White Ensign with an Iron Cross on it and I went down a sap and put up a periscope to look at it. But their sniper (only about 100–200 yards away) hit the top of the sand-bags, spattering me with earth which made me drop the periscope quickly. I put it up again immediately afterwards, but whizz came another shot, which I thought was enough.

Conny is busy trying to find a safe spot for a loophole so that we can snipe the sniper.

September 20th, 1915.   HÉBUTERNE, G Sector Trenches.

I am very busy working all day and night at making my bit of trench a stronghold against the enemy as well as a dwelling-place for the winter, so I don't go up in the front trenches much except to get a cup of tea from Conny at breakfast-time and one at tea-time because, of course, I can have no hot food or drink in my dug-out here. They have got the "Primus" stove up in front and it is half an hour's walk from my dug-out back to the region of cookers. The men get hot food carried up with many groans by the men behind.

Yesterday Alan Gibson came up into the trenches and took my photograph in trench kit, very dirty with top-boots on and no tie: there has been another very strict order about cameras, but he is sending it home quickly before September 30th. After that date all men or officers with cameras will be reported to G.H.Q. if you please. I hope mine comes out well. I will get one for you if I can. He is a useful friend while we are in the trenches: he keeps all our surplus Mess furniture (such luxuries as china plates and glasses, etc.) back at his billet in our rest village.

September 22nd, 1915.   HÉBUTERNE, G Sector Trenches.

I have experienced the joy of finishing off a complete dug-out and feel quite a good builder. I am only waiting for a decent-sized shell to pitch on the top to test it.

We are getting the deuce of a lot of timber out of the old German trenches round here, but there are many unburied bodies about or rather ragged clothing with a few bones inside. Most of the deaths seem to have been caused by French shell-fire, as heads and other important limbs are missing from most of the bodies: smells are beastly round here.

September 22nd, 1915.   HÉBUTERNE, G Sector Trenches.

It is a very grubby Graham that is writing this letter. Here have I been six days in my clothes without a wash or shave till this morning, when I washed my hands in a jam-jar of water. This afternoon I expect to get a shave, but it will be another six days before I get a proper wash or a chance of taking my clothes off.

Conny is quite himself again: in the next list of French's dispatches you will probably see his name. The regiment was told to send in any names for dispatches the other day and I think his was one of them; the Colonel's and Adjutant's go in as a matter of course. It is a farce, and if Conny's name does appear he will be furious, I expect, as he thinks the whole thing rot. All the Staff have their names sent in, as does everyone who is miles away from the trenches.

However, as everyone is full of grievances and spleen against the Staff it is unnecessary to discuss it. But believe this, the further back you get from the trenches the more promotion and plums you get! Even the subalterns acting as R.T.O.'s at different stations—that is a sort of military station-master—get more pay and allowances than a subaltern in the trenches.

Last night we had an amusing but noisy interlude. At 11.30 p.m. precisely I was talking to Conny and Freddie Grisewood at the door of my dug-out previous to turning in, when a most terrific explosion fairly blew our hair up. Then succeeded a devil's own tattoo of shells, large and small, with a subdued rattle of machine guns punctuated every few seconds by these shattering explosions. Fortunately Conny had just come down from the fire trench to see me; all the noise was coming from there. We telephoned up to Rose, the officer on duty, who replied that he was just standing in the trench when this bombardment opened without any warning and that he and the men had been lying on their tummies in the bottom of the trench ever since. The heavy explosions were giant "meinenwerfers" or trench mortars which lob over a great misshapen mass of explosive. They were not coming into our trench, but one went over it and burst behind; the rest were on the troops on our right, the Essex Regiment. The shells were all round the shop, but there were no casualties I think. The same thing was repeated at dawn. We have just been told that our guns are going to bombard the German trenches, emplacements, forts, billets and everything else at three o'clock this afternoon, again at five o'clock and again to-morrow—about 1000 shells. This means holding up all working parties and the end of all quietude for some little time. Of course everyone will have to be in their dug-outs, but that isn't much good, because the Germans won't retaliate till another time, probably not until 8 o'clock to-morrow morning when the breakfasts are coming up. It is a nuisance for us in the reserve trenches, because if they think we are going to attack they will bombard with great big stuff to wipe out our supposed supports.

It is exactly an hour to the bombardment: I must cease at once.

September 23rd, 1915.   HÉBUTERNE, G Sector Trenches.

The bombardment has now been going on for just an hour. The main impression gathered from the depths of a dug-out is of a series of noises never before heard, though faintly resembling what I should imagine a tropical thunderstorm at sea to be like. I say " at sea " because, in addition to a noise like the swishing of the waves, one has that sense of slight but possible danger which makes the sailor thank God for his ship, while anxiously debating its stoutness, just as we thank God for our dug-outs, with the same undercurrent of anxiety as to the strength of the lusty beams and boards above us.

The entertainment (for want of a better word) began punctually to time with a shell from an insignificant little field-gun. Since then there has been a succession of bangs, followed by explosions, some near, some distant: some ending in the wump of a big shell, some with the shattering crash which means proximity, some with the mellifluous squelch which signifies harmlessness and a shell which has gone to earth without exploding, the whole interspersed with the peculiar whistling sound of shells passing overhead to the villages behind. At present there is a continuous sound as of gigantic corks coming from gigantic champagne bottles; here and there the noise of a Little Willie with its report quickly followed by the whirring bang of its explosion and the whizz of small splinters. In fact it is quite a general's holiday, for it is to them that we owe these little interludes of hatred. Everyone has run to mother earth and it is doubtful if a single shell, English or German, has caused any casualty, except perhaps to some wretched stray civilian, unwarned beforehand and with no dug-out in which to take refuge. *But*, and it is a big " but," this will be followed by the inevitable retaliation: whether it will come to-night or to-morrow we cannot tell, but it is sure to come and the only effect will be to dislocate work and to make things uncomfortable. But all we shall read in the communiqué will be:

" Our field-guns opened fire in such and such a Sector on the enemies' second and third line trenches near the villages of —— and ——. We have reason to believe the enemy suffered a few casualties."

The noise is increasing and some really big guns, howitzers, are coming into the game: we can only just hear the shells sighing slowly overhead in a steady stream.

All this has prevented me having a shave this afternoon, as my servant can't get near me or doesn't want to.

September 24th, 1915.   HÉBUTERNE, G Sector Trenches.

I will now finish my story of the bombardment. It was still going strong at 5.30, that is about two and a half hours after it had begun, but by 6 o'clock it was practically over. The wretched village behind Hébuterne seems to have got all the big stuff and the trenches in front were bombarded with Little Willies. No casualties were reported at all!

I walked down to tea with Conny and the others in

the Mess dug-out some way behind me, as the rest of our men have left the front trenches and have come back. They came out fortunately just before the show, which was a great piece of luck. During tea it became very dark and oppressive and the rain started again with an even greater din than before and drenched everything in mud and water. This morning everything is in a horrid state and although the trenches are all boarded, they are frightfully slippery in rubber-soled boots: in fact just now I took a toss which was doubtless very amusing for the spectators.

At 7.30 this morning, while I was sleeping peacefully in my bunk, the enemy rained shells for about three-quarters of an hour, and wounded four of our men in the front trenches, who have only just been brought down on stretchers at a snail's pace. I don't think any of them are badly hurt.

I have just managed to accomplish my first shave and wash for seven days, which is rather a pleasure. Please don't forget the small steel knife. It should have a good blade, a small poker for pipes or nails, and perhaps a corkscrew or tin-opener.

September 25th, 1915.   HÉBUTERNE, G Sector Trenches.

Another day has opened with rain and cold, with the spasmodic noise of guns near by and the continual muffled roar of guns in the distance; the air is charged with electricity, but nothing happens. Yesterday's bombardment killed two men and wounded four others in the front trenches: that is all.

I have had to reduce my kit to the barest necessities, tying the rest up in a bundle to be left with the Quartermaster. You mustn't send out anything till I write for it, except perhaps socks, though I shan't be able to keep with me more than three or four pairs.

There is very little news to tell you. We spent practically all day and night in our dug-outs, as it is too dangerous to start large working parties anywhere. Even the food for the trenches only comes up in the intervals of the bombardment or after dark. But we have a " Primus " stove installed with our servants next door, which makes us independent of food from the village and gives us hot tea, coffee, porridge, bacon, and sausages. We cannot want more.

Of course leave is stopped indefinitely, as you probably have heard in England. However, preserve a joyful and hopeful countenance and we shall doubtless be rewarded in the future.

September 26th, 1915.   HÉBUTERNE, G Sector Trenches.

Everything is now much quieter and after two days a post has at last got through. But I still think it unwise for you to send out anything except socks, handkerchiefs, scarf and helmet just yet. Of course you may not get this letter till October, as I think they are holding them up at the Base. The one I got from you was dated September 22nd, so you see I have no recent news. But if you have heard nothing by October the 3rd or 4th you had better despatch clothes and chance it. I don't think we shall be relieved yet and we shall probably be here for another twelve days. We are all very dirty and ragged and four days' continual rain has brought back our old friend the mud in full force.

How I wish I was in England. It will be queer

sleeping in a comfortable bed again: I haven't even *seen* one for nearly a fortnight, though I have got a model little dug-out just now. The Huns put a shell plum into the street or trench a little further on during their hate yesterday and smashed the wooden pathway; otherwise there was little damage. They blew in a listening post or sap which runs out a little way from our trench, but the fellows in it got away all right. A sergeant was buried yesterday and has gone a bit off his head, but otherwise there is little of interest. We appear to have run short of shells, which may explain the quietness.

October 1st, 1915. COURCELLES.

Alan Gibson and I bicycled over last night to see the " Follies," an entertainment run by our neighbours, the 4th Division. When we got there the cupboard was bare, as the theatre had been closed and removed to another village somewhat nearer the front. I shall go and see it some other time.

This morning we had a grand apple fight in the orchard where the Transport is, and the men were regaled with the sight of six officers all pelting each other.

October 3rd, 1915. COURCELLES.

We have had a glorious winter's day, cold but sunny, and football is in full swing.

All is quiet down our way. From what I can see of the battle, the French and English attacks seem to have been held up completely by the Germans, as they usually are—which means another long weary spell of trench warfare and seems to give the lie direct to those who say that it can and must stop. I am afraid that if this battle fails we shall be here all the winter. Of course if the English and the French *had* broken through we should have had to go forward here with the rest, but I expect they hoped the Germans would have retired hurriedly.

We gave a dinner-party last night which was a great success. We got some excellent Barsac, a cut above the filthy white wine of the country. The chickens were properly cooked, the macaroni cheese was, at any rate, hot, and so were the plates—which was something.

October 4th, 1915.　　　　　　　　　　COURCELLES.

This morning Conny and I borrowed a smart little two-wheeled dog-cart which was unearthed somewhere in Hébuterne and appropriated by our Transport Officer, and Conny's groom drove us over to a neighbouring village to do some shopping. We also paid a call on Major Ovey, who is Commandant of a bombing school there, and brought him back to lunch.

The afternoon has been wet, but a band came over from another Territorial regiment and gave some selections to the men. And now, at 6 o'clock, a large concert is in progress in a barn which our Company got up. I have got Freddie Grisewood to sing, so it will be a great success, I expect.

October 10th, 1915.　　　　　　　　　　COURCELLES.

We return to trenches to-morrow. Conny went up there this morning to look round. We are starting the new winter arrangements, which I cannot explain to you but which will reduce our troubles in the trenches. Conny is as happy as a kid making mud-pies as he is engaged with a large crowd of men in pumping out a filthy pond outside the house such as all French farms seem to possess. He has roused the most foul stench imaginable, and as the pump won't work the water is flowing all over the shop.

October 12th, 1915.   HÉBUTERNE, G Sector Trenches.

I arrived safe and sound in the trenches yesterday afternoon and had the fire trench to myself last night with my Platoon. I also had for instruction fifty Royal Irish Rifles with their captain and subaltern, part of the famous Ulster Division. So I had to post them with my men and take the subaltern round.

We went outside the parapet and stumbled about among debris, shell-holes and barbed wire, and on our way back he tore the seat of his breeches completely off on a strand of wire: I never laughed so much in my life. As he was a dour Scotchman rather than an Irishman, he didn't see the joke and voted trench warfare rotten, more particularly at 5 o'clock this morning when he had to get up for " Stand to."

It was very quiet last night, scarcely a shot, except at " Stand to "; in the evening two little devils of machine guns opened fire just above our trench, which made us duck our heads, but it was soon over.

October 14th, 1915.   HÉBUTERNE, G Sector Trenches.

I am now on my own again for twenty-four hours. There is this difference, that while I am in this support trench I am not allowed to go back for my meals, which is a great nuisance, as it means having half a loaf of bread, the eternal pâté, and some cheese in the privacy and dullness of my little dug-out. At 4 a.m. to-morrow I go up again to the front trench and then come right back.

For the last hour the opposing artilleries have been exchanging compliments over our heads in a formal sort of way; our people sending over some heavy shells which shake the ground, and the Germans retorting with their favourite Little Willies and whizz-bangs.

I am looking forward very much to seeing you all again: it will be nearly six months since that miserable departure in the gloomy darkness of Southampton. How sorry I felt for you then: it was the only thing that spoilt the excitement of going away. I am longing for London with its noise and life.

October 16th, 1915. HÉBUTERNE, G Sector Trenches.

I am more than glad that the dull day I spent yesterday in my dug-out with nothing to do is over.

This morning I went up to the front trench with my Platoon in the grey and misty dawn: so again I find myself alone in charge of two or three hundred yards of the British front. Besides my own men I have got fifty men of the Royal Irish Rifles (Ulster men) under my command.

Since early dawn there has been a thick mist which still, at 11 o'clock, prevails; consequently everything is deathly quiet except for the ceaseless bang of a sniper who I know is in the grass outside our wire; he keeps potting away remorselessly and I have started one or two of my men on to answer him to keep them amused. Of course no guns are firing, as they couldn't observe the effect and there are no aeroplanes up—it seems very curious. Just now a bomb was thrown somewhere down by our trench, but I don't know yet by whom or where.

To-morrow morning I go out again and back to Conny for three days and then back again to our good billets, so on the whole it has been a very comfortable time.

The mist is very chilly and damp and it is getting quite cold at night, but still I haven't yet felt the need either for my overcoat or for winter underclothes.

October 16th, 1915.   HÉBUTERNE, G Sector Trenches.

My twenty-four hours in the fire trench is over and I am clean and refreshed again in the snug little Mess dug-out behind.

It was a miserable day yesterday—very misty till about 12—and deathly quiet. Then at 5 o'clock, while I was sipping some tea, the Germans put a whizz-bang shell into our trench, followed like lightning by nineteen others—as I counted them. Of course Headquarters rang up at once to ask what the noise was about and whether anyone had been hit. As I spoke to the Adjutant the shells kept raining over, but luckily not a scrap of damage was done; it is marvellous where these shells go to, because they were all round and about. They gave us five more later on and then I got the trench mortar battery to retaliate with two shots, which crashed with a reverberating clamour somewhere near their trench and shut them up. We also threw five or six bombs from a new spring gun arrangement, a sort of catapult.

I turned in at midnight and out again at 4 a.m. to send in the report about the enemy. At 5 I was up again and came back with my Platoon to where I am now. After a steaming cup of Bovril I turned in to Conny's dug-out and slept till breakfast. Since then I have had a wash and a shave and taken off my boots and puttees, which is a great relief. Now I have two days of rest before me; then I go in again and then we shall all troop back to our little village and resume civilised life for a week.

October 18th, 1915.   HÉBUTERNE, G Sector Trenches.

Last night I had to move back again to the horrid little support trench and the lonely dug-out—very dull. I have just eaten my miserable breakfast, a cold kipper, a boiled egg and some tepid coffee.

Since then we have had a very trying hour. The Germans began firing on the ground between us and the front line with some large shells—stuff which the guns behind usually get, not the wretched infantry. They came over every three or four minutes with a stately sighing noise, growing gradually louder till they burst with a frightful crash about fifty or a hundred yards in front of our trench; most unpleasant, as it was impossible to be sure that one wouldn't pitch on top of it. Of course it is the noise that is really so terrifying, combined with the shaking and concussion of the explosion. It is difficult to imagine what the really large shells, used against fortresses, must be like.

It was miserably cold last night and it is pretty cold to-day. Even sleeping in all my clothes, with a blanket and overcoat, it was bad. But my winter things will soon be here, I expect. We go out of these trenches to-morrow for a short rest.

October 19th, 1915.   HÉBUTERNE, G Sector Trenches.

Thank God, in two or three hours' time I shall have left these trenches for billets.

Since I wrote to you yesterday we have had a ghastly time. The German bombardment, for so it became after lunch, grew extremely violent; they were using some of their largest shells, which shook the earth and sent splinters flying hundreds of yards away.

At 4.30 p.m. a white-faced officer, one of our subalterns, came up to my trench from somewhere behind and told me that the front line trenches were completely wrecked: the officer in charge buried and killed in the signallers' dug-out, all the telephone wires were cut, and that I, in fact, was virtually the front line. This news was certainly depressing and I gave up Conny for lost as he had gone up there a few minutes before.

About a quarter of an hour later the Colonel came up, called me out and ordered me to take my Platoon down to the front line as quickly as possible, as it had been reported that the German front line and saps were full of men; they might be in our trench now for all he knew. I hastily turned them out and rushed down the communication trench with only about two men at my heels, hearing appalling explosions ahead of me.

The trench was blocked in one place by a stretcher with a wounded or dead signaller on it, and this delayed us until I got him removed. Finally, when I reached the front trench the most terrible scene of destruction confronted me; it was impossible to see the old trench line. Then Conny came running up very dishevelled and shouted to me to take my men down one of the front trenches at once and stand to, ready to be attacked. As it was impossible to get to this trench except overland—the communication trench being filled in—it was a nasty job. The Huns had turned on to the spot which we had to pass their most appalling of all engines—the meinenwerfer or mine-thrower. As I was about to go across I saw a blinding flash in front of me and a great column of flame and earth rose into the sky: the concussion hurled me backwards into a deep German dug-out. I felt shaken to pieces: it was a most horrible feeling of being absolutely dazed and helpless just at the wrong moment. A corporal who was with me pulled me up and we went back to get the rest of my men up, as they were straggling behind and getting lost in the confusion. As we were waiting about a few minutes later Conny saved our lives by yelling out " Look out for the meinenwerfer!" He had just heard the faint sound of its discharge. There was a rush backwards and everyone flung themselves face downwards under any sort of protection that offered. There was another terrific explosion and we were covered with filthy smoke and falling mud and earth. However, after this I ran the gauntlet and got safe into the trench, which I found quite intact, thank Heaven, though it was cut off at the end. It was now mercifully too dark for the shelling to continue, so we had the meinenwerfer instead. About three fell in it, all of which, by some extraordinary chance, did no damage to life. I felt most frightfully shaken and pretty rotten, but after about half an hour it passed off.

Two other Platoons had by this time reinforced the front line; the enemy had ceased every kind of fire and there was dead quiet. We posted sentries all the way along and the rest had to work like niggers to try to rebuild the trenches before daylight— luckily we got plenty of sand-bags. A large party of R.E. came up and a few Gloucesters. The men worked splendidly. We were on duty all night without a stop, building up to the front line, renewing the wire in front, and clearing the entrances to the trench so that we could get out when it became light.

The wreckage was awful, dug-outs completely smashed in and everything pitched up all over the shop. It is a miracle how few the casualties were. Captain Treble, who was taking charge of our Platoon in the front line, as we had an officer away, was killed sitting by the telephone in the signallers' dug-out. The shell scored a direct hit on it and his head was smashed in by the timbers. The signaller was, I think, mortally wounded and one bomber broke down. There were no other casualties.

During the worst part of the show I saw a young subaltern of the Seaforths, the battalion on our right, who had actually come round to have a look. They had had it as badly as we had, but had only three casualties. He seemed pretty cool and was wearing a squash hat—a Homburg. We fraternised over the wreckage and voted the Huns rotten beasts.

Twenty minutes later.

I thought this letter would end abruptly at " beasts." For just after I had written that word I heard to my horror one of those awful explosions which made yesterday so hideous, followed by two or three others. They were again firing, away to the right this time. I telephoned back to Conny to ask him where the shells were actually falling, and he said that it was a good way over to the right on the next Division. It turns out that they were not the heavy guns as I had thought, but only that formidable meinenwerfer firing from the German front trench. Our heavy guns then put shells into their front trench with wonderful accuracy; the ground shook, huge clouds of yellow smoke arose and some of the fragments flew back to our trench. Since then we have had peace; it looks like raining and I pray that it will pour. We have only another two hours here and then freedom.

The row these things make is incredible and I can hear nothing but the low whistle of heavy shells; every puff of the wind startles me and I feel as nervous as a cat. It is the sitting still throughout a solid day listening the whole time to shells and wondering if the next will be on the dug-out or not which is so unnerving. I cannot understand what sort of men they are who can stand three or four days of continued bombardment. Of course, at the end the ones who are alive are absolutely demoralised.

October 20th, 1915. COURCELLES.

At last we are back again safe and sound and have recovered from the horrors of the last thirty-six hours. After I wrote my yesterday's letter to you I had two long hours to wait alone, hungry, tired out and cold before being relieved, and the Germans started shelling again, but not with their biggest guns.

I have never been so absolutely cowed before as I was when I was sitting in my dug-out, which I knew was no good against a direct hit, listening the whole time to the whistle of shells, a noise which I couldn't get out of my ears. However, we got out finally and joined the rest of the company back in the old billets. I was quite done up by the last day and a-half, as I had had no sleep and very little food.

We picked up some enormous pieces of shells and a base the size of a plate and weighing the devil of a lot. The general opinion at Divisional Headquarters, which I visited this morning with a friend, is that this was a travelling circus, a big gun (one of the "Jack Johnsons") which is brought up by rail some two or three miles behind and is intended to cheer the Germans up a bit.

But now after a really excellent English breakfast of porridge, kippers, and eggs and bacon, I feel a new man.

October 23rd, 1915. COURCELLES.

Good news for you! The Orderly Room has just sent round for Conny's address and my own, but Freddie Grisewood, the Adjutant, has just told me that Conny goes off the day before me, and that I shall arrive in town at 3 a.m. on Thursday. I shall clean up at the Grosvenor and walk in to breakfast. Conny will probably turn up on the Wednesday if you will put him up.

FIRST LEAVE. 10 Days.

November 5th, 1915.   COURCELLES.

Here we are again in the rain and gloom, but still in a billet. When I got to Boulogne I ran into Conny and another officer, Tim Griffin, who left the battalion four months ago with flat feet; he had been in the Flying Corps for three weeks, and was now coming back with us to try and get leave to return to England and start learning a pilot's job. We all three travelled together with a Gunner Major who offered us a lift in his car from Amiens, so we got back at 7.30 this evening after a furious drive at top speed.

I find the battalion in much the same state as when I left it, except that they have had an awful time in the trenches, rain every day and mud up to their knees!

November 6th, 1915.   COURCELLES.

Another day gone by since I left you and home, and already the holiday seems like a distant and happy dream.

To my great joy Alan Gibson has got me as his understudy for Transport Officer, and I am learning the job with him, so that I don't have to go on fatigues or parades with my Platoon. I am very much pleased and this morning went off for a ride with him across country from 11 o'clock till 2 o'clock, which was splendid fun. This afternoon I have been round the horse-lines; it is great fun, and if ever Alan goes away I may get the job.

November 7th, 1915.   COURCELLES.

To-day I was detailed by the Colonel to go over to the Expeditionary Force Canteen and buy the food for all the canteens in the regiment—a most frightful job: Conny came with me and we started to do the ten miles on foot, but soon got a lorry, then a private car and then an ambulance. I am now frantically trying to make the accounts balance—an impossible task, as I have been catering for about six different sets of men, with millions of different articles from Beecham's Pills to bloater paste. Also we are giving a dinner-party in a few minutes—two very nice Engineer officers are coming: the dinner is very elaborate and I hope it will be a success. We have got stacks of food.

Poor Freddie Grisewood went down with a temperature of 105° yesterday and has gone to hospital: Deacon also has departed on account of eye trouble, so we have no Adjutant. The Second-in-Command has gone, and as four or five officers are on leave we are very short-handed.

November 13th, 1915.   HÉBUTERNE, G Sector Trenches.

Please forgive me for not writing yesterday, but we came up into the trenches, which is always a long business. Moreover, they are in an awful state, filled with mud and water up to the knees and most of the dug-outs derelict and dangerous. It took us about four hours to take over from the Worcesters, who came out literally soaked in mud from head to foot. It makes one bitterly remember the remarks heard at home that the trenches were to be drained and none of last winter's mistakes repeated.

The wretched Huns opposite are even worse off, being deeper down the valley. They were seen this morning quite openly on top of their trenches throwing up the mud and water. Our men didn't shoot, though ordered to do so. All last night everyone was working hard to get the long three-quarters of a mile of communication trench clear, but with very little result. And now to-day it is raining again.

To-night I have to go up in the front trench for thirty-six hours, then back again to dug-outs behind which are just as bad as those in front.

It is a ghastly business and it looks as if we shall have to abandon the front line or build little disconnected breastworks relieved at night every twenty-four hours, as it is practically impossible to get food up.

November 15th, 1915.   HÉBUTERNE, G Sector Trenches.

I am so sorry I couldn't manage a letter yesterday, but we have been having rather a trying time for the last forty-eight hours: in fact we are beginning to taste a little hardship. The whole of the night before last I was up with my men in the front trenches floundering through the most appalling mud and water, over the knees in a great many places: you can believe how glad I was to be relieved at 8 o'clock after the long weary winter night of fourteen hours, during which I had had little or no sleep. But when I got back, an artillery bombardment began and I was unable to do more than lie down till 3 o'clock without shutting an eye. At 3.30 I had my first and only meal of the day—hot sausages, bacon, and tea.

Last night I was again up in the trench from 6 o'clock till 6 o'clock this morning. During the night there was quite a hard frost, the mud hardened and ice formed in the trenches: I was pretty cold, as I only had a light Burberry overcoat on—but my waders were useful: you needn't bother to send any—they are an article of issue. It was too cold to sleep. I went down for a time into one of the deep German dug-outs where the sentries go after their spell in order to rub their feet with anti-frost bite grease: they were bitterly cold, poor devils, and it was indeed a curious sight to see our ungainly, mud-caked figures going down the steep steps of the dug-out.

Conny came up and relieved me this morning at 6 and I have since been back here and have had two good meals and a rest on a bed.

To-night I shall only go up for an hour or two and then we shall be out for ten days.

The conditions are terribly hard at present and are likely to become worse when the cold increases and the mud becomes more uncontrollable. All systems of drainage absolutely break down. Only the artillery show any signs of life and they continue the daily shelling. We spend our time fighting the weather.

There is a yarn that the other night a German officer gave himself up to the Brigade on our right saying that he was fed up with it.

November 16th, 1915. HÉBUTERNE, G Sector Trenches.

The winter reveals itself in many ways, and this morning's dawn has brought a new enemy and horror. After a bitterly cold night, with a beautiful moon, we woke this morning to find the whole countryside white with about four inches of snow. And it is still snowing! This is quite a novel aspect from which to view the trenches. Everything is deathly quiet; occasionally there is a rifle shot and still more occasionally a shrapnel shell from a field-gun. I have just finished rubbing my feet in hog's lard—some kind of anti-frost bite grease, which stinks vilely. I think it does a little good, but my feet are once more like lumps of ice. The indiarubber gum boots not only keep out water but air, and consequently one's feet get very numb.

I was up in the fire trench last night till about 10.30 or 11 and one of the men came in with frost-bitten feet: I think he is a shirker and didn't look after them on purpose: however, he can't walk this morning. If you begin sending them off to hospital with that, lots of them will develop it. Another fellow last night got the jim-jams and I found him leaning against the side of the trench with a white face trying to look ill. I discovered he was posted in the sap which goes out from the trench and which has acquired a bad reputation lately, as the Huns chuck bombs at it to amuse themselves. Last night there was a lot of shouting and talking across the lines, especially between the Scots on our right and the Germans opposite, which wasn't very complimentary. One Scottie said he was going on leave, and the Hun called out, "That's where you all ought to be—with your mothers." Someone yelled out "Oxford's at us," and then "You English are all rich!"

We have got another four days up here, but have finished with the fire trenches. We have unfortunately run out of sausages, but if you sent any now we should be out of the trenches by the time they arrived. Bovril and beef tablets are very welcome and can be easily sent and carried. A good ham timed to arrive in four days' time from to-day would be welcome, but you won't have time to send it off till after we come out, and they are wasted while we are in the trenches.

November 17th, 1915. HÉBUTERNE, G Sector Trenches.

Gradually getting filthier and filthier: we are back behind in a support trench but go up from time to time to clear the communication trenches. I have got to go up from 2 a.m. till 6 to-morrow morning—which is a rotten hour to be out though it isn't much of a dug-out to leave.

November 21st, 1915. COURCELLES.

We are at the end of our first day of rest; curiously enough, I think it is a Sunday.

We had the usual kit inspection this morning, and this afternoon Conny, Bridges and I walked over to a neighbouring village to see the latest horror from Woolwich—two eight-inch howitzers with enormous great caterpillar engines to drag them along. The shells take two men to carry and are about two-foot high! They are of a similar type to the beast that levelled our trenches just before I came home. I think that they will fire to-morrow for the first time and that they will probably break all the windows in the village. They are being turned out at the rate of thirty a month, but they are by no means our biggest guns though they fire a shell weighing about two hundred pounds. We have already got a decided superiority in artillery and enormous guns are coming over continually: it will make all the villages round here very unhealthy and quite spoil the winter quiet.

The new journey for men going on leave from France, *via* Havre, has caused a tremendous row and scandal, and Major Ovey has just returned miserable at the thought of the discomfort, fatigue and hunger with which officers and men have to put up. During the journey of two days they only get two meals of bully beef and biscuits, which we never get issued to us here, and some pretty strong reports have been sent in about it—one from an officer in our regiment. The carriages are neither lighted nor warmed: a few biscuits are placed on the floor underneath the seats with an occasional tin of bully beef. On the boat, which is crowded, there is neither food nor accommodation. Many people are therefore avoiding leave at present.

November 25th, 1915. COURCELLES.

A piece of good luck for me to-day.

I have been detailed to attend the bomb school for a course beginning to-morrow for twelve days, so I am off in a minute to the next village to report to Major Ovey.

By going there I shall miss our next tour in the trenches and shall return here just as the Company are coming back.

November 26th, 1915. COURCELLES,
SAILLY-AU-BOIS Bomb School.

It is most fortunate having this twelve days' course, as it is interesting work with nice regular hours—all the day's work over by 4.30 instead of those terribly long, cold nights in the trenches from 5 p.m. to 7 a.m.

You will be glad to hear that I shan't be back in the trenches for eighteen days.

Thank you so much for sending the cigarettes—the men will love them.

November 29th, 1915. SAILLY-AU-BOIS Bomb School.

The fatal day, Kaiser Bill's birthday, has come to an end without bringing anything worse in its train than a break in the weather and the most dismal day of rain and slush.

Everything seems to be going well just now and the last week has seen a great change. I am at last convinced that the Germans are absolutely done and would make peace at once. The next month ought to see the English in Baghdad, the Italians in Gorizia, and the Bulgarians wiped off the face of the earth between the 500,000 Russians and the French army, also perhaps a peace with Turkey; in fact I think anything may happen before I see you again.

December 3rd, 1915. SAILLY-AU-BOIS Bomb School.

You can tell my friends from me that Northern France in winter is one of the dullest and wettest spots under the sun when it isn't freezingly cold. There has been rain again for two or three days, heavy and continuous: the poor devils in the trenches are having a wretched time and to-day I heard that we had lost three or four men, killed by a dug-out falling in and suffocating them: it is a most criminal thing and makes one rather sick: they were supposed to be in rest dug-outs too.

I am enjoying my stay very much; we all get on excellently with Major Ovey's successor, Waller, of the Gloucesters. He has already invented a very clever improvement to the lemon bomb which enables it to be fired from the rifle, and he is altogether a very interesting chap, a friend of the late Lord Armstrong and of old Noble who died the other day. Incidentally he is a grandson of Professor Huxley.

December 5th, 1915.   SAILLY-AU-BOIS Bomb School.

It has been fairly fine to-day for the first time for many days, which was, of course, signalised by considerable shelling begun by us: as a retort the Huns had the confounded cheek to start shelling the village just as we arrived home for tea this evening, and about a dozen shells came footling along our street and burst more or less harmlessly somewhere round by the church. In fact I have been listening to a series of loud explosions all day long.

This morning we threw the hand grenade: each man being carefully instructed. The Instructing Officer and myself have to stand in the little trench with the man who throws, so we take good care he doesn't make a fool of himself, though some of these yokels are sufficiently alarming.

I am glad to say I passed the final test all right, and so have qualified on the whole course.

This afternoon we threw another sort of grenade, a most attractive affair called the " Light Friction " bomb; it only has a killing radius of five or six yards, but there is a tremendous concussion with volumes of black smoke which is very effective at night against an enemy who isn't prepared. In fact it doesn't kill by the bits at all, but only by concussion and shock, which stops the heart beating. We threw volleys of ten at a time, so you can imagine the row. If the men throw them rather short, which, of course, a lot do, you can feel the strength of the things.

December 7th, 1915. COURCELLES.

I have just returned to Conny and our billet, after a ripping time at the bomb school.

The weather is too awful for words: the trenches are a wash-out and no dug-out is standing at all. The poor devils have had four days in the wet with mud up to their knees and without any cover at all. The communication trenches are impassable; it takes six hours to get down to the trenches from the back, so you can imagine the state of everything. I am dreading going back there next week: it is going to be very bad.

December 7th, 1915. COURCELLES.

To my delight I have been told off to act as Transport Officer in Gibson's absence on leave for eight days, so I am now temporarily a mounted officer in charge of seventy horses.

To-day I headed a long trail of horses off to water.

My mind is deeply engaged with a grand dinner-party I am giving to-morrow night, among the guests being a most amusing fellow, Georges Marochetti, an Italian Baron, who was wounded at Neuve Chapelle and is now acting as interpreter to some heavy artillery in our vicinity.

The eight days of comparative peace and comfort we enjoy in our billets go far to making up for the vileness of the trenches. How I long for those dear old summer days in quiet clean trenches in beautiful sunny weather with a short six-hour night.

December 11th, 1915. COURCELLES.

The dinner-party last night was a great success and the cheese straws beautifully hot, instead of tepid. Our cook is a treasure. I think I told you he was one of the cooks at Magdalen before the war.

To-day Conny, Major Rowell, Marochetti and I went out riding together, and of course the two experts played tricks on Conny and me the whole time. Marochetti nearly pulled me off my pony once or twice and Rowell jumped clean off his own horse on to the back of Conny's, much to the discomfiture of the latter. He slid gracefully off the back of it when it began to buck and retrieved his own horse from an amused dispatch rider.

This afternoon Alan Gibson came back, so I am no longer Transport Officer.

December 15th, 1915. HÉBUTERNE, G Sector Trenches.

We all arrived here safely again in trenchland yesterday evening with the usual noisy muddling and changing of troops.

The first two days we are in quite a good little cottage, one that has so far escaped shells, and there are ten or twelve of us all messing together and six of us sleeping in one room.

This morning I had a hot bath, but otherwise I have had nothing to do all day: there was considerable " strafing " all this morning, quite an orgy of din from all sides, but no particular damage was done.

Last night Conny and I were out till 1 o'clock this morning wandering over the ground by the trenches, trying to find the overland routes by which all traffic has to be conducted. You cannot imagine the vast stretches of mud and water and the desolation of the trenches. To-morrow at 4 a.m. we go up for our forty-eight hours. It is still fairly cold, but I am afraid that it is trying to rain again.

There is no news of any kind, except the unceasing boom of guns, the all-pervading presence of mud and the usual monotony. However, the thought of seeing you all again next month keeps me cheerful and well: in fact, in spite of everything I have never felt healthier or stronger.

December 18th, 1915.   HÉBUTERNE, G Sector Trenches.

My hands are caked in mud, my body is bathed in it, my soul is full of it. I can hear nothing but the steady drip of water, gradually washing away the remains of this dug-out.

I got my men somehow into the front trenches last night, dumped them in small parties with bombs for each of them and struggled through the night till 6 this morning, soaked in mud and water. Poor Father's gloves are an unrecognisable mass of filth inside and out; mud inside my waders and inside my Burberry.

This morning at 6 I was relieved and came back to join Conny in this dug-out behind, where we have sat over a brazier all day listening to the falling mud and drying our clothes. To-morrow at 4 a.m. I go up again till the evening. All reliefs have to be carried out by night; none of the trenches can be used at all, and we have to walk across the top.

By day we are all isolated from each other and can only sit still and exist. It is the longest forty-eight hours I remember. Nothing seems to happen at all, though the guns still fire every day. But from the wretched infantry there is scarcely a sound.

Last night all I had to report were two salvoes of bombs during the night (four each time), thrown somewhere near our trenches, otherwise the silence of the grave.

Even Conny and I were feeling a bit depressed this afternoon. After all we have been sitting in this miserable dug-out with nothing to do since 6 a.m. this morning and it is now 6 p.m.

We live for the most part on sausages and cheese as, of course, we cannot cook anything else here. The Primus stove is in the dug-out with us and a solitary servant (the faithful Goring) turns up to fry a sausage every few hours.

Conny is now engaged in emptying the contents of a waterproof sheet suspended from the ceiling to catch a little of the water.

This absolute barbarism for forty-eight hours is very queer; to-morrow night we shall be back in the little ruined village with a comfortable dinner and a white tablecloth. A life of many changes!

Marochetti motored up here yesterday to see me, just before I went up to the trenches. He has been very good to me and has got me all sorts of things for the household from Amiens and Doullens—wash-hand stands, cigars, a turkey, and lamp oil, a most precious commodity. He has got leave from a Provost Marshal to take me into Amiens next time we come out if Major Ovey will sanction it, so I am looking forward to a jolly time at Christmas. We are trying to give the men a good Christmas dinner and two hundred chickens have been ordered, but I don't know where they will come from.

The rank smoke from the brazier is making my eyes smart rather: I think I shall drop off to sleep for an hour or two.

December 25th, 1915. COURCELLES.

Many happy returns of this wonderful day.

I had a jolly time in Amiens yesterday: I motored in with Marochetti, Alan Gibson and Conny and did a lot of shopping and then had a dream of a lunch cooked in splendid French style which would have delighted your heart. Marochetti ordered it. We started off with dozens of oysters, then had some scrambled eggs with truffles, then some chicken done in a new way floating in a glorious brown sauce, followed by a lobster.

When I got back I found a concert in full swing and was told that I had to play football at 9 o'clock this morning.

It was raining hard when we started: it was bitterly cold and the field deep in mud, but we played for twenty minutes and I got caked from head to foot.

Two friends from the Sussex Regiment have just come over from another village to see me and have asked Marochetti and me over to tea there. On Monday we are dining with some of them.

My turkey from Amiens has come and is a beauty, but the Christmas posts have all been delayed and I don't expect to see your turkey for a day or two, though the mince-pies have arrived.

Everyone is agreed that next Christmas will

probably find the war still going strong, so perhaps there is a chance of it ending. But I am looking forward only as far as the end of January, when I hope to see you all again. Marochetti has put off his leave and he says he will arrange to motor me to Havre, which will be splendid if it comes off, as it is a seventeen-hour journey by train.

I do hope you all had a cheery Christmas at home and are not worrying too much over me. Things are very quiet now.

December 25th, 1915. HÉBUTERNE.

We had the unpleasant news to-day that we have got to return to the trenches to-morrow instead of two days later; they have altered the length of the tour of duty from eight days to six as conditions are so bad.

There are certain regimental changes in progress: Major Ovey having been in command for a month, becomes, I believe, automatically a Lieutenant-Colonel to-morrow and another new batch of subalterns is expected from England.

I was out all day to-day from 9.30 to 3 with a party of seventy-five men under an R.E. officer digging up flints from the most muddy soil imaginable for mending the roads: it is impossible to conceive a more dull, dismal, wet, cold, dirty and dispiriting job. However, the last week of January shines always like the evening star, and cheers the otherwise dull landscape of life.

December 26th, 1915. COURCELLES.

I didn't have such a bad day yesterday though the confounded Bosche did their best to spoil it.

Marochetti and I went over to tea at a village some two miles away with a mutual friend, a Captain Duncan of the Sussex Regiment, and, if you please, at 5.30 when it was quite dark, blowed if we didn't hear loud explosions outside. Someone said " By Jove! Some arrivals " and a bombardment went on for about twenty minutes, rather unpleasantly near our house.

The C.O. of the Sussex had the windows of his kitchen all blown in and his Christmas dinner wrecked by a shell, much to the disgust of the officers with whom I was having tea, as they were to have been his guests. Another barn was wrecked, but I think only three artillerymen were killed and none of the Sussex. It was really a most impudent thing for the Germans to do on Christmas Day, though our guns did fire on them a bit in the morning.

My Christmas dinner was very dull without Conny. I escaped soon afterwards and went up to the headquarters of the Artillery to see Marochetti's old Colonel who was in a very good humour. Having left them I went on to our headquarters to call on Major Ovey, where I found a whole crowd of officers having a tremendous rag.

The room was more or less cleared for action. I was asked to propose the toast of the Headquarters and was handed a glass of what looked like crème de menthe, though I knew it wasn't: at once everyone stood up and I raised the glass and pretended to drink, much to everyone's amusement. The medical officer and some others thought I had drunk some of it (it was green cracker paper soaked in water) and told me to spit it out quickly, as I was holding my tummy and rolling about as if poisoned. However, they soon saw me laughing. Major Ovey was in very good form: it only wanted Conny there to complete the party.

December 29th, 1915.   HÉBUTERNE, G Sector Trenches.

I have had rather a trying day, twenty-four hours in the front trench since 5 o'clock last night. Myself, another officer, my Platoon sergeant and two stretcher-bearers huddled into the only gimcrack dug-out that is left in the line and which acts as trench headquarters. All went pretty merrily during the night except for the dismal news received at 4 o'clock this morning when I was sending in a report that we had lost another officer, a young subaltern called Doyne, lately from England, who was in the trench on my right and who apparently was shot clean through the head at about 2 in the morning, when examining the barbed wire.

At 9 o'clock this morning shelling started on a pretty heavy scale on the trenches opposite and we lived in an inferno of noise till 5 o'clock this evening, when I was relieved. We landed some heavy stuff into the trenches just opposite, which made the ground rock. In fact I have got rather a headache from it all and am quite glad to get twenty-four hours' rest in the village.

December 30th, 1915.   HÉBUTERNE, G Sector Trenches.

We had a difficult business getting a wounded corporal of ours out of the trenches last night. He was hit rather badly in the back yesterday by a shell and lay in the mud for some hours. Directly it got dark the medical officer got up there, bound him up and dosed him with morphia, but I don't think they expect him to live, as he unfortunately got some corrugated iron on which he had been sitting into his wound. Curiously enough he was one of the new drafts, who have been uniformly unlucky since their arrival.

December 31st, 1915. HÉBUTERNE.

I am too weary and fagged to do more than scribble my usual line. I came out of the trenches about an hour ago after a really hateful day. Shells are still whistling in my ears as they whistled all day, accompanied by deafening explosions which seemed to be all round me.

It is really too annoying, to put it mildly, for our artillery to carry out these prearranged programmes of bombarding the enemy's trenches when our poor devils are literally without a stick of shelter. To-day we have had five men knocked out and four have died already. It is sickening and I can only thank God that they were not my men, but belonged to the trenches on our right where our Company has been hitherto.

1916

January 1st, 1916.   HÉBUTERNE.

Marochetti sent me up two bottles of champagne for the New Year, which cheered everyone up tremendously, and the doctor, after a very rough time of it in the trenches getting the poor devils out, was very much pleased to find it waiting for him.

To-day has been rather wet and gusty, and very quiet; this evening I go in again with Bridges for my last twenty-four hours this trip.

Another subaltern of my Company, Brooks, left us yesterday with very severe gastric trouble: I don't think we shall see him back for some time. That leaves me Senior Subaltern and Second-in-Command, as there is only one Captain now that Conny has gone.

There is no more news of a divisional rest, but I think it will come soon; the Colonel of R.A.M.C. here said that the Oxfords would all go sick if they went on much longer; we have had up to the present a fairly small percentage of sick, but we have had a worse time of it in the trenches than the rest of the Brigade. Lots of the men are suffering from rheumatism and lumbago, and fifty reported sick this morning with various complaints; at least twenty-five were really ill, I believe, so our strength is getting sadly weakened.

January 3rd, 1916.   HÉBUTERNE.

Sorry about the grubby post-card I sent yesterday, but it was all I could manage from the grime of the trench.

I spent a miserable twenty-four hours, as I fell into a deep hole over the top of my thigh gum-boots about 1 o'clock in the morning, while wandering round, and consequently I had to spend the rest of the night and all yesterday caked in mud and water from my waist downwards.

On my way out last night it was pitch dark and raining hard, and I nearly lost my way going over the top. However, once in the village again I soon got warm and clean and happy at the thought of being relieved by the other regiment this afternoon, when we go back to our comfortable billets.

There is little news of interest to you except that another man was wounded in the leg yesterday, which makes our tenth casualty during this tour in the trenches.

January 5th, 1916.   COURCELLES.

For two days I have been commanding the Company, as Rose has been sent off on a course.

Yesterday afternoon Marochetti took me for a walk, right out of our area to the top of a high ridge, where I could look down on to a valley (the Y Ravine) in which the two lines of trenches run. Our guns were bombarding the German trenches, and we could see the whole thing in panorama; it was most interesting. We were in a very desolate spot near a *sucrerie* which has been shelled to pieces, but as it was a very dark and lowering afternoon, there was little chance of our being spotted, as the Huns were too busy keeping their heads down.

After tea Alan Gibson and I drove over together to see the "Follies," which were really splendid: they have now got a full-sized orchestra, which makes the show go thoroughly well. It is quite the best and cheeriest performance one would wish to see anywhere and is crowded every night with officers and men from every regiment for miles round.

I am looking forward to leave with straining eyes, and hope to get home for your birthday. Also Marochetti has promised to save me the hideous train journey to Havre, as the commander of the artillery brigade, Colonel Jenour, has lent us his car.

January 10th, 1916. HÉBUTERNE.

Perhaps you remember that in the good old days I used to look on returning to Winchester as a rest cure after the holidays. I am now feeling the same about the trenches. We came up last night, and I find myself in an excellent trench, sunk deep in a hollow road, an old French trench with nice hard chalk sides and a bricked bottom, also well behind the line; so, you see, I am quite happy. Among other comforts there is a good dug-out, with a table, a wire bed and the usual dug-out picture gallery on the walls, or rather on the back wall, the sides being of cast iron.

At night I take charge of working parties up in the trenches under the guidance of Conny who is now Second-in-Command, but I manage to turn in about 1 o'clock; it is literally "turning in" where a woollen sleeping bag is concerned; they are splendid things and I slept like a top this morning till about 9 o'clock, when I was awakened by the roaring of the Primus stove and the goodly smell of sizzling bacon and sausages. It is so convenient to be able to wriggle out of bed right on top of a hot breakfast without the civilised nuisances of washing, shaving, dressing, etc. So you see by all this that I am in a particularly contented mood, not commonly associated with the trenches in winter.

I gave a most successful dinner-party the other night. Gibson and Conny from headquarters, Bridges and Fream of the Gloucesters from the Bomb School, all came: the cooking was certainly good. After the usual grumbles to be expected from first-class chefs reduced to rather inadequate utensils, our cook produced an excellent dinner—five courses! The jam omelette and the mushrooms on toast contended for the chief honour.

January 11th, 1916.   HÉBUTERNE.

I was up very late again last night with a working party and then had a poor night's rest on a cold wire bed; also I have got a heavy cold on me which has given me a very bad headache to-day, so you must excuse a long letter as I know Conny is expecting me to crawl round some trenches this afternoon.

Three new officers arrived last night: one an old friend who was with the regiment all the time at Writtle, but got bad bronchitis just before we came out; the two others are Newman Hall of Oriel and Enoch.

January 15th, 1916. COURCELLES.

Safe out of the trenches again, and back to peace and comfort for six days—where we were met with the latest list of honours in *The Times*. Major Ovey has got a D.S.O. and three officers in our Battalion have secured Military Crosses; in fact everyone who was mentioned got a cross—senior officers getting D.S.O.'s.

January 16th, 1916. COURCELLES.

I am frightfully busy arranging a grand dinner-party for to-night to celebrate the Military Crosses. We have evolved the following menu:

Oysters,
Consommé Courcelles,
Rôti de Veau de Sailly: Möet et Chandon, 1906,
Poulet Conybeare,
Asperges des tranchées,
Rum omelette à la Q.M. et Macédoine,
Welsh Rarebit.
Coffee. Liqueurs. Cigars.

That should be a success if only everything goes well. I have got some very good champagne for them, but a bombshell has just fallen on me as I find that there are no chickens to be had. However, I shall get some somewhere.

You will be delighted to hear that we are not going into the same trenches next time, but are exchanging with another regiment whose trenches are quite dry, much safer and very near the outskirts of the village, thus saving many a weary trudge through the mud of the communication trenches. Everyone is overjoyed.

SECOND LEAVE. 10 Days.

February 9th, 1916.   LOUVENCOURT, A.S.C.H.Q.

At last Conny and I are in sight of the end of our journey.

To our disgust on arrival at Southampton we found the loathly little *Viper* awaiting us and looking all the more insignificant by comparison with the *Mauretania* which was moored just beside her. However, we crowded into the minute eating cabin and had a high tea of fish and ham.

The crossing was, I suppose, a bad one. We started by sitting in the cabin, but it grew so stifling and the rolling was so bad that two officers, who were unwisely lying on seats in the centre were flung right across the room, which created a faint amusement. From the beginning everyone behaved admirably and departures from the cabin, though hasty, were never too late. I felt frightfully ill suddenly after about two hours, and got up to go outside; the 'tween decks was the most ghastly sight I have ever seen; no one could stand up because of the rolling, and the sides of the boat were literally a mass of men groaning and swearing. I managed, with another officer, to clamber up on to the upper deck, where there were only two or three others, although the beastly little cockleshell rolled like a rocking horse and one had to cling to the gangway to stand up: it was glorious but very cold. We got in about 2 in the morning and had a cup of tea and bread and jam in the cabin before landing. Half an hour's walk through Havre brought us to the train which didn't start on its all-day crawl till 4.30.

Conny and I met a lot of friends in various regiments and six of us travelled together the whole way. I managed to sleep all right till about 10 a.m., when we reached a small place called Douchy, where we all rushed out to the "Café du Nord" and had omelettes and coffee. By 2 o'clock we reached Amiens and carried out another raid, securing three lunch baskets; Conny and I rushed into the town and bought a huge "Paté de Canard" sausage.

We reached Louvencourt, the headquarters of the A.S.C. for our Division, at 9 o'clock last night and got into this café from which I now write, where we devoured the sausage and some more omelettes, retiring to rest at 10 p.m. on stretchers, in an upper room. We breakfasted leisurely at 11 a.m. and then wandered round for news of the regiment. It seems we are still in the old trenches, but for twenty-eight days and without rest billets, which seems a feeble sort of joke.

February 10th, 1916.   HÉBUTERNE Trenches.

I went on duty in the trenches on the evening of my arrival from 9 p.m. till 2 a.m. Everyone seemed very depressed; poor Ovey is looking very sick with life: apparently they have had the deuce of a time the last two days—heavy shelling all over the village and trenches and our artillery can't reply.

Also we have got to stay in this village for a month without a rest, though God knows what the men will be like at the end of it.

Conny will be commanding the Battalion for the last three weeks of February, as Ovey is going on leave.

The wind seems to be very bad in high places and

Hun attacks appear to be expected anywhere. There is a ghastly din going on now all round, enough to make a saint swear. However, we look forward to March bringing a rest.

February 12th, 1916.   HÉBUTERNE.

We had a very bad day yesterday. Among other misfortunes we lost our Adjutant, Tim Griffin, severely wounded by a shell, and the Regimental Sergeant-Major killed by the same shell.

Marochetti and another artillery officer came over to see us for tea, and before they had been in the room a few minutes rather a large shell fell about fifty yards from the house, so we took to our cellar for half an hour, much to Marochetti's disgust.

I think the shelling will gradually quieten down; it has been much better to-day. I must say I am slightly fed up with the whole show; however, there is always leave to look forward to.

February 15th, 1916.   HÉBUTERNE Trenches.

I was on duty from midnight till 4 a.m. last night. The first two hours were rendered hideous by a German " stunt." I was just going down into a narrow little sap leading out of our trenches when a hail of shells came whistling over, interspersed with a few large meinenwerfer and a shower of bombs, quite a tremendous din for about twenty minutes. As the same thing had happened earlier in the night at 11 p.m. I wasn't very much surprised. Most of the stuff went over on to the Warwicks on our left, who are always getting " strafed " by the Huns.

The last two hours were embittered by a hideous

storm of wind, sleet, snow and rain, so that I can tell you I was glad to be relieved at 4.15 and to creep back to my comfortable flea bag and cellar in the village. In two minutes I was soundly asleep and didn't wake up till 1 o'clock, in time for lunch-breakfast, which is one way of making the time go in the trenches.

My Platoon now only numbers about twelve men for duty owing to sickness, and the gunners have also been very much reduced, so we have hopes of being taken out of the line in March.

February 17th, 1916. HÉBUTERNE.

Again no letters from home last night, but I am not perturbed, knowing the vagaries of the military postman. I wish, however, that he would refrain from delivering a solitary bill when there is nothing else with it to help the digestion.

We managed to get the trenches back to normal condition last night; they had been reduced to the state of canals by the rain, and every few yards one met a luckless wight who had stepped on what looks like an innocent and firm piece of boarding only to prove a floating raft covering a deep hole. I myself have twice in the last few days had this trying experience, followed by a rush of icy cold water over the tops of my gum-boots.

I was on duty in the trench this morning from 11 to 1, when whom should I meet, down an unpleasant little sap, but the faithful Marochetti, strolling round armed with a pair of field-glasses to observe the Bosche. I took him back to lunch and astonished him with all sorts of Piccadilly luxuries, ranging from boar's head (cold) to grape jelly (from

Robert Jackson), an Italian confection which is delicious and which I strongly recommend to your notice.

It is settled, I think, that we go back to rest somewhere about March 3rd: I may be able to spend the next four days in Courcelles; if so, Marochetti is arranging for me to mess with the R.G.A. headquarters, and has promised to take me over in a car to see a friend of his, one of the Thesigers, who is back at some place far behind on the staff. But as we shall probably only have two officers including myself, I may not be able to go until the next time out of the trenches.

February 18th, 1916. HÉBUTERNE.

We came out of the trenches this afternoon for four days. I am not going back for a holiday, as we have only two officers, but it will be quite a rest here.

At 2 a.m. this morning when I was on duty the Germans suddenly started a tremendous "strafe": hundreds of shells, meinenwerfer like the crack of doom, bombs, machine guns and the whole bally chorus at once directed, thank Heaven, on to the Warwicks on our left. I watched the whole battle from our trenches. We opened fire with our machine guns and rifles on the German trenches far away to the left, as we thought they were going to attack; the din was colossal, and twice the signallers came running up the trench to fetch me to speak to Conny on the telephone. The authorities were very windy in the village, wanting to know if our trenches were getting bombarded and where the row was. Finally, our guns opened rapid fire just over the German trenches.

It was a bright moonlight night, but the scene was lit up with the flashes of the explosions. The whole show died down about 3.30 and I believe the Warwicks only had seven or eight casualties, though there are rumours that the Huns got in and bagged a machine gun and some rifles   At any rate it was a bright little show.

February 21st, 1916. HÉBUTERNE.

The Germans have been making so many little night attacks against the trenches to the right and left of us that we are getting a bit jumpy. The night before last, at about 7 p.m., we heard the usual din and uproar going on towards the further side of the village, and later heard that a large body of Huns had got into our trenches, but had been completely surprised by the awful mud and that after a brisk hand-to-hand scuffle they had surrendered. But this information is very unreliable, and it is quite possible that they got away again. A lot of wounded came through the dressing station, but only suffering from whacks and bangs on the head.

As you probably know, the shrapnel helmets are among the latest freaks of fashion at the front; hitherto they have been treated rather as a joke. Now, according to the latest orders from Conny, officers and men will *always* wear helmets night and day, though they need not sleep in them! So I suppose we have got to resign ourselves to these hideous green things; they are abominably heavy and shaped like soup plates rather than helmets—altogether most unpleasant.

Our Adjutant, poor Tim Griffin, died on the 19th

under the operation for removing his arm. It is very sad. Quite one of our best and most useful officers and a very good fellow. I liked him awfully.

February 22nd, 1916.   HÉBUTERNE.

I was delighted to get a letter from you last night and to hear that the fall of Erzerum had cheered you up, though I can't see that it will have any great effect on the war.

It has been snowing heavily for about an hour and looks like continuing, which is annoying, as we are going into the trenches again this afternoon for four days.

Apparently it was true that a German patrol which got as far as our trenches two nights ago were badly scuppered: quite a number of corpses were discovered in the barbed wire, and the Huns who actually got into the trench never got out again. So that may damp their ardour a bit. However, "Minnie" was extremely active again last night about midnight and disturbed my peaceful slumbers with unholy crashes, though she was operating on the village about a mile to the north of us.

February 25th, 1916.   HÉBUTERNE Trenches.

This morning I was on again from 4 till 8 a.m., as I like that time better than 9 to midnight or midnight to 4 a.m., the moon being up about 1 a.m. this week. I have never known it so cold, even in Switzerland, but my Selfridge 35*s.* outfit was a treasure; with a big leather jerkin on and my blizzard helmet surmounted by the steel contraption I kept quite warm.

However, about 8 o'clock it began snowing again and the wind freshened to a gale. When I went into the trenches two hours ago, at 3 p.m., the whole place was deep in snow, more than a foot deep in most places, with a hard stinging sleet coming down the wind. There wasn't a sound from either side the whole afternoon; absolutely dead silence. It is a great blessing that we are not in our old trenches. What will happen when the thaw sets in is a question that terrifies the boldest hearts; the trenches will be a sea of mud and most of them will fall in. While the frost lasts it is rather fun.

We are going out to-morrow just to the back of the village, but Conny told me last night that I could go back to Courcelles for the four days, so I wrote off and told Marochetti at once. He will arrange for me to mess at the Artillery headquarters I expect, as the Colonel asked me to last time, and I hope we shall get a motor drive to Albert, Amiens or Doullens and some dinner-parties. I shall get into respectable clothes again for the first time since I left home, and shall get a bath and a few other luxuries. So you see I am fairly cheerful—I mean very cheerful.

But at present there is no sign of a move back for the long-expected rest.

February 26th, 1916. HÉBUTERNE.

As it is rather a busy morning I am afraid this will be a short letter. But we are being relieved at 2 p.m., and soon after I go off to my little village behind with a pass for Amiens from Conny which he gave me last night; so I am going to enjoy myself for four days.

It wasn't very cold last night after all, but the

trenches are full of snow and the countryside is virgin white. The village is quite pretty, as the snow effectively conceals the ruins and always makes trees look attractive.

Leave has been stopped suddenly for the whole Expeditionary Force I think, or rather for the fighting part of it. There is the deuce of a big battle going on to the south at Verdun; I believe the Germans are attacking on a huge front of something like twenty miles. If so, they must mean business this time.

February 27th, 1916. COURCELLES.

Here am I back at Courcelles enjoying a short rest.

Last night I dined with Marochetti and the Gunners; the old Colonel was in very good form and most genial. To-night I am dining with some friends in the Sussex Regiment back at another village about two miles away: the day after to-morrow I hope to go off for a joy ride somewhere in a car, and then back to the trenches again. But I think we really may get a rest soon.

The post has been awful and for two days I have not heard from you nor have I had any papers since Friday. But through private wires I hear that the Germans are making a tremendous push at Verdun, but have lost a great many men. Leave, of course, is still stopped and is, I think, likely to be for some time.

March 1st, 1916. HÉBUTERNE Trenches.

Here I am back at the trenches at the old address: I am afraid that there are no signs of being relieved yet, but no doubt something will come through soon. I have enjoyed my four days very much indeed: we had a jolly motor drive to Doullens yesterday and a good lunch. The place was simply crammed with troops marching through and the staff were very much in evidence.

The K.D.G.'s, Household Brigade and Indian Cavalry are digging trenches behind the line here and another lot of cavalry are in trenches at Ypres, which isn't much fun for them.

March 3rd, 1916. HÉBUTERNE Trenches.

Poor old Marochetti came up to tea to-day to say good-bye to Conny and myself. They are off to-morrow to Arras. I can tell you now, as it can't be a secret much longer, that we are taking over another large slice of the French line. Thank Heaven there is no chance of our going north to that beast of a district. His Colonel is to be Brigadier-General in charge of a very large command of guns and he is keeping all his personal staff; Marochetti hopes soon to be made his A.D.C. with a commission in the British Army, but he is very sorry to leave here and has promised to motor over whenever he can.

I am afraid there is very little chance of leave being started again for some time; only special cases are getting it. As for our move, I think it will not come off and that we shall not be taken out of the line completely at all, though we may get a week's rest soon.

A new officer has joined our Company, Carew Hunt, a friend of the Oslers and an Oxford man, quite a good fellow, I am glad to say.

Colonel Ovey returned last night, so Conny is no longer C.O.

March 4th, 1916.   HÉBUTERNE.

Rose has just returned from London and says that on the whole it is dreadfully dull there and that it is difficult to amuse oneself; also, like most of us, he seems rather disgusted with the general public at home, who don't seem to take any interest in anything much and are frankly bored by the war.

Conny is very well. Colonel Ovey thought he had undertaken rather a lot in his absence, but Conny is nothing if not go-ahead and initiated a lot of reforms, schemes and orders in the three weeks during which he commanded the Battalion. I had a splendid dinner with him at headquarters two nights ago; the Medical Officer had just returned from a trip to Amiens, so we had fried soles, chickens and new potatoes, with some other delicacies, which wasn't bad as a fortification against trench duty afterwards from midnight to 4 a.m.

March 7th, 1916.   HÉBUTERNE.

Carew Hunt, our new officer, is a very welcome addition to the Mess—he is about seven foot high, languid but very amusing and knows a lot of people; also he has many of the same tastes as myself, including literature, in which he is very well read; he also appreciates good food keenly, which pleases me. Our cook has really done very well lately. He makes the most wonderful soups out of nothing and scorns the simple method of boiling cubes and squares in water. He pours all sorts of queer things into the pot like an ancient alchemist at work and produces something quite savoury. But he is always complaining of the inadequacy of the materials and demanding all sorts of impossible utensils.

March 12th, 1916. HÉBUTERNE.

In order to save our lives Conny has put us all to the most hideous discomfort and misery. Incautiously talking to him the other day when he was having tea with us, I remarked on the good target our house presented on the very outskirts of the village with only a few bare trees to screen it from view and directly in the line of fire of the shells. Conny continued the conversation, and looking round our small and dirty little room, which has one wall buttressed with sand-bags, said: " I think it would be a good thing to build a wall of sand-bags inside the room all round and place upright beams at intervals to take three or four cross-pieces and have another ceiling of sand-bags on top at a distance of six feet from the ground," thus reducing the size of the room, which now has to contain seven officers, for another arrived to-day, to the size and appearance of a dug-out, and shutting out half the light. I did not suspect that this would ever come to much, but next morning round came Conny with measuring rods and ordered us to put all the servants on to filling sand-bags outside and to start work right away. Off came the door, and the room has been full of sand-bags, beams, logs, iron stakes and men ever since, and it is likely to be about a fortnight's work!!!

When I unwisely hazarded the remark that I wished old Conny had to live in the beastly place himself, he was exceedingly sharp and I was told I could go and live in the trench if I liked. Of course one can't help admitting the wisdom of the precaution, as our chimney must be easily visible to the Huns, and a shell might lay out five officers at once before we had time to go to the cellar; but still it is rather annoying.

We are now absolutely crowded with new subalterns, far more than our establishment. This slightly relieves the work but diminishes space. Fortunately it brings me in plenty of money for the Mess.

Another sergeant in my Platoon is, I think, getting a commission in this Battalion; he will be the second, as Early, who was my Platoon sergeant, has now joined us as a second lieutenant. The latter is the head of the largest blanket firm at Witney and is a thoroughly good fellow.

March 16th, 1916.   HÉBUTERNE.

Yesterday Rose and I started off on our two horses in the most glorious sunshine we have seen since September. I rode Conny's horse, thanks to his kindness. We rode right away from the *sacré* " Front " and its eternal noise across the glorious downs, which are now drying again. It was really an ideal day. We stopped for lunch at La Rossignol Farm, the headquarters of a Field Company of Royal Engineers. Then we started off again and had some splendid gallops. To end up we had tea with Gibson at the village where the transport live and walked back to trench-land in the evening.

The first thing that greeted our arrival was a little Bosche battue which caused us to go into the cellar for ten minutes. Fortunately it was all over by dinner-time and Conny and Bridges turned up for Brook's twenty-first birthday dinner, which was a great success. At midnight Conny and Bridges left to go round the trenches.

March 18th, 1916. HÉBUTERNE.

Conny has just this moment been in to inspect the work of fortifying our billet, which doesn't get on very quickly. A shell will probably bash the whole thing in before completion. He is fairly well but I think is rather feeling the strain of living in a dug-out four or five hundred yards away from the front trenches since February 2nd, and is looking a bit haggard. He came round last night after dinner for a talk and I thought then that he looked as if he needed a rest.

A new German gun has been firing in our direction since breakfast time, but each time the shell falls short in an orchard on the other side of the road to our house. Last night while trying to get some sleep before going on duty at 3.30 a.m. my rest was disturbed by the loathly crump of the dreaded meinenwerfer. She started at her usual time, 11.30 p.m.: about fifteen of the beggars fell about one hundred yards behind our trenches and three hundred yards from the cellar where I was trying to sleep. However, one gets so used to these unearthly interruptions that really I didn't take much interest in them beyond cursing the noise. Once you know where the things are going, or rather that they aren't directed against your particular spot, you cease to take any interest unless you have reached the deplorable state of being upset by hearing someone else getting shelled. When this point is reached and shells have begun to get on your nerves, it is time to apply for permanent leave. Sooner or later you are bound to be affected by always living in this din, but it makes a world of difference if you can keep your mind occupied and take as much exercise as possible when out of the trenches.

March 19th, 1916.   HÉBUTERNE.

Such a night of alarms and excursions and a wonderful firework display by Brother Bosche. Unfortunately it was my night to be off duty till 7 this morning, and I had retired to bed in the cellar at 10 feeling very satisfied and sleepy after a good dinner. At 2 a.m. I was awakened by the most frightful din imaginable, a really heavy bombardment. I knew at once that all was up with sleep and leapt out of bed: in two seconds I had my respirator, revolver and gum-boots on and was ready for the world in arms.

On looking outside the door I saw shrapnel bursting over the village at our back, but nothing much on our trenches, the bombardment being on our right. The sky was full of red, green and white lights sent up by the Huns as signals and in order to prevent our artillery from seeing the S.O.S. signals sent up from our own trenches to ask for support. But within a minute of the first German shell our artillery had opened rapid fire, making what is called a " barrage " or curtain of fire to prevent the Germans leaving their trenches. We were all ordered to " Stand to " in the various alarm positions, behind the front line. My Platoon had a good trench for a view of the proceedings and were quite immune from shells or meinenwerfers. The whole thing was over in an hour: starting at 2 a.m., both sides kept up a ceaseless bombardment till about 2.40: then it slackened down and at 3 o'clock I was inviting Conny in to have a drink of beer or tea.

We have not had any definite news of the affair yet, but I don't think the Huns got any prisoners this time and there were, I believe, only a few casualties. No one could understand how they managed to clear a few prisoners each time they did a raid. About one officer and six men was the usual number. But the other night a curious little glass bulb containing some liquid and fixed to the end of a short handle was found in No Man's Land between the trenches. It had been suggested that they may have used gas and that this liquid generates it when the glass is broken and it is exposed to the air; again it is thought that it may be vitriol or something of the sort. At any rate the Hun has been super-wily. I trust he got a smack in the eye last night.

March 20th, 1916. HÉBUTERNE.

You will be glad to hear that the Bosche were rather badly scuppered the other night. Our guns were quick enough to prevent them getting into our trenches; I believe that they lost a good many men in the barbed wire, and one raw youth of sixteen years of age gave himself up. We also lost a lot of men—I am told as many as seventeen—but lies grow up like weeds in this atmosphere. Rumour has it to-day that the Huns have proposed terms of peace to our politicians: this too is, I suppose, a lie.

We come up out of the front line to-morrow for the usual four days in reserve. I am going back with Conny and shall enjoy myself.

March 23rd, 1916. HÉBUTERNE.

I had only just got back for my rest with Conny when a wire came down recalling me the next morning; so here I am, back in this beastly village, but detached from the Battalion. I have been made Adjutant of the Keep, which is the inner part of the village and is under the command of an R.E. Major. I am to act as his Adjutant for about ten days. It will be rather fun, as there are all sorts of people there; a company of Oxfords, one of Sussex, some R.E., some trench mortar people, and machine gunners. And I shall escape our next tour in the trenches.

We were all kept up to 3 a.m. this morning by a vigorous battle which was started by ourselves at 12.15. Three large patrols were sent out to get into the German trenches and the artillery were to open fire at 12.30. Everyone in the Keep was ordered to stand by in cellars and dug-outs in case of retaliation. Of course, typical of the British Army, the whole show was nearly an hour late; the patrols couldn't get through the barbed wire and the Huns put up a devilish smart bombardment, all over the village, bashed in a few houses and killed and wounded a few men. Unfortunately we had a corporal killed just as I had turned in about 3 a.m. and another man wounded. I was the only one of the six officers who slept upstairs last night; but really I had such a comfortable mattress I couldn't face a cold hard cellar. As it was, I had just got to bed in my pyjamas when a few whizz-bangs seemed to advise retreat, so I went to bed again dressed, so as not to be caught. As the Tommy says: " Gawd! what a life! "

March 25th, 1916. HÉBUTERNE.

No news for you to-day except that I have spent the morning wandering round this blessed Keep registering wells with a map, plumbing their depths (in most cases foul) and making notes about winches, chains and buckets; rather dull, but still the weather is fine again and the snow is beginning to melt.

March 30th, 1916. HÉBUTERNE.

My Company has gone into the trenches and left me behind, so I am living with another Company in the same old place at the back of the village.

I walked down to the trenches this morning to see them and met old Conny walking round energetically. I also met the General and his Brigade Major, who inquired most tenderly after my eye. When they last saw me two days ago, I was well bandaged. The General laughed at me when I told him that it would be all right next morning, but I had the laugh of him to-day.

A sad sight this morning; a British aeroplane, hovering over a German observation balloon just behind their lines was brought down, crumpling up completely and turning over and over. But that is the fortune of war. So curious it seems to live more or less peacefully in this village and to see people killed a mile away with no noise, no fuss, no excitement and very little interest.

I get a good deal of society even in these remote quarters; dining out with different people and visiting friends ensconced more or less comfortably in dug-outs and cellars. But oh! the terrible monotony and boredom of it. As I write, a wheezy gramophone with bronchial catarrh is banging out the well-known strains of the Tango and Maxixe and life is on the same plane. But, thank God, I am only nineteen and am still capable of getting a lot of amusement out of life even out here. After all one sleeps like a top, and feels more healthy than ever before, two blessings that many people at home might well envy.

April 3rd, 1916. HÉBUTERNE.

The weather is grilling: I am sitting in shirt-sleeves again—it is quite like the old Plug Street days.

I had a terrible business all to-day billeting R.E. in the most filthy hovels imaginable. I can tell you I am not very popular; but I imagine that it is the Adjutant's job to do all his Commanding Officer's dirty work. But Major Clissold is a ripping old chap and it is a relief to be independent of the Company for a time.

Conny is giving up his commission to continue his medical career and qualify as a doctor, which the War Office is allowing medical students of over five years' standing to do. I don't blame him; he will lose an awful lot of ground if he is still unqualified at the end of the war.

April 4th, 1916. HÉBUTERNE.

All is going pretty well and I am getting quite a lot of enjoyment out of life at present.

We gave a dinner last night: it was a great success: Conny was in splendid form. We sent round to another Company at the last moment for Maurice Edmunds, so we were quite a gay party.

The Battalion is going back for eight days soon, but I am going to stay up here. The Brigadier met me this morning and gave me my choice, so I asked to be allowed to stay up, as I do not want a rest very badly and here I can always get away for the day if I want to.

April 10th, 1916.   HÉBUTERNE.

I don't know how long this job of mine will last, but the former Adjutant has stayed in England and got married; also he is not, I believe, very popular, so I may be fairly permanent until, of course, our Brigade leaves this part of the world.

April 14th, 1916.   HÉBUTERNE.

I am very much depressed to-day. Conny has gone off for good; his orders came quite suddenly. I happened to walk over to see the Battalion yesterday afternoon and he asked me to stay to dinner at headquarters Mess; just before dinner the Adjutant handed him a chit from G.H.Q. ordering him to report to the War Office forthwith. I think old Conny was very sorry to go in the end; he told me that he didn't expect anything would come of his application. He walked all the way back to the trenches with me after dinner, and just as he arrived in the village about 11.30 p.m. we saw the flash of German guns and five or six big shells burst on the trenches. We thought a raid was on and hurried into our dug-outs, at which we had just arrived. We told old Conny that he would be caught at the last moment if he wasn't careful, but it was only a piece of casual shelling.

He is back in England by now, lucky fellow, just at the right moment too, as there is a nasty time coming; all leave is stopped and everyone on leave has been recalled at once.

To-night I am dining with some friends of mine in the Sussex up here. I hope there won't be any shelling. If bad, it is rather apt to upset a dinner-party.

April 19th, 1916. HÉBUTERNE.

The entire Brigade is going out for a short rest very soon, but I think, if possible, I shall elect to stay on up here.

I had a letter from Conny yesterday: he went to the War Office, and as no one took much notice of him, he just went off to Guy's Hospital and is busy at work again there. I am so glad for his sake that he is safely out of it all. I only wish I was, but I expect I should want to get back again after two or three months. But two months' complete rest would be simply delightful.

This morning I had to lie flat down in the mud. I had rashly strolled down to the trenches with a friend, and on our way back we were caught by a Hun machine gun. The bullets zipped viciously among the trees behind which we lay flat and tried to get flatter. I was furious, as I had a pair of light breeches on which got filthy.

April 26th, 1916. BAYENCOURT.

Summer has arrived; the heat is intense, the sun is glorious and everything is green.

I am enjoying the most splendid holiday, which

began last night. My two Wykhamist friends, Hill [1] and Alan Gibson, took pity on me and put me up with the officer on whose hospitality I have been living for the last fortnight in the line. We occupy a bell tent again, which is really delightful after being so long in dug-outs. We mess with them in their wooden house just opposite, and it is really likely to be the pleasantest week I have spent in France for a long time, as I have nothing to do, not being attached to the Battalion. So I can sit all day in slacks in a nice armchair in the garden reading a book, and can have a ride whenever I like.

Unfortunately this morning at 5.30 we were woken up by a very sustained German " strafe " on some guns about a mile away from here; as we were in the direct line behind, they all seemed to be coming in our direction: it went on solidly for about an hour. About one hundred and twenty shells were fired, which by the greatest good fortune hit no one, only just touched one gun and blew up a limbered wagon with some shells in it.

Gibson and I have just walked across to see them, and the whole ground in front and behind is simply dotted with shell-holes. I don't suppose the guns will stay there much longer, as the Huns seemed to have discovered them pretty well.

When is the war going to end? We actually have got some real Russians in France at last; with snow still on their boots, so they say.

April 29th, 1916. BAYENCOURT.

This holiday is simply idyllic and now there is

[1] Captain J. S. B. Hill, M.C., Bucks Battalion, Brigade Major.

every prospect of it being prolonged for another week.

It is doing the men a lot of good and it is splendid to see them playing football again or resting peacefully in the shady orchards after having had for so long to tramp backwards and forwards from the front line to a hovel in rear, both equally dangerous.

Yesterday I was out all day riding; starting at 11 o'clock with a friend of mine, Scott-Williamson of the Bucks; we rode quietly under a blazing sun to a very pretty village some three or four miles away where his regiment is resting and where Divisional Headquarters are housed in a pretty château.

There we called on his elder brother who is Second-in-Command of a field ambulance in our Division.

As my friend was going to be inoculated, I thought I would do the same. So the elder brother jabbed us both, but unfortunately in the neck, which I think is a worse place than the arm. At any rate it began to hurt immediately, and by the time I had ridden home I felt quite ill and shivery. However, I went to bed pretty early and slept soundly till 4 a.m., when a Hun 'plane disturbed everybody by an early morning display of bomb dropping. As we have only got about half an " Archie " gun just here it did much as it liked.

I really believe we are all going into reserve soon; but I distrust every rumour.

May 3rd, 1916.   HÉBUTERNE, G Sector.

Here I am with the suddenness of fate pitchforked back again from the delicious comfort of my country retreat four miles away to the front line trenches, and worse still to our old enemies, the ones we held in the winter. One gets very antagonistic to front line trenches after a prolonged absence from them and I have now been out of them for over a month.

All I can say at present is that we shall be in till about the 10th May; then we may look forward to a complete change, but no one knows anything definite yet.

It seems very curious and dull to be living again in a dirty damp dug-out alone and right up in the front trench with just a cold snag of meat and bread and cheese for food. But I hope that it won't be for long. Every day brings me nearer to you. Yesterday two officers went off and two should go now every six days. There are now only six to go before me.

May 4th, 1916. HÉBUTERNE Trenches.

This is the second letter I have written to you to-day, but since writing this morning we have had some bad luck: two officers killed in the Company on our right, one of the officers in my Company who was doing his first twenty-four hours up wounded through the palm of the hand and a sergeant in my Company killed. Bad work for the twenty-four hours we have spent up here.

I have just been relieved from the front line and have gone back to a fairly comfortable dug-out where I hope I shall be able to sleep to-night if all is quiet, as I was up all last night, and am doing another twenty-four hours to-morrow evening.

I am feeling very tired, but I daren't take my boots and puttees off, which I have now had on for thirty-six hours, because the night is still young and the Bosche may be up to some devilry at any moment. Thank Heaven the dawn comes at 3.15 a.m. and gives the weary warriors the signal for sleep. The peace that reigns from 3.30 a.m. till about 9 o'clock passes understanding; all the staff are in bed, the gunners are asleep and the intense atmosphere of the night of watching is relaxed; you can almost hear the Hun sausages sizzling over the way!

May 9th, 1916. COUIN.

Yesterday was relief day, and to-day I had to rise at 7 a.m. and take a working party to work three miles away in the pouring rain. We are in some vile, cold, hideous, bare huts in the most beautiful woods imaginable in the grounds of a very attractive château, occupied by the staff. But the rain and the cold have spoilt everything; let's hope it clears up soon, as it will be great fun then.

I got the most splendid parcel from you to-day, containing eggs, cakes and cigarettes, for all of which I was deeply grateful. Parcels are more welcome than ever just now, as the Mess has got to economise tremendously and I have had to close my account with Harrods and with Robert Jackson owing to financial straits. As if to mock me I am, as Second-in-Command, running the Company pay and am drawing thousands of francs every week.

May 15th, 1916. COUIN.

Through a lucky combination of circumstances I am able to proceed on leave on Wednesday, and shall arrive at Waterloo on Friday at about 10 o'clock as before. The Adjutant asked me this morning if I would like to go either to-morrow or Wednesday, and I decided, of course, to do so while leave was still open.

THIRD LEAVE. 10 Days.

May 27th, 1916. CANDAS.

I have just got back after the usual terrible train journey from Havre, starting at 5 a.m. this morning and arriving here 9 p.m. But we have had an excellent dinner and to-night I shall get a comfortable bed and shall motor over with two friends to the Battalion to-morrow. You need not worry about me for at least a fortnight; this should cheer you all up. If anything we are likely to go still further back during the next month.

June 1st, 1916. ONEUX.

Please forgive my not writing for so long, but we have had two very busy days. Yesterday at 3.30 a.m. we paraded at Beauval and marched eighteen or nineteen miles to this place, which we reached about noon; the men stood it splendidly and we only had very few casualties.

I think that we shall probably be here about three or four days for training and that we shall then move on somewhere else for another four or five days; then back to Beauval, and thence I suppose to the trenches unless something unexpected happens to prevent it.

June 4th, 1916. AGENVILLIERS.

Here we are in another village about three or four miles away from the last and in a very comfortable billet. I have secured an excellent bed in a nice big clean room next door to the Mess.

Yesterday we had a big practice attack from 6

in the morning till 12 noon, and afterwards I arranged with a friend to go into Abbeville, but was unable to get a horse. We walked as far as St. Riquier, where we tried to catch the local train for Abbeville, but it had just gone and the cows had been turned out on to the line again for the next twenty-four hours. So we contented ourselves with looking at the church, which is remarkably fine, and buying food for the Mess.

Eight new officers have arrived; fortunately my old friend Carew Hunt, who has been ill, has now returned and is again posted to our Company with one other officer, so we are now seven and I have given up my Platoon and am doing Second-in-Command's work only.

Did you see that Conny has been awarded the Military Cross? I am delighted. Do write and congratulate him.

We shall be going back towards trench-land in about the second week of June, but just now anything may happen. At present we are thirty miles away.

Our new Commanding Officer[1] has just arrived, but I have not yet seen him.

June 9th, 1916. AGENVILLIERS.

I feel rather a wretch for failing to write yesterday but really this " training " is beyond a joke. Yesterday we were out from 1 p.m. to 9 pm.—soaked through to the skin; this morning we were up again at 5 a.m. and have just come in at 1 p.m.

To-morrow we march twenty miles starting at

[1] Lt.-Col. A. J. N. Bartlett, D.S.O., 52nd Light Infty., late Adjutant Bucks Battalion, commanded with intervals until the end of the War.

4 a.m. on our way back to the trenches; we are to do about fourteen miles the next day; we then bivouac, reach the trenches on the third day and *REST* at last.

Maurice Edmunds has just been gazetted Captain and to-night we are having a dinner party to celebrate it.

Since I gave up the Mess Presidency we have fed like Gadarene swine on ration beef and tinned fruit without alternation. To-night two other gastronomic experts and myself have done our best to produce an eatable dinner. Herewith the menu:—

Consommé
Œufs à la poche aux petits pois
Gigot de Mouton
Choux Fleurs: Pommes nouvelles
Omelette au confiture
Sardines aux anchois
Dessert. Fraises, à la crème
Café.

I do hope that the cook won't make a muck of things.

June 12th, 1916. HÉBUTERNE, G Sector Trenches.

This paper and the pencil tell their own tale, I expect; at any rate we are back peacefully in the trenches under wintry conditions, thanks to perpetual rain, and are thoroughly tired out after two days of hard marching and a week of this beastly training. We marched sixteen miles the first day, as I said in my note of yesterday, and about nineteen yesterday, arriving in the vicinity of the front exhausted. I slept uncomfortably in a tent last night and was up at 7 a.m.: I had an egg and then came the weary march up to these vile trenches, which I reached about midday. From 12 to 3 Edmunds and I have been wandering all round the most filthy muddy trenches putting the men into their places, looking at bombs and ammunition, etc., in fact doing all the work which the new officers have not yet learnt.

In the short month we have been away everything has changed amazingly and it isn't difficult to see what is going on.

June 21st, 1916. HÉBUTERNE.

I am rather pleased with myself this morning as our Company cooker has just won a competition which was judged by Alan Gibson. This is a feather in my cap, as I was responsible.

June 23rd, 1916. Camp near COUIN.

Life is very busy just now and everyone is on the " qui vive." I am enjoying the excitement.

I am now commanding the Company for an indefinite period. This morning the new Colonel had a talk with me; he said that I was very young, but that he had himself once commanded a company when he was the same age, though not on active service. Thank God the responsibility doesn't worry me and seems to give me a new interest in life; but it may be rather a trying ordeal at first.

June 29th, 1916. Camp near COUIN.

I am a wretch for writing so little at such a time as this, but really I am off my head with work, trying to supply my Company (200 strong) with everything from iron rations, wire-cutters and bomb bags to waterproof sheets and Balaclava helmets.

I too am loaded. I have to carry *six* maps, a huge field telegraph book of forms, and a large sort of musical comedy watch supplied by Government to be carried by the Company Commander. But remembering Lord Napier, I am taking nothing besides these official things, except a tooth-brush and my iron rations. Everything else will be left behind and I expect lost. I shall manage to put my Burberry coat on to the back of my horse.

Yesterday I was out riding from 6.45 to 8 a.m., then again from 9 a.m. till 3 p.m. with an interval for lunch. It simply deluged with rain, but we had to spy out the country and find cross-country tracks to avoid using the road. God knows what it will be like when we move, as the tracks are already deep in mud. Everyone is extremely busy and to-night we are sending a raiding party of fifty men and two officers up to the trenches to discover what the Bosche is feeling like after four days' steady bombardment.

BATTLE OF THE SOMME.

June 30th, 1916.   Camp near COUIN.

To-morrow I believe will see the lifting of the curtain on one of the biggest shows in the war. You can imagine what we are feeling like here. Our raiding party got off last night with no casualties, as they couldn't penetrate the German wire at all. Crowds of Hun prisoners are being captured already and seem glad to be caught. I don't wonder at it; we have been giving them hell for about a week both night and day, and there's plenty more to come.

I really think it ought to be a great success this time. You will have to excuse me if I don't write much, but I am so very busy and in these beastly draughty bivouacs there isn't room to sneeze; at present I am sprawling over the luncheon table with my writing pad on someone's valise.

July 2nd, 1916.   Field behind MAILLY MAILLET.

I don't know when you will receive this letter, but I hope it won't take long. I cannot give you much news, but the great battle began yesterday, as you probably know by now.

We were moved yesterday to our allotted position— a large field behind Mailly Maillet. I rode over with the Battalion and was never so thankful for a horse. The march was very hot and dusty, but the various pieces of news received *en route* of the capture of villages and of different positions bucked the men up tremendously. It was a wonderful sight to watch the guns and ammunition limbers galloping up into action. We met motor ambulances bringing back the wounded, and the excitement became intense when some Hun prisoners passed us. Having reached our field we made our preparations to move into the inferno at any moment: meanwhile we listened to the din and watched the heavy guns firing.

Night came and we dossed down with a waterproof sheet and a mackintosh: it was miserably cold and the noise became worse than ever. However, I warmed myself up with a tot of rum and got a little sleep.

We breakfasted at 6 a.m. and are now waiting for news!

All the wounded who are coming back are carefully

interrogated by inquisitive Tommies, but reports are very conflicting and we can't make out what has actually happened immediately in front of us, though I am afraid we have a lot more work to do over again. I should think, from the quiet which, but for casual shelling, now prevails that there will have to be a further bombardment before any more progress can be made. We had good news from the French last night, but it is difficult to make out what has actually happened.

I am awfully glad that I have survived to take part in this show. What a tremendous experience it is, and what a change from the old life.

Six more officers turned up last night from England, attached to us from the Middlesex Regiment. I have now eight under me—so we are pretty full up; as a matter of fact only twenty-two officers out of the forty will be allowed to go into action with the Battalion when we move from here.

Thank Heaven the weather is splendid and looks as if it will keep fine. I only hope it does.

I am feeling very fit in spite of the load we are carrying. We are more like Christmas trees than ever: two bombs per man; tin discs on our backs; white tabs with a number on our fronts; wire-cutters and wire breakers; tools and sand-bags; maps and note-books.

I have managed to glean these few sheets of paper from a friend, but for the next few days or even weeks most of my letters will probably be written on message or telegraph forms. But do not worry: I shall get off some sort of letter or card whenever it is humanly possible.

P.S.—We have just had our orders for to-morrow; it will be a great day in my life; if I live, I shall never forget dawn on July 3rd, 1916. Don't expect another letter for a day or two—writing will be quite impossible.

July 3rd, 1916.   Field behind MAILLY MAILLET.

Quite safe still after a most mixed affair last night. As I told you, we started off about 6 p.m. full of buck for the fight. We had a march of about three or four miles up to the trenches. I had my horse and he stood the roaring and banging splendidly and didn't care a bit when guns went off under his nose. We finally got into position for the night in a sunken road in front of our guns, which were making a colossal noise. Here we prepared to wait until the dawn; but at midnight we suddenly had orders to fall in and march back to our original position. Apparently the Huns had retired from the trenches in front and to the right of us, and the other troops which had such a hot time two days ago had walked into the trenches which we were ordered to capture.

At present all is rumour; we have no definite news though the battle still seems to be going on.

July 4th, 1916.   Bivouacs near COUIN.

Another curious development. Yesterday, after writing to you, we had orders to march back to our original place of bivouac seven miles away, which we did in a boiling heat and on dusty roads. It was awful for the men and I felt it myself very much though I only marched for one stage, during which I put my groom up as he has very bad flat feet. Also I sprained my ankle last night again, which gave me considerable pain this morning. I have had it bound up very tightly and painted with iodine.

I suppose you noticed in the papers that on the left of the British attack we met with very strong resistance north of the Ancre. That was our front. To-night I believe we shall be sent up to relieve a broken Division in the line; at least there is a very strong rumour to that effect. We are not so optimistic now about the battle, as we seem to have stopped now and to be held up as has always happened before.

July 5th, 1916.　　　　　　　　　HÉBUTERNE, G Sector.

Here we are again, back in the trenches, or rather the canals, as the water is over our knees. My Company Commander has returned, so I am now again Second-in-Command. There is no news of the battle except that the French are supposed to have captured Peronne, which is very important. In front of us everything is again quiet, as we seem to have come up against something unpleasantly strong. there. We are now waiting for better news from the south.

July 6th, 1916.　　　　　　　　　HÉBUTERNE Trenches.

Many thanks for your letter of July 1st, which I see was written just before you received news of the great battle.

The papers have come out with huge headlines:—
" Attacks on Gommecourt," which is described as the " most heroic deed of the War." This has amused us very much, as we are sitting nearly opposite the beastly place.

The return to trench life is perfectly exasperating, though we are told it is only temporary and is not to be regarded as ordinary trench warfare. The Bosche opposite is quite subdued; all his trenches and engines of destruction have been destroyed and wrecked by our bombardment. But of course our own trenches are also in a pretty bad state and have been badly knocked about.

A small German village opposite us has been levelled by our bombardment and all the trees which up to a few days ago completely sheltered it have been stripped by gun-fire. In front of it we can see lying out the bodies of our own men, and there are rumours that some of our people are still holding the place, as we actually captured it at one point in the battle; but I am afraid that by now they have all been taken prisoner or killed. According to the authorities the Germans were expecting the main English blow to fall at this point, which explains the number of Divisions which we came up against.

July 8th, 1916. HÉBUTERNE.

This is the most depressing time I have ever spent in France: nothing but ceaseless heavy rain—the trenches are like rivers and are falling down when they are not shelled down. The guns never stop day or night and we can hear the devil of a battle going on at the moment just south of us, though things are quiet where we are. But we are only waiting to be at it again, and the sooner the better. I am absolutely fed up with trench warfare, especially now when we thought it was over.

I heard from Conny last night; he was very anxious about the Battalion. The village he mentions is an old enemy of ours and our dead now lying in front of it between the lines testify unmistakably to the fierceness of the fight they put up though they couldn't hold it. Yesterday one poor devil crawled into our trenches in an appalling state: he was wounded in three places and had been lying out for five days. The doctor thinks he will live all right, though he will probably lose his arm through poisoning.

I think we shall probably be relieved to-morrow, so don't worry; look out for the next fighting north of the Ancre.

July 9th, 1916.   Bivouacs behind SAILLY.

We were relieved at 6 o'clock this morning by a sister Battalion, and although now a dismounted officer,[1] I succeeded in wangling my sprained ankle and borrowed a horse from a friend who doesn't like riding: I was thus saved a three-mile trudge over mud-sodden country. In the whole course of my time out here I have never known the trenches worse: it poured tropically for three days, and the men came out caked in thick yellow mud from head to foot. Their feet had not been dry for four nights and they could scarcely walk. Now we are in bivouacs as before and have been ordered to send five hundred men out to-night to work in the trenches. Lord knows how they will do it.

I am told that the betting in London is six to four on the war being over before November 1st. But I still see no reason to suppose that it won't go on for at least another year: we cannot hope to drive the Germans back at one blow and they will undoubtedly fight bravely to the bitter end. However, the unexpected usually happens, in war as in most things.

[1] Brooks returned from Hospital and took over command of the Company.

July 14th, 1916. HÉBUTERNE.

I must write off a line to you to-night, as I may not get a chance to-morrow. I think that we shall leave these trenches about 1 o'clock to-morrow morning for more exciting scenes.

Our Army Commander, Sir Henry Rawlinson, says that the biggest success of the whole show has been scored to-day—the advance to Longueval and Bazentin—and now the Armée de Chasse may get on the move.

If it is true that the Indian Cavalry are in action we shall have an exciting time of it.

Thank Heaven we are to be taken out of the trenches: I wouldn't miss this show for anything.

July 16th, 1916. HÉBUTERNE, G Sector.

We are still in the trenches but are being relieved by an entirely new crowd this afternoon. It is now pretty certain that we shall move off almost immediately. This is tremendous news about Bazentin le Petit. If only we can hold these places against counter-attacks. . . .

Yesterday afternoon I had a good look at the battle-field of July 1st through a telescope at a splendid observation post. It was a very interesting sight: it lies just to the right of us; the whole plain sloping up to a village called Serre held by the Germans is visible; our troops attacked it after six days' bombardment, and after getting into the village were driven back to their original trenches. Heaps of their bodies are still lying out there unburied, but the Huns and ourselves have been sending out stretcher parties each night.

The three lines of German trenches in front of the village are absolutely shattered and are almost levelled; their thick wire is absolutely wrecked, but their machine guns did appalling damage in spite of everything. The village itself is one mass of ruins with a few gaunt trees standing up; before the battle it was thickly wooded and almost invisible. Far away to the right I could see our guns shelling a large German railway centre well behind the line—a good sight.

July 19th, 1916. BOUZINCOURT.

The regiment did an attack last night. At 7.30 we got orders to move off at 8 through Albert to the trenches. The scheme was to take a German trench suspected of being occupied. My Company was in the attack, but I as second in command of the Company, stayed behind with seventeen other officers and five per cent. of the men, to act as reinforcements. This morning the Battalion marched back to this village, having done their attack, lost direction and got into an old communication trench full of dead Germans. They fell back on the English front trench, a ditch with no cover at all, and were shelled for two or three hours while they tried to dig themselves in. Each of the three companies (the fourth was in reserve) had about thirty to thirty-five casualties, about eighteen killed and the remainder wounded. No officers were knocked out though two were cut about the face with shrapnel: the men are dead beat.

I saw a few Hun prisoners wounded and lying on stretchers this morning just next to our lines. They looked on the verge of starvation and collapse, as indeed they were; they had been for three or four days without food in their deep dug-outs. But plenty of them are getting killed all right, and our casualties are not so enormous when you consider the armies which we have now got. Only one army out of four is at present concerned in this great battle. All the three northern armies are peacefully carrying on trench warfare.

July 20th, 1916. BOUZINCOURT.

The Battalion went off last night and are in bivouacs the other side of Albert; they were not in last night's fighting, which I regret to say was another failure and rather a costly one for our sister regiments. A great friend of mine, Fream, of the Gloucesters was killed. He had been instructor at the Brigade Bomb School for nearly twelve months and had just returned to his regiment.

I am riding up this afternoon to see the Battalion with the Padre, who is a thorough sportsman and good rider. I'm afraid this is going to be an unpleasant little corner for a bit; already it has proved very expensive. I think that some time this evening our people will probably relieve one of the Battalions who were in it last night. I am still among the non-combatants, very bored with life, with nothing whatever to do except to wait for bad news.

July 22nd, 1916. BOUZINCOURT.

There is little to report except that I am still living in comfort back here while the regiment is bivouacked nearer the trenches: another small attack was made last night and again failed. They will have a further go at it to-night on a larger scale.

I enjoyed my ride with the Padre yesterday very much; it was a most glorious afternoon. We rode up to a high ridge from which we could overlook the whole battle-field and see the remains of Bazentin le Petit and Ovillers la Boisselle. It is an extraordinary sight, absolute ruin and desolation and not a foot of wall standing anywhere in the last-named village. Shells of all sizes were bursting over the country, but nothing much was doing as we are busy getting the guns up.

I don't entirely share your optimism about a march on Berlin; the days for such gallivanting have departed; but I think that the Russians will soon be back on German soil if we can continue hammering here, and that should make a great difference. Also I cannot help thinking that the Germans will soon have to fall back a considerable distance to shorten their front. At the same time their resistance is extremely tenacious and they have plenty of machine guns, which, when properly handled, can hold up armies. This is indeed no exaggeration and you would despair of ever making a big advance, especially with cavalry, if you could see the way in which troops are mown down by these little devils, worked by three brave men.

Somewhat dejected-looking Huns keep coming in, mostly starving and wounded: some of them have wounds which have not been dressed for three or four days, during which they have had no food. Artillery fire is ceaseless all night but is much quieter by day. It is an extraordinary sort of battle and I wouldn't have missed it for anything. I think we shall soon enter upon another violent phase. I hope so, as one cannot stand still—it is fatal.

July 23rd, 1916.   BOUZINCOURT.

I have just walked round to the Field Ambulance Station where the motor ambulances unload their wounded. There I saw one or two of our fellows who say that our Division has gained its objective all right, but I am afraid that some Battalions have been practically wiped out. Our own must have suffered very heavily if our men's casualties bear any relation to those of the officers.

Four of us and the Padre are back here and I expect we shall go up any moment now. There was only one officer left in my Company early this morning, as Maurice Edmunds sent a note down to let us know who had been hit. Since then I believe we have advanced even farther. The Anzacs have gone right through and, according to all accounts, have taken Pozières.

Apparently the first line of attack met with very stubborn resistance from machine guns, but the second line found no resistance from the Huns in front who surrendered. I saw a young German officer who was wounded; he said that our bombardment before this last attack was too heavy for them and that the noise was something colossal.

Last night I walked out towards the hills behind Albert, from which the whole front appeared as one bright illumination of flashes of all sizes, with German star shells going up in hundreds. At midnight the bombardment became intense and every gun for miles round was firing.

July 24th, 1916. BOUZINCOURT.

The regiment has returned this evening to camp: Brooks, who was commanding my Company, has been killed; two other officers were wounded and all the N.C.O.'s except the Company Sergeant-Major and four lance-corporals; the strength was sixty-three men instead of one hundred and fifty. But the men, thank God, are in tremendous spirits. Still it is sad work looking at the gaps and trying to make up the casualty returns.

Only five men seem actually to have been killed in my Company, but a number are missing, though a great many of the wounded have been got in. I have much to do writing letters and trying to get what evidence I can from the few men left. Although no one saw Brooks killed, there is little doubt that he was.

One Company returned with no officers, and the other two with three and two apiece instead of four. However, the fight goes on well; there are more attacks to-night, and the men have got their tails up properly. We still have three hundred odd and with a new draft we shall soon, I expect, be in it again.

July 26th, 1916. ARQUÈVES.

Here we are once more on the " trek," marching away from the great battle; yesterday afternoon we came into this village, about ten miles back, at 4 o'clock and I found some quite good billets for the Company in barns. It is a fairly large place and plenty of " doulay " and " oofs " for the men. I succeeded after a lot of hunting round in persuading an old girl to take in my three officers and myself in one small but well-furnished room with one bed in it.

We had an excellent high tea after our servant had entered and taken possession of the stove, a sort of household god which every cottager and farmer possesses, and which occupies a conspicuous position, brightly polished, in the middle of the parlour-kitchen.

We thought that we were going on this morning, but we are not moving till to-morrow morning: however, now that I am again mounted, these marches do not worry me at all. We are going back to Beauval and I hope we may get the same billets. We are, of course, very much reduced, but plenty of Derbyites may turn up at any moment to fill the gaps and then I expect we shall go back to the line.

Things are going pretty well, but slowly and steadily; you mustn't expect too much at first, as every step has to be fought, won, consolidated and then held against fierce counter-attacks. The Hun is still going strong and is up to every devilry imaginable. During our attack, while our men were pressing on, two men were seen to light and throw smoke bombs, shouting "Gas! Retire! Put your smoke helmets on." These ruses still work very successfully, and the other day a regiment retired at the order of a German without knowing it. I was told by a friend this morning that two German officers were captured, one with the watch and the other with the revolver of my poor friend Fream. I don't think either of them lived very long: feelings run a bit too high to make the unwounded prisoner's lot a happy one. A whole crowd who came towards our own trenches with their hands up were mown down by their own machine guns as well as ours.

July 29th, 1916. AGENVILLE.

We have been constantly on the march for three days. First back to a small village from which I last wrote to you and where we stayed one day: then from there to Beauval, the large town where the Battalion was taken at the end of May while I was on leave: this to the immense joy of everyone, especially when we heard that we were going to the identical billets we had vacated over a month ago. The civilians were delighted and rushed into the men's arms, demanding stories of their battles and doings and asking after all the missing faces.

Unfortunately we only stayed there one night and moved again this morning at 8 o'clock for a five or six-hour march under a broiling sun. The dust and heat were terrible, but I was simply delighted with my Company: only four men fell out, all absolutely exhausted and whacked, three of whom had returned only the night before from hospital with trench fever and enteric. All the rest got in and are now lying absolutely fast asleep in the orchards of this pretty little village. I went round to see them just now, and except for a few who were having their feet tended by stretcher-bearers there wasn't a sound or movement. I marched for two stages, that is two stages of an hour each, and found it quite hot and unpleasant: it really is a triple blessing being mounted, especially when you get into billets and have to buzz round putting the different Platoons into their billets.

The officers' billets are rather inferior. We are billeted in an " estaminet " which was, of course, mobbed by our men on arrival; we didn't go into it until they were turned out at 2 o'clock by the military police. We had some excellent omelettes there and have evidently found favour in the eyes of the owners, who are a very decent lot: a cheery old man and his wife, equally cheery daughters and some pretty little kids, who filled our laps with tame rabbits during our *déjeuner*. I have a most clean and pleasant room with large bed and sheets. Carew Hunt, again returned to us, has another bed in the same room and my three other officers sleep upstairs. We mess in another house next door, and I think we shall be very comfortable.

The weather is glorious, I am very well satisfied with life in general and have got some nice officers in the Company with me: all ranks in the Battalion are on good terms with each other: altogether things are going well and it only wants a little leave to start to make everyone thoroughly contented.

July 31st, 1916. AGENVILLE.

I am enjoying the job of training up a new company from the wrecks of the old and am fortunate to have four good platoon officers under me who are all really good fellows, though quite different:—

CAREW HUNT: Was at Merton: is an excellent Mess President: speaks French fluently and secures wines, pigeons, salads and fruit with the greatest ease.
C. LAKIN: Was at B.N.C. Very competent.
PEARSON: A typical schoolboy: full of go and brave and keen.
KING: An attached boy from the Middlesex Regiment: very very young, but not a bad kid.

Altogether we are quite a happy family and the C.O. and Second-in-Command, Captain Schomberg of the East Surreys, both regulars, are also very popular and good soldiers: so I think we shall do well in the future.

August 2nd, 1916. AGENVILLE.

The vile old beast from whom we rent our Mess is a thoroughly Zola-like character with a bottle of rum always under his arm: I call him Dubosc. He provokes the most horrible scenes, wandering in sideways with unkempt beard, filthy old clothes and raucous voice. We all exclaim that we have most important business and must talk of " les affaires," but he points at one officer reading the *Tatler* and another eating gooseberries and flies into a passion.

But yesterday it seems that we bought some salad and fruit from a woman who turns out to be a cousin and arch-enemy against whom he has a vendetta. He rampaged into the house, swore he wouldn't have the woman near the " estate," flew round gesticulating and expostulating and said that we had only to ask for anything and he would get it for us himself. Finally, I got so annoyed that I told him to go to the devil or I should have an escort in. I told him that he must make all complaints to Monsieur le Baron as we call Carew Hunt. At this he disappeared, murmuring apologies.

However, he came back later with an enormous goose flapping under his arm. Carew Hunt, to pacify the old beast and get rid of him, signified that he would buy it, on which he suddenly whipped a small pocket knife out and cut off its head in the middle of the room. He is a proper old swine and is at his best when lying flat on his face incapable.

August 8th, 1916. AGENVILLE.

Our pleasant holiday in this village is drawing to a close and to-morrow we move to a destination at present unknown. This may mean many things and I will not speculate upon whether we are going forward or backward. At any rate we have had a very good rest; the men are much refreshed and the new drafts are settling down. To-morrow's march will test their real strength. But although we shall never see such lads again as the ones who came out at the beginning of last year and who are mostly gone now, these fresh men have something of the same keenness.

I have given Carew Hunt standing orders that two presentable guests are to be invited to dinner every night: he is quite up to it and we have had excellent dinners since we have been here, mostly cooked in the French style and without any recourse to bully beef or even to ration meat. He is a perfect marvel as Mess President and I trust we shall keep him.

August 12th, 1916. BOUZINCOURT, SOMME.

Here we are again back in the area of " The Big Push " just where we were a fortnight ago.

This little village, which is the sort of ante-chamber to the Chamber of Horrors beyond, presents a scene of intense activity—troops of all kinds, lorries, guns and supplies, all going the same way.

We were bivouacked on arrival and only supplied

with the waterproof sheets without sticks for putting them up. However, I sent off the whole Company to cut sticks and we soon had a little encampment up. Unfortunately the Bosche started shelling us at long range, which frightened our Brigade and they ordered us to move camp further back, which we did with much grumbling.

We expect to go up and relieve some troops tonight or to-morrow. It will be very nasty, but it can't be helped. Meanwhile I am busy seeing that gas helmets, goggles and iron rations are all complete in my Company.

August 13th, 1916. OVILLERS Trenches, SOMME.

In the midst of the most ghastly surroundings I can only bring myself to write you a mere line.

I have just taken over some trenches, such as they are, full of equipment, filth and bodies and am being heavily shelled. I have had four casualties already, one killed and three wounded: my poor men are rather windy I am afraid, and I can't really blame them as most of them have only been three months in the army and this is their first introduction to the trenches.

The village we passed through just now is literally abolished, absolutely flat, not a sign even of a wall and the stink is awful.

The Huns are in a miserable state, absolutely craven and disheartened: some prisoners have just passed down the trench, rotten specimens. But they have a devil of a lot of guns here which give us hell.

One of my boys has just come down rather badly

wounded and whimpering, but he will be all right directly he gets back to the dressing station.

August 14th, 1916. OVILLERS Trenches, SOMME.

I have seldom felt such a miserable wreck. I have had my boots on since 8 a.m. of the day before yesterday and have had no hot food for thirty-six hours, only a small piece of bread and cheese and a hunk of melted chocolate.

We were heavily shelled all yesterday without a stop and I had a few more casualties. The bombardment increased in violence about 9 p.m. and the Germans attacked our front line, the garrison of which had been hopelessly reduced by the afternoon's shelling and by our own shells falling short. Our men were driven out and back, and receiving an urgent message for reinforcements and bombs, I sent up two of my subalterns with their Platoons and two bombs a man. They appear to have lost their way and couldn't find anyone except the Anzacs, who were also having the devil of a time.

I then got a message from King that they believed the trench in front of them was occupied by the Germans, and the next thing I saw was the boy himself, with his whole face bathed and streaked in gore and roughly bandaged. He said that Lakin, my Second-in-Command, was killed and that a good many of the men were casualties. I passed him on to the dressing station and then went round to Battalion headquarters to get some information. I was told to remain in my trench and hold it with the remaining Platoons of my Company, reinforced by a party of Berkshires who had turned up carrying bombs.

Later I saw Pickford—who had been in charge of the front line all day. He said he has lost nearly all his Company and all his officers—among them Leslie Hunter, a Wykhamist and a Fellow of New College who has only just joined us.

I got my officer out: he was wounded in the head and leg and was suffering very severely indeed from shock.

The Berks counter-attacked the trench at 4 a.m. to try to regain it and I was present at their conference at my Company headquarters just before. I don't know what has happened to them, but a friend of mine, commanding one of the Companies, has been killed and another badly wounded. I believe they are having a pretty bad time of it up there.

The Bosche is still shelling us, but not quite so heavily.

I took over as my Headquarters a deep German mine shaft, but it isn't a very good place and I have chosen instead a narrow little sap running out of the main trench—as safe as anywhere can be, I think. The whole place simply reeks, and I am filthy from head to foot. I am hoping we may be relieved to-night or early to-morrow morning, as this will be our third night without sleep and some of the men are rather ill I'm afraid. Carew Hunt and I are the only officers in the Company at present, but I have one lad whom I left behind on a machine gun course and who will rejoin afterwards.

Your letter quite cheered up the whole evening when it unexpectedly arrived yesterday amidst this awful desolation. I can't describe the awful destruction and the litter and waste: shattered trenches and dug-outs with equipment, bodies, food, bombs and rifles everywhere. But I hope to be out of it to-night: if so I will write and tell you.

August 15th, 1916.   Reserve Trenches behind OVILLERS,
SOMME.

Out of it again and thankful for small mercies.

After writing my yesterday's letter to you we settled down to the most awful hell of shelling I have ever been in. I thought I should have to take my men up to the front line and relieve our other Company there, but by the grace of God they arranged for another Battalion to relieve us at 2 a.m. From 11.30 a.m. to 2.30 p.m. the Germans shelled like the devil with big stuff; it was a most trying ordeal; I was in a shaft full of filth and flies with my servant, bugler, sergeant-major and a wounded man (with a huge gash in his back and wounded in the leg), a stretcher-bearer and anyone who happened to blow in. The wounded man was very good and cheerful though his arm was nearly off and his lung pierced.

We spent the time getting hold of iodine and dressings and trying to patch up his wounds. Finally, the other Battalion came up and I began to pass my men out of the trench back through what is left of the village of Ovillers.

The trench was all blown in and littered with filth and bodies. I think the awful stench is much worse than the shelling. My men told me that this thirty-six hours in the trench was far worse than their attack on July 23rd. But I had only twenty-two casualties in my Company and two officers wounded.

Lakin is very seriously wounded and King rather seriously.

Hunter was seen to be hit and is either a prisoner or dead, probably the latter. He will be a great loss, as he was a most brilliant man and a splendid officer. Another Company Commander, Willie Wayman, is missing and probably killed, and two other officers wounded slightly. The regiment had nearly one hundred and forty casualties I'm afraid—of course a few men are still unaccounted for.

We found our cookers, with tea waiting behind Ovillers. There I formed my Company up and called the roll. A groom came up to me as I emerged from the trenches, saluted and said: " Would you like a horse? " Of course I was delighted: they hadn't brought my own up but I got the Padre's—a little polo pony full of buck, but I was so delighted to get on again and not to have had to walk a step further that I would have ridden anything.

It was curious to ride all through our old line of trenches and the old German front line. The Huns have already got a superiority of artillery here and give our people the most ghastly time of it; they know the exact range of all our trenches as they are their old ones. However, each night we push on a bit somewhere; unfortunately it is very expensive.

We are now back in some trenches cut in the chalk hills instead of bivouacking in the bare field which was allotted to us. I slept as soundly as I have ever done till 12 o'clock this morning and now feel as cheerful as possible.

August 17th, 1916.   SKYLINE Trench, OVILLERS, SOMME.

You wouldn't be able to conceive the filthy and miserable surroundings in which I am writing this note—not even if you were accustomed to the filthiest slums in Europe.

I am sitting in the bottom of an old German dug-out about ten or twelve feet under the earth with three other officers and about ten men, orderlies and runners; the table is littered with food, equipment, candle grease and odds and ends. The floor is covered with German clothing and filth. The remains of the trench outside is blown to pieces, and full of corpses from the different regiments which have been here lately, German and English. The ground is ploughed up by enormous shell-holes; there isn't a single landmark to be seen for miles except a few gaunt sticks where trees once were. The stench is well-nigh intolerable, but thank God I have just found the remains of a tube of frozacalone Bridge sent out, which I have rubbed under my nose. Everyone is absolutely worn out with fatigue and hunger.

Yesterday while trying to find the regiment we were relieving, I was very slightly wounded by a piece of shrapnel to the left of my left eye. It knocked me over and stunned me a bit, but was only a flesh wound and is healed now except for a bruise.

I wandered on round these awful remains of trenches with my bugler, simply sickened by the sights and smells, until I found some poor devils cowering in the filth, where they had been for forty-eight hours. I moved them back. Soon after this I felt rather dizzy and went back to Battalion headquarters where the Colonel was very kind and made me lie down on a German bed for a rest. Later in the afternoon I went down to the doctor, who has a fine dressing station in a huge German dug-out. There I rested and spent the night and came back here this morning.

Thank Heaven we are due to be relieved in an hour or two, when we shall go back to some trenches behind, though they will, of course, be only comparatively better. To-morrow morning I hope the whole regiment will be relieved and go back.

I will knock off now and continue after the relief is over, if it comes up. I hope this may get off with our ration party to-night.

I shall never look on warfare either as fine or sporting again. It reduces men to shivering beasts: there isn't a man who can stand shell-fire of the modern kind without getting the blues. The Anzacs are fine fellows, but they say Gallipoli was a garden party to this show.

August 18th, 1916.   AVELOY, SOMME.

Back to civilisation tired out but joyful: filthy but safe.

Received three days' post just now and delighted!

I will write at length when I have had some food and sleep.

I think we may get a rest now.

This " pushing " is a little too hot.

August 22nd, 1916.   Reserve Trenches, USNA Redoubt, SOMME.

As we have returned to the region of trenches, I find I must use up my valuable Field Message Book for writing-paper.

Last night just as we were going to sit down to a good dinner—two guests—a message came through ordering us to parade in fighting order as soon as possible. There was the usual hurry and skurry and half an hour later we moved off into the night on our way back to the line.

However, we were stopped at our old halting-place about two or three miles behind the battle and put up for the night in some old dug-outs and gun-pits where we had been before two days ago. We were in divisional reserve and got a night's sleep all right, but no baggage or food came up till this morning. Now we have been told to be ready to move at a moment's notice—direction not stated, but certainly forward I expect. I think we shall only be up for two or three days more at the most, but am afraid we shall have to put in another day or so in the front trenches. However, you never know your luck, so don't worry.

I don't suppose I can possibly get this off this morning, but will leave it with my cooks, who stay behind when we move.

There have been slight outbreaks of dysentery here among the men, which is rather annoying, but nothing serious.

August 23rd, 1916. OVILLERS Trenches.

Here I am again seated about thirty feet down in a late German residence surrounded with maps and papers and trying to convey to Battalion headquarters what piece of captured German trench I am holding.

But really it is most difficult to discover where one is: the ground is honeycombed with old trenches and maps are published every day, each giving different versions. Of course the situation changes every hour owing to small attacks and bombing stunts—in fact everything is loathsomely unsettled compared to the dear quiet old days of proper trench warfare.

You can scarcely hear a sound at the bottom of these mined shafts except a dull booming. The stink is rather bad, but these trenches are a positive paradise compared to the ones next door which we had before, no corpses and comparatively deep and clean.

I really hope we shall go back after this tour for a rest: this is our third go in and quite enough.

I am bucked to death with my lads though I have got a poor chap who has suddenly gone groggy with shell-shock. He can't keep his hands still and waggles them the whole time. I have brought him down here and he is buried somewhere in the depths of the dug-out.

I have just had to interrupt this letter on receiving three messages from the Adjutant and a visit from a strange officer who wanted to find some obscure trench in my area in order to do some digging at 1 o'clock to-morrow morning. I was up at 3.45 this morning in order to go round with the Colonel and look at the trenches, and of course I shall be up all night to-night and probably to-morrow night as well; you can imagine one gets slightly fatigued. Living on bread and jam and bully, lemonade and water, doesn't make one's spirits exactly bound; however, it's all in the day's work.

August 24th, 1916.   OVILLERS Trenches.

It is about twenty-four hours since I last wrote to you. We are still in these vile trenches and I am feeling rather more tired than before.

Thank Heaven we had a quiet night and day, but of course I was up all the time receiving and sending messages until I dropped asleep over the table. All I can get to eat are dog biscuits (rations), which are very hard, but still do fill up the gaps.

I have been relieved from the responsibility of the front line and am just a little bit further back in another flea-invested German dug-out. It isn't much of a change or rest and we shall have to work all night I think. There is a faint chance of relief to-morrow, but I am afraid only a faint one—and we shall probably have to stick twenty-four hours more of it.

Just on our left there is a strong point to which the Bosche is clinging passionately and our C.O. has determined that we have got to have it. Bombing goes on round it all the time and we are constantly withdrawing our men in order to shell the spot; but the Hun sticks there, and as our left Company can't make much of it we shall perhaps be given a try if there is no relief to-morrow.

But there is a strong rumour that we are to be relieved, and soon undoubtedly we shall be; I hope this time for good, as really we have had a bit of a " rough house " this time.

Your letters continue to arrive regularly with the rations even up here, which cheers me up tremendously, not that I am a bit depressed or downhearted: I never felt better in my life, though the surroundings are revolting.

August 25th, 1916.   OVILLERS Trenches, SOMME.

Still in the trenches for the third night and feeling filthy and tired.

Plagues of flies, but still going strong.

Hope to get relieved to-morrow.

I have run out of writing-paper and everything else.

This is a disgusting hole: if only the people at home could imagine a tenth of the vileness of this part of the world that figures so gloriously in all our cold official communiqués!

To-morrow's letter I hope will bring you good news.

August 26th, 1916.   Reserve Trenches behind OVILLERS, SOMME.

At last I can write to you in comparative safety again, though scarcely in peace or comfort.

After another night up in the trenches we were relieved at 8.30 this morning and got out of it without accident and I felt delighted with myself, especially when I found my horse waiting for me in the old spot, although we are only just in some rickety dug-outs and trenches about a mile behind. I can't tell you how tired and filthy we all are and hungry too—much too hungry to want to go to sleep at once.

Your dear anxious letter about my " wound " arrived in the trenches with a parcel containing—oh! sacred joy! a Fuller's cake and some Haversack chocolate which dropped like manna from Heaven in our midst. The cake reposed—a veritable Snow Queen—among the variegated litter of the German dug-out which was my headquarters—a huge place in which I was able to crowd forty men and which was most useful, as my stretcher-bearers were able to work there in safety. We had a comparatively quiet night and I only had about five casualties in all, together with a few shell-shock cases.

I had a lot of letters last night. Two of my late brother-officers have died of wounds, Newman Hall, who was wounded in the battle of July 23rd has died at Rouen, and now I have just heard that Lakin, who was my Second-in-Command, has also died, as I was afraid he would. I can't help feeling more and more like the survivor of some great disaster, when I look back a few weeks and remember that we had nine officers in this Company alone, and of them only myself and two others are left.

I must say that my two officers are the best I could have had: Carew Hunt is a marvel. Can you imagine a tall, very delicate man, suffering constantly from laryngitis and neuralgia, living more or less cheerfully up in this hell and taking patrols out into the outer darkness in search of vague Anzac regiments on our right; entirely devoted to the amenities of University life and respectable comfort, he has managed to throw himself entirely into this new and really horrible job: to me it is quite extraordinary.

My other officer, Pearson, is quite a lad and is really worth his weight in gold. He is exceedingly cool and brave, which is saying a lot now-a-days when the oldest and strongest of the soldiers get affected by the constant shelling: and he is very cheery and eager—just like a schoolboy. You would have loved to see him walking into your cake last night when he came in for a rest after four hours in the open trench. It went down splendidly with a dollop of rum and water. I should certainly like to recommend both these officers to the C.O.'s notice and I have already sent in a report on a young lance-corporal of mine who did some splendid work reconnoitring last night.

There has been a big attack again this afternoon, and as we are near the guns, the noise has been loud and incessant—but nothing will stop me from sleeping to-night.

I really don't think we shall be put back into these trenches again—we are so very reduced and exhausted, and are expecting in a day or two to go right back. I must really knock off now and have a little dinner before a blessed sleep—my first for four nights. I had quite a respectable beard this afternoon.

August 28th, 1916.   BOUZINCOURT, SOMME.

You remember how joyful I was when I last wrote to you yesterday. Well, that same evening just as I was waiting for the savoury to be brought in for dinner, I got an urgent order to parade my Company at once in fighting order and to proceed to the trenches. Can you imagine anything more hateful? We were tired out, we had at last got clean and we had hoped to have seen the last of the trenches for many days.

Two other regiments in our Brigade had, we knew, done an attack at 7 o'clock that evening; it was clear that our job would be to go and support them if not actually to take over the captured trench from their wearied soldiers, a most dangerous and unpleasant task.

We arrived panting hot after groping our way for miles and miles behind a guide along the old German trenches in the old nauseating surroundings and with plenty of shelling. I reported to the O.C. of the Gloucesters, an old friend of mine, a younger brother of their Colonel and actually Second-in-Command but who was now acting C.O. He told me to make my way to advanced headquarters and carry up bombs, lights, tools, aeroplane signals and rockets to the captured trench: to start a digging party on getting communication through to the captured trench and to hold myself in readiness for a German counter-attack, which was, of course, expected.

The trench was full of men, wounded and stretcher cases blocking the way, Bucks and Oxfords carrying bombs and tools, German prisoners being brought down, and runners trying to get through with messages.

I was up all night, but at 6 this morning I came back with the whole Brigade, the Division being at last relieved by an entirely new lot; so now we are at last free of this awful battle and to-morrow we hope to march away to quieter climes.

But you can imagine how I loathed that last long night in the trenches. I may add that the attack was a brilliant success and not very costly, though I am sorry to say I lost a friend of mine in the Gloucesters, Winterbotham, who was killed.

I see that I figure in *The Times* casualty list—what a ridiculous farce! And they call me " 2nd Lt.," much to everyone's amusement; it is really rather hard lines, as I am now entitled to put up a Captain's stars, having commanded the Company for over a month! In fact I suppose that in a day or two I shall be gazetted, as I think my name went in some time ago. The extra screw will be rather jolly, though, as there is no opportunity to spend it, I suppose I shall have to save it.

August 30th, 1916. Bus.

Here we are again back in a more normal part of France and only a mile or two from the village where we spent last winter so happily. Thank Heaven for small mercies; we are encamped in a wood in huts and tents. I am living in a tent with Carew Hunt and Pearson. We are messing alone; it is much pleasanter, as we get on so very well together.

It has poured with rain steadily all day, which makes life very cold and miserable. I have been writing reports for men whom I want to get decorated with the D.C.M. or Military Medal. Really my stretcher-bearers have done the best and I have very strongly recommended three of them, they have a perfectly awful time, as they have to be in the open trench the whole time dressing wounds and carrying the men off.

The battle is going awfully well, but very slowly and I am afraid we shan't do very much more this winter than capture Thiepval; at the same time I shouldn't be surprised at a sudden German retreat now that Roumania has come into the field. It must make an appreciable difference.

September 1st, 1916. Bus.

I am still enjoying a peaceful existence here; yesterday I had a jolly ride and revisited the scenes of our pleasant rests in the winter, when Marochetti, Conny and I used to have such good times; but it has been badly blown about now and all the civilians have been sent away since the Great Push.

We are really very comfortable here in our little tent; we feed outside in the open as the weather has improved. But it is a terrible thought that winter is nearly upon us—only one more month of rapidly fading summer and then the horrors of long black nights and wet days. I only wish something decisive would happen, but nothing does.

I should like to be able to take you up as far as those two captured villages which are now well behind our line—it is a perfectly marvellous sight; the ground is a mass of tangled wreckage—not even a wall to be seen—a village after capture is now simply a mass of bricks. We still talk of the church at Ovillers as a a meeting-point, but it is only the largest heap of bricks to be seen and stands about six or eight feet high. Huge masses of wire-stakes, equipment and rifles lie all over the place with clothing and uniforms. The mine craters caused by the explosion of underground mines are extraordinary sights.

The first attack on July 1st must have been an appalling affair. I shouldn't think many Huns lived through it without going mad. But to-day they think nothing of putting 20,000 shells on one small piece of trench which happens to be wanted; and now that the Hun hasn't got his deep dug-outs he is feeling the strain. You hardly ever hear now of any hand-to-hand fighting because when the infantry reach their objective the few remaining Bosche surrender at once. Some of them haven't had any food for four or five days owing to our incessant gun-fire. Altogether guns are getting too much of a good thing and will soon, in my opinion, make the work of infantrymen impossible. But that will not be till the next war I expect!

September 1st, 1916.   Bus.

This morning we were inspected by General Fanshawe, commanding the Division, and were complimented very highly on the doings of the last month. He ended by saying: " Of course we are going into it again, and this time we shall be fighting more in the open still with no trenches at all." All the same I am very much afraid that it will be a long time before we see any open fighting.

September 2nd, 1916.   Bus.

Early this morning, another very big battle started, with a prolonged bombardment of great intensity. After breakfast I rode over with a friend to see if I could find out about it. We went to a casualty clearing station where the wounded were coming in pretty thickly; two hundred and fifty had gone through already. There had been some pretty big attacks on a wide front and some more German territory had been captured.

We rode on to a small prisoners' camp and saw some of the captured Huns in devilish comfortable quarters, nice clean white tents and with good army rations. Those that work here always get bread while we, more unfortunate, often go without and have dog biscuits. Also they get 4*d.* a day, with which they can place orders with the Y.M.C.A. huts and canteens—and are supplied with paper and writing materials free from the Y.M.C.A. huts into the bargain. Many of the prisoners have been found with letters on them from friends who are prisoners in England in which they say how well they are treated.

The Prussian Guards are no better than the other troops once you get at them: we had them up against us, and though the prisoners we got were certainly for the most part very fine men physically, the best troops can't stand the awful strain of acting on the defensive against modern artillery fire.

One German who came down the trench the last night I was up after the attack suddenly saw a dirty bit of old bread while he was waiting outside the officers' dug-out, made a grab at it and hogged it off in about two seconds. One of the men called out: " Hullo! Fritz! What cheer! " or something of the sort and he replied: " Angleterre bon." They are very sick when they hear that they are not going back to England, but are being kept for work in France. They are a rum crowd, but pretty human when they have got off their high horse and have had a bit of a rough time.

September 5th, 1916.   AUCHONVILLERS Trenches, opposite BEAUMONT-HAMEL.

Here we are snugly ensconced in some first-rate trenches, quiet, clean and deep with plenty of dug-outs. We are only in as a stop-gap and, as I hope, for a fairly short time—so please don't worry.

There is a little village behind us, though nothing is left of it except a few cellars into which some of our men are going. Personally I think it is more comfortable here.

We let off some gas last night, or rather our predecessors did. This made the Hun a trifle windy and he shelled us for about two hours; it was our reply to a little dose of 2000 gas shells which he sent over the day before, causing our fellows to wear their stinking helmets for seven hours on end. So the stupid war goes on!

September 6th, 1916. AUCHONVILLERS Trenches,
opposite BEAUMONT-HAMEL.

This is a very pleasant quiet existence after our experience of former trenches.

This morning I have been acting as President on a Board of Enquiry about some beastly live bombs which unfortunately got mixed up with some practice bombs and caused a scandal for which the Brigade desires to fix the responsibility. As the result of the enquiry is, as far as I can see, to incriminate the Adjutant and the Assistant Adjutant, both of whom I called as witnesses; we shall now expect to hear of their Court Martial for negligence. As a matter of fact everyone connected with the matter seems to have been pretty thoroughly careless; but I expect the report will get pigeon-holed all right at the Brigade office if the General is busy.

We are in a sort of rabbit run of a dug-out. I have my headquarters in one compartment and the medical officer, Lewis Gun and Bomb officers come and sleep here, as we have about eight beds. Then further along to the right are the servants, five of them, the sergeant-major, four orderlies and a platoon and half: about thirty-five men in all! Further down to the left are half a dozen headquarters' runners. There are four entrances down deep narrow shafts, and the whole place is as dark as a coal-mine. However, it is pretty safe, which is the great thing.

Schomberg [1] said he would like to see the state of chaos inside when the gas alarm goes! So should I. With dug-outs of this type you have always to post sentries at the top of the stairs at each entrance to give instant warning of gas when the men are sleeping.

Thiepval takes a long time to fall, but according to the papers we are all round it and Guillemont has gone. The latter was a tough nut and cost many lives. They say Delville Wood is the worst sight of the lot and is perfectly ghastly. I was talking to an officer who had been there the day before yesterday. In fact, a General who walked up a communication trench into what remains of the wood, was so horrified that he remarked that something must be done at once, as it was so depressing for our men. There has been fighting there almost since July 1st without a stop, so you will have a faint idea of its state. Of course the trees are all completely shattered by shells; at one time the wood was very thick.

We have seen a lot of the Anzacs. Most of them were annoyed and contemptuous at the way in which they have been boosted and advertised in the Press, They are wonderful fighters but most casual devils. We used to see them, wounded and unwounded, wandering about all over the shop even in trenches half of which were held by the Bosche, and this without either arms or equipment.

[1] Lt.-Col. G. St. G. Schomberg, East Surrey Regt., acting Second-in-Command.

September 9th, 1916.   Bus.

Yesterday we came out of the trenches to the most delightful billets imaginable. My Company headquarters are in a nice little red-bricked house standing well back from the road with a little garden in front.

An old man and woman, both very genial and kind, run the house and have placed at my disposal one sitting-room for the Mess, with a clean tiled floor, lamps, plenty of chairs and a large bedroom with a feather bed, where I sleep: my other subaltern has a mattress on the floor and Carew Hunt is sleeping next door. He is unwell, " flu " I think.

We are likely to be out of the trenches for some considerable time and probably in a day or two we shall go right back. Already I have sent four of my war-worn veterans to a camp at the seaside for a holiday; I wish I could follow them.

This morning I sent in my application for leave to go to Rouen (to stay with Charlie [1]) from September 18th to September 21st: the C.O. is passing it on all right so I hope the Brigade will grant it: they have been sending round all sorts of chits to the effect that officers and men may be recommended for a " rest " and that everything will be done to grant leave on reasonable excuses. As a matter of fact we are all expecting to get some proper leave soon, so things are looking very bright.

September 13th, 1916.   Bus.

We are busy training—six hours a day—eight to twelve and two to four. What with route-marching,

[1] My uncle, Lt.-Col. C. O. Greenwell, Durham Lt. Infty., G.H.Q., 3rd Echelon.

drilling—physical drill—bayonet exercises, shooting and bombing, I am pretty well employed with my Derbyites. Unfortunately the weather is so vile that we get very wet; this morning it has rained nearly the whole time. I have stuffed my breeches with newspapers, an old dodge to keep the damp clothes off the skin.

I think we are going to be here for at least another week or ten days; yesterday I met the Brigadier on horseback, and he asked me about my application for leave. He has sent it on to the Division, so I hope to get it when it has passed through the endless meshes of red tape.

September 17th, 1916.   G.H.Q., 3rd Echelon, ROUEN.

My holiday at Rouen is drawing to an end and I leave this afternoon for the regiment, arriving at about 10 o'clock to-morrow morning.

I have had a very jolly time here; the night before last we went to the theatre: it really was most amusing: the audience were quite as funny as the performers. The place was full of English and French soldiers in all kinds of uniforms and the show was a sort of hotch-potch of English and French " turns." Yesterday I went to church with Charlie in the private chapel of the Archbishop's Palace, where the officers of the 3rd Echelon are.

Everyone here is debating whether something really decisive may not happen before the winter comes on, or whether we shall stick on with trench warfare again. It is difficult to say at present, but I can't imagine that the Bosche is in a very happy state.

September 24th, 1916. FIENVILLERS.

To-day I have been out since 10 o'clock. I rode over with Pearson to Doullens and lunched there at rather a jolly hotel. It has been very hot all day, quite like summer again. I do hope it will continue and give us a chance of killing a few more Huns before the protecting cloak of winter gives them the rest they want so badly.

The old woman in our billet is rather a nuisance, frightfully motherly and talkative. I found her scrubbing my bugler's breeches with ammonia this afternoon, the bugler being slightly embarrassed at the situation. Her store is in our mess-room: consequently she hops in and out from the kitchen where our staff of eight servants also congregate. Whenever I go through on my way out, I see about four servants trying not entirely to fill the kitchen, the portly old girl well developed fore and aft, her eldest daughter lapping up tinned fruit, her youngest kid cuddling the cat in one hand and a Tommy's bayonet in the other, and probably some decrepit male visitor—the few males remaining are all decrepit— smoking a foul old pipe in the chimney corner.

October 2nd, 1916. WARLENCOURT.

Another day's march has brought us nearer the line but not, I am glad to say, to the part we were in before: in fact we are very near the place where we spent last winter and summer, so it won't be so bad if we can take over a permanent piece of line and settle down for the winter outside the " Push " area.

At the present moment I feel rather fed up. We are billeted in a single hut with another Company and I am furious, as I got my officers an excellent billet last night in a cottage out of which the C.O. has turned me on various inadequate grounds. I protested and consequently am very much in disgrace at headquarters. But it will blow over pretty quickly and the Colonel is really a sportsman.

October 4th, 1916. WARLINCOURT.

To-day I was told to put up three stars pending gazette, as it has taken such a long time to come through. I am arranging a large dinner-party to celebrate it and have secured some chickens and plenty of champagne—Veuve Clicquot too!

October 9th, 1916. WARLINCOURT.

I am frightfully busy just now and every moment of the day seems to be filled.

I am making use of my excellent billet to entertain every night, and we always sit down eight or nine to dinner. Poor old Carew Hunt has to work very hard.

To-night the C.O. and Adjutant are dining with me and a great friend from the Bucks, Captain Reid, who has got the D.S.O. and Military Cross: he is a splendid chap, looks about twenty, is absolutely fearless and always the cheeriest soul alive. He deserves any honours he gets.

To-day a Scotch Major [1] gave a lecture on bayonet fighting to all the officers of the Oxfords and Bucks and N.C.O.'s. You cannot imagine the enthusiasm this chap raised: he was full of stories of the Bosches and of the most cold-blooded yarns. Of course he reiterated the fact that cold steel alone would win

[1] Major Campbell.

the war and that now that our men were beginning to come to close quarters with the Germans, the game was up. As a matter of fact he is only too right. But the failure of morale among the Germans makes it difficult to use the bayonet, though, as the Major said, when you do get near them, they always have their kidneys exposed—the best place for that weapon. He was a great success.

October 10th, 1916. WARLINCOURT.

The dinner-party to the C.O. went off very successfully; he is excellent company and suitably young for the job, which is a great thing; it prevents him fussing and worrying his Company Commanders when the time for action comes.

October 16th, 1916. WARLINCOURT.

I have been out riding since 2.30 with a friend and returned to my billet for tea to find the usual crowd enjoying the hospitality of B Company, the Second-in-Command, the Padre and Alan Gibson. We are now called the " Smart Set " by headquarters, and the " Exclusive Company " by the other Companies, which is rather absurd as we entertain nearly every night, always having two or three officers to dinner.

October 20th, 1916. WARLUZEL.

Soon after I had written my letter to Bridget last night the post came in and brought me your letter, B.'s mittens and the papers. Please tell her that as I already had a pair of mittens which came out with my winter clothing I made a present of them to Carew Hunt, who was delighted with them as they matched his Indian " Chuddah " or shawl, which he always carries round with him to our great amusement.

We are back in this village in which we stopped two nights on our way up a fortnight ago; we have the same Mess, a large clean room with two windows opening on to a sort of back garden. The good lady is a very sporting old girl; she likes us and we are very comfortable. However, we are certain to move on again to-morrow.

This afternoon I shall try and get leave from the C.O. to ride into Doullens and do a little shopping.

October 21st, 1916. WARLUZEL.

We have had some more officers sent to us and I have had a Second Lieutenant, a schoolmaster, posted to me who is over forty. He was left behind by our Second Line Battalion and has now been pitchforked out by the Third Line. But it is a little difficult: I have four Platoon commanders already, all good fellows, and with one exception quite young: he will have to be supernumerary to one of them. I can't put him with a boy half his age, though I am myself young enough to be his son. Poor old man, I expect he will soon find his way back to England.

October 25th, 1916. LA HOUSSOYE.

We are in a wretched village full of Flying Corps and Motor Transport: the noise of the heavy lorries is never silent and the roads are ankle-deep in mud. However, we are not very far from Amiens and I hope to get a trip there if we stay long enough.

Five of my officers have to sleep in a huge, bare loft with about twelve more officers and my poor schoolmaster is absolutely miserable and depressed. He knows literally nothing about soldiering, has never done any bayonet fighting, bombing, musketry or even drill for the last six months and they had no right to send him out. He is a victim of chronic neuritis, has a sad lack of a sense of humour and can only express his horror and detestation of the whole business and his opinion that he and most of us will all be dead in a fortnight. In vain do I point to my own longevity, in vain tempt him with five-course dinners, in vain lure him on with unlimited booze. Cards do not distract him: a lively argument on the subject of Socialism may possibly fix his wandering attention for a while, but he soon relapses into a morbid state of self-pity and recalls the long tale of his woes. In fact I felt so sorry for the old boy that I spoke to the C.O. about him this morning and he has been sent to see the doctor. His kit alone was a monument of stupidity, containing a folding bath, an enormous eiderdown quilt, a Gladstone bag, enormous woollen bed stockings and, crowning folly, a Dayfield body-shield of steel weighing the Lord knows what and quite useless.

October 31st, 1916. MILLENCOURT, SOMME.

There is again great difficulty to-day in writing or rather in posting letters, as we have moved forward and shall soon be in the trenches. Once more the horrible comedy of shivering soldiers crouching over inadequate braziers in filthy mud-holes with frost-bite and all the other accompaniments of trench warfare in the winter will be played over. It is a wretched prospect.

I returned just now from riding over with a friend

to a canteen to find one of my nicest Scotty [1] subalterns prostrated by an epileptic fit: apparently it was a very sudden seizure which came on while he was playing Poker. In five minutes he was breathing evenly again and asking what had been the matter with him. Now he has just gone off in an ambulance and I am afraid we shall not see him again. This is the second time it has happened since he has been in France and the authorities are naturally very strict about anything of this kind. The curious thing is that he feels perfectly fit again within an hour or two, and it is this which puzzles the doctors, who have hitherto reported him to be quite sound.

I shall be losing my old schoolmaster in a day or two as the Colonel has recommended him to be returned to England as unfit. So that will leave me with five officers again, a less unwieldly number than seven.

November 2nd, 1916. Bivouacs near CONTALMAISON, SOMME.

Just a hurried line written amidst the filthiest surroundings to let you know we are just off to the trenches. Last night we camped on what was German ground before July 1st in a filthy, muddy camp of tents and bivouacs: outside the remains of what had been a famous village during the " Push."

The mud is perfectly ghastly, never have I seen anything like it: men and horses are caked in it from head to foot. It takes ten horses to get the smallest guns about. I am afraid we may have three weeks or a month of this at the least. However, it is the fortune of war; someone has got to do the dirty work.

[1] Officers from the Scottish Rifles had been posted to the Battalion as reinforcements.

We start at 4 this afternoon, so I have scarcely a moment to spare.

Will try and send a Field Post-card daily.

November 4th, 1916.   Trenches behind LE SARS, SOMME.

We have been here for thirty-six hours now, living like dogs or rats far from any sign of civilisation. For miles behind us there are nothing but ruined villages on which to pitch wretched little camps in the slush for rest billets. The trenches are absolutely impassable, sometimes waist-deep in liquid mud. Everything has to be carried for miles across country and at night. No one knows the way, all landmarks have been removed by shells and mud; and not for a single moment are the guns silent. Such food as we can get is gritty with mud, our clothes are caked with it; we think mud, dream mud, and eat mud. Last winter I thought was bad, but this winter in the Battle Area is quite unimaginable.

How long we shall remain here we cannot tell, but I suppose for three weeks at least, unless we do an attack.

Your beef rolls arrived on the very eve of leaving for this swamp, and provided us with a last good meal, for which I was awfully grateful. But I think you should use tins as far as possible when sending parcels now as the posts are rather uncertain.

Please don't think from this letter that I am at all depressed: thank Heaven I have got four young fellows with me and we are quite cheery, even playing vingt-et-un yesterday with matches and an old dirty pack of cards. Besides which everything sooner or

Working Party of British troops on muddy ground, Somme area. November 1916.
Courtesy Imperial War Museum. (*Facing Page* 178)

later has an end and I hope this may mean that we shall be out of the trenches at Christmas time.

November 6th, 1916.   Trenches at LE SARS, SOMME.

Writing in dark to say " Fit as a Flea " but fagged out and absolutely filthy.

Having a very rough time this go, but ought to be out of it to-morrow.

Haven't had clothes off or proper sleep for three days.

November 7th, 1916.   Trenches at LE SARS, SOMME.

Got out of it last night all right but had a good many casualties through shelling.

Back in a support trench or rather mud ditch. Heavy rain. Everything caked in mud.

Spirits: High.

C.O. very sporting—sent us a bottle of whisky last night on arrival; mud pouring in, and here are five of us sitting down here, simply a flight of narrow steps.

Carew Hunt, whom I left behind at Albert, has sent us up plenty of food, thank Heaven, and the other night a bottle of fizz actually reached us at 2 a.m. after twenty-four hours in the front trenches: we were simply done and soaked through. It saved our lives. The very best too, Heidsieck '06: can't think where he got it from.

Great difficulties in getting food and water up, but still it's a wonderful war.

Guns never cease.

This is our fifth day up. Hope to get back to a bivouac to-morrow night and then a night's sleep.

I enclose a private note the C.O. sent me yesterday

when I had written rather a depressing report and was having a rough time. Very good of him.[1]

We are nearly out of the wood.

Feet as cold as ice and five days' beard. You wouldn't recognise your first-born!

November 8th, 1916.   Reserve Trenches, MARTINPUICH, SOMME.

Yesterday was a typical Somme day, it poured with rain and the remainder of our trenches got filled in. Perfectly hopeless.

I was relieved at about nine o'clock and came back through the most appalling mud and slush I have ever seen. We went back to some old German dug-outs here. It is the largest village captured in the Big Push with the exception of Combles, but it is nothing but a mass of ruins with its streets knee-deep in mud. However, I got into a warm dug-out belonging to an artillery headquarters and managed to get my first uninterrupted sleep for four nights, soaked through as I was.

Fortunately the Huns had installed an oven, so I roasted in front of that for some time and then wrapped my feet in sand-bags. I am quite used to sleeping in my clothes now with only a light Burberry as a cover, my British Warm being an impossible garment to carry round in these desolate regions.

We have, I believe, to spend two days here, which will make seven days without a wash or a change of clothes. Then we shall go back to a bivouac or camp.

[1] Captain Greenwell: Very sorry about those casualties. I propose putting you back to-night into same places as before you went into front line—one of your orderlies refused a tot of rum just now—d . . . bad taste. Cheer up.—A. J. M. B.

Horse and motor transport in difficulties. Aveluy - Albert Road. December 1916
Courtesy Imperial War Museum. (*Facing Page* 180)

However, I still get your letters. I got one this morning which arrived with last night's ration party. The vicissitudes they pass through enhance their value!

Two nights ago three Germans gave themselves up, to everyone's joy, as Brigade headquarters were very keen on finding out the identity of the Germans opposite. They were Prussian Guardsmen! I was in support and was standing outside my headquarters dug-out about eight o'clock on a moonlight night when I saw three quaint-looking figures with long overcoats and funny-shaped helmets moving aimlessly about accompanied by a youthful Tommy with a fixed bayonet and almost in tears. I gave them a hail and brought them back. The boy then told me that he had had the three Bosches entrusted to him and to a pal, but that his pal had been wounded by a piece of shell and he had therefore been left alone; now he couldn't find Battalion headquarters. I asked the Bosche if they spoke English, beamed on them and gave them a guide to take them along. They were very cheery and quite resigned to being the victims of British stupidity before profiting by their generosity.

My legs are wrapped in two sand-bags to keep them warm while my boots get dry and I haven't been out all day, so I am feeling a bit muzzy; that's the worst of this trench life. At any rate we are warm and dry here, which we haven't been for four days. How I long to get back to billets again, we have been spoilt for the last two months.

November 10th, 1916.   Reserve Trenches, MARTINPUICH.

I am writing from the comparative safety and quiet of a " reserve position "; mud-holes which were once trenches.

This is our eighth day up. I am filthy and the cold is bad. My boots are split from toe to heel and I have had nearly enough of it.

To-night we move back to a village or rather to a point where a village and a wood stood before the " Push "; so you see we are not going back to any rest billets; we shall have to collect any old pieces of wood and timber we can get hold of and use them to put up bivouacs with waterproof sheets!

I would give anything just now for a change in England—it seems such ages since I saw you all. However, I firmly believe that the darkest time precedes the dawn.

Fortunately Carew Hunt has been keeping us very well supplied with food, which is the main thing. He also sends me up all your letters each night, which helps to cheer things up.

I must knock off now to see about the " move " this evening.

November 15th, 1916.   Bivouac in BAZENTIN Wood.

I have just been sent down to hospital, but probably only for a week or two, so don't worry.

It is very annoying leaving the regiment like this and I shall take the earliest opportunity of rejoining them. Meanwhile I must resign myself to a fortnight's inactivity; but at times like this one is moved on very quickly and I expect I shall get shunted off to the

British soldier cleaning his rifle in the trenches, Winter 1916
Courtesy Imperial War Museum. (*Facing Page* 182)

Base pretty soon.[1] I am afraid that last very unpleasant tour in the trenches did for me, it was so very long and the weather was vile. It is frightfully cold at present but nice and sunny.

[1] Carew Hunt took over command of the Company until he was invalided to England at the end of the year.

1917

January 13th, 1917. Base Camp, ROUEN.

HERE I am in a very comfortable Base Camp where I have met two of my oldest friends—Maurice Edmunds, just back from England after being wounded, and Colonel Ovey, with whom I had a long talk; he is not at all fit and is marked " Permanent Base ": he will be getting some sort of job here soon.

I shall almost certainly be going up the line the day after to-morrow, as to-morrow I have to be " gassed " —a formality which has to be gone through by all officers passing through the Base.

January 21st, 1917. CERISY BULEUX.

I left Rouen the day before yesterday at 3 p.m. and had the most ghastly journey I have ever had even in France, travelling in third-class carriages with no light or heating till ten next morning—I was frightfully cold. On arrival I picked up a motor supply lorry in which I travelled for another hour across very flat country two or three inches deep in snow to a small village. Then a five-mile walk to another village where I got home at last and found the Battalion. The C.O. was very kind and to my delight has given me back my old Company, although a Major was commanding it—I am billeted in an enormous bare château and have a comfortable room with a good bed—it seems very quiet after Rouen and Havre, but it is icy cold.

To-day there has been a big Brigade Field Day. The C.O. told me to get a horse and come out as a sort of galloper to him as I had not heard anything of the scheme. We started at 8 a.m. and have only just got in—5 p.m. Not bad for the first day. It was jolly to be on a horse again and I enjoyed myself thoroughly. I am so thankful to be back again and with my own Company: the only trouble is that someone has sneaked my horse! But I hope to get it back soon.

January 22nd, 1917.   CERISY BULEUX.

Another very energetic day: out on horseback from 9 a.m. for a seven-mile ride to a big pow-wow of Brigade officers (C.O.'s and Captains) under the Divisional General, who tramped us over miles and miles of country while elaborating a scheme of attack against the Huns. He kept us out till 3 p.m. without lunch, and of course I had missed my breakfast, thanks to my comfortable bed. I have never known such piercing cold, the snow has been on the ground for over a week. I came back by motor lorry and got colder still: in fact I am only just beginning to thaw. But I feel as fit as a flea. It is a great joy being among my old friends again, and I am as happy as a schoolboy: there is really no life like it.

January 26th, 1917.   CERISY BULEUX.

I have been frightfully busy since returning to the Battalion, and now we are just on the eve of another move: it means a great deal of work. We have rather an interesting journey in prospect to regions famous but hitherto unvisited. I cannot say more at present, as you know the military regulations.

I am still feeling extraordinarily fit and am thoroughly interested again in the old game.

February 4th, 1917.   HERBECOURT.

Amidst great excitement we arrived yesterday at another little camp of huts, and I was photographed with one of my officers by a funny little French Captain who kept telling me that it was quite " tranquil " in the trenches and that there were " beaucoup d'abris " (dug-outs). He was very much interested in my Scotty officer with his Glengarry and began to discuss Sir Walter Scott and to try to talk Scotch though without much success.

Our huts here are pretty comfortable: eight officers sleep and eat in each of them. The only problem is how to keep warm. Fuel is very scanty and looting strictly forbidden.

We are a very happy little party here, and regimental life is most pleasant. I think we shall now settle down into this sector for the rest of the winter and have these huts as our rest billets. If so, we shall be quite satisfied, as it will be more comfortable and restful than constantly moving about.

February 8th, 1917.   SOPHIE Trench, HERBECOURT.

The weather is still arctic with a cutting blast and to-morrow we have to move up to the trenches. The authorities think that the Hun is up to some game or other, so to-night we are all on the " qui vive " and stand ready to march off at any moment. It is a great bore, but I shall turn in in my clothes after I have written this—Huns or no Huns.

To-night B.'s parcel with the waistcoat arrived, for

which grateful thanks are returned. Every little helps in this beastly spell of cold weather. Everything freezes hard and at each meal we have to thaw the bread, the mustard, the butter, and finally the wine, which is frozen in its bottles: pretty stiff, isn't it? We do nothing all day but trot round to the nearest stove to thaw something.

This morning I spent unprofitably sitting on a Court Martial on some poor devil who had tried to keep warm by drinking a pal's rum ration as well as his own, with disastrous results: I sympathised with him sincerely.

Oh! Geewhiz! I was forgetting the great event of the week! What *do* you think of the great Amurrican people coming in to tackle the old war? You bet they have some good reason for it.

February 9th, 1917.   Trenches opposite
LA MAISONNETTE.

I am frightfully tired, as I have been on the go since 9 this morning, when I started out to walk up to the trenches, nearly five miles away, through an interminable communication trench. I didn't get back till 2.30 and after a bite of lunch started up again with my Company at 4.30. When I tell you that I didn't report the relief complete till 9 p.m. you will understand what a long and arduous business taking over trenches is even under ideal conditions, for these trenches are a "joy-ride" compared to the ones we were in last November. I think we shall probably be in for three or four days this time. I hope not longer, as I have a lot of new men and I don't want them to start off with a bad time, as they are very keen.

I wonder what you would think of my surroundings? A small square chamber like an Egyptian tomb, deep in the bowels of the earth (sixteen steps down), lighted by a candle, and surrounded by the usual litter of a Company headquarters. Revolvers, cigarettes, maps, plans, orders, illustrated papers, a cake, a few dirty cups, three or four bottles, tin hats, Balaclava helmets, respirators—any old thing.

I had to break off this letter for an hour or two to compose several reports, a boring adjunct of trench life. Meanwhile my Scotty subaltern has just rolled in from the fire trench pretty tired and is composing himself for slumber on a pile of sand-bags in the corner. I hope he will keep warm: I feel pretty cold, as my coat hasn't arrived yet. I simply wear an ordinary Burberry with a thick leather jerkin under it and a warm scarf, much more convenient than a British Warm.

I can just hear the buzzing of an aeroplane. Poor devil, he must be colder than any of us. I can't think how they stick it in this weather. God knows what it will be like when the thaw does come: I shouldn't think there will be anything left of these trenches at all: they will all come down with a rush.

The ration party has just arrived after a tedious journey—laden with rum and bully beef, etc.

I shall sit up till the blooming dawn—go round and dish out—RUM—and then I think turn in myself. Unfortunately the dawn doesn't arrive till nearly six at this time of the year.

Hurray!!! I have just heard that my coat has turned up safely, also a batch of Tommie's cookers—which heat a cupful of tea with a great effort, after which they die a natural death. However, it all helps.

I hope you don't mind me rambling on like this, but it's a good way of spending the night.

No mail seems to have made its appearance with the rations for some reason, also no oil has turned up for our Primus stove, which is the sort of tragedy that makes us all philosophers. I don't know when I shall get this letter off—sometime to-morrow I suppose. Fortunately I have my pal, Alan Gibson, behind to act as go-between when I am in the trenches.

I have just remembered that I must do something active about our water before morning, as we haven't got much, and it has to be fetched from somewhere at the back of beyond in petrol tins!!! What a life!

I really must shut up now.

February 11th, 1917.   La Maisonnette Trenches.

I am just two days dirtier and more tired since my last letter, but I hope to get relieved the day after to-morrow.

I get very sick of living in these cold dug-outs without being able to get any water to wash in or any other light except candles. But it's no good worrying and time seems to pass somehow. Last night like a silly ass I gassed myself by sitting too near a coke fire. It gave me a frightful head for about two hours and I had to lie down, feeling rotten. They are very dangerous things to have in dug-outs and I am constantly warning the men about them.

The Huns seem disposed to behave quite decently here, and except for a machine gun strafe at intervals throughout the night, he keeps pretty quiet. We let off a shoal of bombs at him last night and shut him up. One of my subalterns is very keen on " strafing," and lugged me out to watch him shoot a Hun he had spotted. He only just missed him.

February 16th, 1917.   Trenches DÉSIRÉE Valley.

To-night I am alone, as my three officers are busily employed. I have had the unpleasant job of detailing one of them for a reconnoitring patrol between the lines preparatory to greater things later on. So I have been very busy studying trench maps of the German lines and organising the business as well as possible. They have just gone on up to the front line (we are back in support) and I shall sit up for their return, which will be at about midnight if all goes well.

Things haven't been too quiet, and yesterday Battalion headquarters were shelled continuously for two-and-a-half hours. As they were only about four hundred yards away from my headquarters I could watch the whole show. It was wonderful shooting and I expected to hear that they had a bad time. About lunch time I got through to them on the 'phone and found that their kitchen had been smashed in and nearly everything destroyed. They had had a very rough time of it and when I walked over to see them after lunch they were a bit dazed. The whole ground was littered with wreckage, but comparatively little real damage was done though they must have had nearly five hundred shells on them. By ill luck one officer, Vokes, was killed. He was standing in the entrance of a dug-out without his helmet, watching a bomb dump go off which had just been hit; a piece of bomb seems to have come right through the doorway and caught him in the head although he was standing just behind two other men. He was a good officer, I believe, just out from England; I hadn't met him yet.

But on the whole we have had a very easy time and our four days in the front line were wonderfully quiet. I had no casualties except one man, who dropped a sand-bag of French bombs he was carrying and was very severely blown about. He died almost immediately, poor fellow. I was very sick about it although really the accident was not due to carelessness on anyone's part except perhaps his own. To-morrow we are being relieved and go back to some huts behind, where we shall be in reserve for eight days, which will be rather jolly.

I am afraid there is little news; life is very uneventful in the winter here. But I am in excellent health and spirits and so are the men. I have a ripping lot now as I have had some drafts from the cavalry, chiefly from the Oxfordshire Yeomanry and the Bucks Hussars. They are as keen as mustard, very cheery, and have thoroughly brought back the old spirit.

February 18th, 1917.   Camp 56, CAPPY.

We returned to our rest billets yesterday afternoon. I found my pony waiting for me on the side of the road, and very welcome was the sight of it. We came back to an encampment of huts—bare and empty. Fortunately they are divided into small cubicles and we have been getting the Pioneers to work, with the result that we have made ourselves fairly comfortable.

Your letter tore my heart-strings because I know how much you must look forward to this leave. I am naturally getting very restless, but it's no good worrying: it must start again soon. But at present the whole traffic system is badly disorganised. Be sure I shall write and tell you directly it opens again.

By the way, please don't ever stop parcels, they are very precious and my friends will joyfully eat their contents even if I don't. You see we share everything in the Company Mess.

February 24th, 1917. Camp 56, CAPPY.

We have had no post from England for five days: no potatoes or fresh meat in rations: we are short of bread; it's raining and leave is still stopped: and now we are just off to the trenches, or rather to what's left of them. This business of going into outer darkness for five days armed only with a haversack and a raincoat is rotten, to say the least of it. I can't make out what's gone wrong with everything. However, the darkest hour precedes the dawn and I hope matters will mend a little.

Our new Brigadier, among other fads, has insisted on all officers providing themselves with Tommies' uniforms as a sort of disguise: they are to be worn not only in the attack but in the ordinary trench warfare; it is a sad departure from the " Nelson touch "—all decorations won in battle and worn in battle.

Trench feet are going strong and the authorities are yelling themselves hoarse with bloodthirsty threats. Each man in my Company has to be responsible for the feet of another: so that A looks after B's feet and vice versa. If B goes to hospital with trench feet A is crimed and brought before the C.O. A good idea. We wash and powder and change socks at every turn; unfortunately in the trenches, where the trouble starts, this is almost impossible.

A muddy trench. (*Facing Page* 192)

I must shut up now and arrange the details of the move. Good-bye. Don't think I am really as gloomy as I sound.

February 28th, 1917.   LA MAISONNETTE Trenches.

By the time you receive this many things may have happened on the Western Front. As you will see by the papers the old Hun is at last beginning perceptibly to weaken, which is a good and cheering sign. There is no talk of anything save of retreat and evacuation and we are preparing to rush through, though I don't expect it will come to much just yet.

We were unexpectedly relieved from the front line trenches last night after only two days up. I was rather annoyed, as I suppose it will mean going up again to-morrow night. But I was so frightfully tired that I could hardly tramp along the three or four miles of awful roadway thick with mud, back to the old Sophie Trench. Although I was relieved at 8 p.m. I didn't get back to my headquarters till nearly 1 a.m., which gives you some idea of the conditions. But it is most comfortable here and I thankfully sank to rest on my box bed and didn't get up till 12.30 this morning !

We are again running very short of officers: one was wounded the other night while starting out on a raid, and by our own guns too. He lost a thumb or something of the sort. Maurice Edmunds got a sudden attack of pleurisy in the trench and had to be carried out. I am sorry to say that he is rather ill.

March 2nd, 1917.   LA MAISONNETTE Trenches.

About 5 o'clock yesterday evening as I was parading my Company on the road about four or five miles behind the line, we saw a wonderful sight. A Hun aeroplane came over and was greeted by more than the usual gunfire from " archies " all round. About two miles further back we had a " sausage " observation balloon up. The old Hun came steadily on, flying very low, and I began to get a bit nervous lest he should spot all the men on the road. Presently the gun-fire became more and more violent and the whole air a mass of white puffs. Suddenly the plane made a swooping dive downwards and onwards: we all thought that she had either been hit or was going to have a whack at us with a machine gun. However, her objective became clear—she was going straight for the observation balloon. There was a perfect tornado of shells all round her, but she went straight on, and while we held our breath she swerved just over the balloon. There was a little rattle of machine gun-fire and she swung off, pursued by shells but triumphant. Two seconds later the balloon descended in a mass of flames and black smoke. As we watched, its two observers jumped out on parachutes and began gliding slowly down, as we thought, safe. But the balloon seemed to come right down on top of one of them and must, I think, have killed him. The other descended into safety. A long trail of black smoke went up to heaven and the show was over. We went on to the trenches feeling that at times even the men behind the line may have a bit of the war thrust upon them. It isn't often that the infantryman looks on. The German should get an Iron Cross all right: it was a marvellous performance.

There is practically no news. Our Adjutant, Bridges, to complete his extraordinary good luck, stopped a bullet in the arm early this morning while wandering round my trenches. He got a compound fracture and a Blighty wound, the lucky dog.

I don't think that I have ever been so tired as when we got out of the trenches at 8 o'clock last night. I had had no sleep at all the night before. I was up at 2 a.m. and had a five-mile tramp through slush and mud till 6.30. I was called up again at 9 and had to ride three miles back without breakfast to Divisional Headquarters to give some evidence. I got a hurried lunch at about 2 o'clock. Then I went up to the trenches again—a three hours' journey. I was up all night and finally, at 6 o'clock this morning, I sank on to a pile of dirty sand-bags to sleep like a log until 2 o'clock this afternoon. I shall take care to be over forty in the next war. But we never know what is good for us and I can imagine myself sitting at home fifteen years hence bitterly regretting the days when I was a Captain in the Army, free, with plenty of money and sport and with no worries about food or habitation. After all, it's a gay life sometimes and full of change.

I should like to apply for special leave when I get out, but to tell you the honest truth there is rather a lot in the wind just now and as we are so very short of officers you must bear up and help me to hold on philosophically. I hate thinking of you at home waiting for me and your letters make me very home-sick.

March 9th, 1917.   Camp 56, CAPPY.

I am up to my eyes in work and frightfully excited: a great chance has arrived and to-morrow will be a red-letter day for me.

I shall be in charge of two companies and am to run a little show of my own which, if successful, will bring great credit on the regiment and on all concerned. But it involves a lot of organisation, detailed instructions and practice, and the staff as usual have rather rushed things.

Two other companies of a sister regiment are also engaged, so it will be a much bigger affair than usual. To-morrow morning I shall be busy weeding out incapables and putting on the finishing touches. Only the keen boys will do for this job and, thank Heaven, they are all as pleased as Punch at the idea. Unfortunately, it is bitterly cold with an east wind, driving snow and sleet, so that we may have to wear night-shirts.

I must get to bed early to-night and have a good sleep. I shall be up pretty late to-morrow, though the whole business ought to be over in an hour if all goes well.

March 12th, 1917.   Camp 56, CAPPY.

The Army is wonderful. We were worked up to a feverish pitch of excitement and enthusiasm over our raid, but at 4 o'clock in the evening the show was put off for twenty-four hours.

Yesterday our preparations had gone even further. Most of my men had blacked their faces with burnt corks and looked like nigger minstrels. They had received a few words of blessing from stray Padres, and were just putting the finishing touches to their outfits, when I was summoned by telephone to Battalion headquarters, where the Adjutant greeted me with "the show's off—we go into the trenches to-night." Rather sickening wasn't it? But frankly I am glad it didn't take place last night: I think that it would have been a fiasco as the trenches are thick with mud. We should have had to assemble on top, always a dangerous proceeding, and as the barbed wire had not been sufficiently cut by our guns we should have had to find a gap for the whole bunch to go through—which means disaster if the Bosche happens to be watching it. But I am sorry that it didn't come off earlier during the frost.

March 15th, 1917.   Camp 56, CAPPY.

We are out of the trenches and to-morrow the Corps Commander is going to decorate various heroes with D.C.M.'s and Military Medals. I am busy selecting a suitable party of men to represent the Company on parade, and am recalling to their memory the various accompaniments of long-forgotten ceremonial parade—clean buttons, boot polishing, etc.

Your reference to my coming 21st birthday reminded me unpleasantly of the flight of time. As to presents, your good wishes are sufficient. It is always difficult enough to think of what one wants on ordinary occasions without the additional solemnity cast over the matter by the fact that one is twenty-one. Really I can't conceive what I should like. The usual gifts on such occasions—gold watches and so forth—would be embarrassingly out of place in these days, and this applies equally to the other articles of the pre-war male trousseau—dressing-cases with ivory brushes, etc. A good cigarette case I have got already.

To descend to a humbler plane, what I do *really* want are a dozen small-size white handkerchiefs with my initials on them and a small suède case in which to keep them, the sort of thing which I bought with B. in Bond Street when I was last on leave. The case should hold about a dozen handkerchiefs. But I like small ones, not the table-cloths men usually have.

We live in daily expectation of a Hun retirement, and this hope is strengthened by the numerous large fires seen behind their lines in a large town in front of us. Every time a new fire is sighted, the Generals for miles round leap out of bed and begin babbling of pursuit, open warfare and cavalry manœuvres. But after upsetting the well-earned rest of all the battalions in their immediate neighbourhood, they once more subside and content themselves with lengthy pow-wows on what to do when the Germans do start recrossing the Rhine, and how best to run a subaltern's Platoon for him from a château fifteen miles behind the line. But it doesn't make much difference, as one can and does run one's own show when in the trenches without much interference save over the telephone wires, and they, thank God, are often cut.

March 17th, 1917.   Camp 56, CAPPY.

I am bursting with news, but dead tired; physical infirmity is doing battle with the spirit.

Your two letters of the 18th and 11th lie just beside me; the first came the night before last: the second, in which you mention the raid, came to-night.

On the night before last at practically a moment's

notice I was ordered to carry out the same raid at 1.30 a.m. Motor lorries would start at 7 p.m. to take us to the trenches. The only modification was that we were *not* to return but to hang on, as in the opinion of our General the Bosche was almost certainly preparing to retreat.

We went up, but owing to the short notice we had been given everything was a ghastly muddle. No guides were provided to take us to the front line and it was pretty dark. As we moved forward the Germans started putting up lights all the way along their front trenches almost without intermission, and as soon as they saw us coming along they began a bit of harmless firing. At 2.20 a.m. I was still not in position to kick off and the time for starting had carefully been put off from 1.30 until I reported that I was ready. However, just as I was making my way to the C.O. to get him to put off the artillery bombardment till 3 a.m. the show began. There was a ghastly racket and a Bosche bombardment descended promptly on our front and second lines, cutting me off from my men. I was furious and thought the whole business had been irretrievably muddled and that we should never even start. I rushed into the C.O.'s dug-out and told him he must stop the artillery and put the show off, but he said it was impossible and that I must push on somehow or anyhow.

I came out of the dug-out into the trench feeling that the best thing I could do was to get hit as quickly as possible, and when I saw the Bosche " barrage " on the very trench I was in I realised it would be murder to take the men through it over the open.

So risking Court Martial I stayed where I was until the row had died down a bit. Then I ran down to our front line and found my Company mostly intact and all together, with my best subaltern—a dear boy, Pearson—knocked out.

I then got into touch with the two companies of Gloucesters on the right and found that they were all in confusion, but that some of them had got over to the German line. I therefore sent over at once my remaining officer with a Platoon. I got a message back to say that he was in, that the Bosche were gone and that he had a prisoner. So I came over with two more platoons at once and sent back for the other Company, which also came over. We pushed on to the second line and then to the third line. I got my telephone going and telephoned through to the C.O. to say that I could take a fourth line too, if required, and that we had patrols out all round searching for the Bosche.

I looked down on burning Peronne and couldn't see a soul. After their last piece of bluff the Bosche had disappeared completely. I stayed up there all next day and got back here to this camp at 2 a.m. this morning dog-tired.

The next thing we heard was that our Division was holding the famous Peronne. We captured two little German machines for bomb-throwing, which are being despatched to Oxford, and everyone seems very well pleased. Immediately our reports got back, the Divisions on the right and left of us which had refused to take the initiative, as they did not believe that the Bosche was retreating, pushed forward; it was a score for our General.

So trench warfare is over just here. We are miles away and cannot hear a gun: it seems absolutely extraordinary. I personally think the Huns will fall right back on to the enormously strong Hindenburg Line, and that we shall not dig in in front of them, which would be suicidal madness, but simply keep in touch by cavalry patrols.

We had about five casualties in the two Companies and only one man was killed. But I am simply miserable at losing Pearson—I just had time to see him in a dug-out, and then he was in some pain, with a cut over the eye, and badly wounded in the thighs. The shell was almost on top of him, and a corporal who was with him was badly shaken up. I rode over to-day to the Casualty Clearing Station, where to my joy I found him, but in bed, poor little devil, and awfully low. Thank God his eye is all right and will heal quickly. I saw his wounds, and the doctors told me that he was going on all right, though they are always very much frightened of gas gangrene. But God knows we got him attended to as quickly as we could, and he has since had several anti-tetanus injections. To-morrow I shall try to see him again, but I have to attend a Court Martial in the morning.

March 19th, 1917.   Camp 56, CAPPY.

Here we are still. We have not yet started in pursuit, as there is such a lot to do in the way of road-making and bridging. But we shall be off very soon now. It will be strange to do open warfare for a bit, and rather exciting. Mr. Beach Thomas of the *Daily Mail* has a lot of hot air to get rid of, but the Huns did certainly put arsenic in the wells at Basleux, and they have left all sorts of little booby-traps behind them. I quite forgot to look for them the other night when I got into their trenches, until the C.O. sent me up two Sappers the next morning to examine the captured dug-outs.

The cunning dogs half sawed through some bridges across the Somme and put bombs underneath which promptly blew up. They have left stoves in the dug-outs all ready for lighting which also blow up—in fact they have done this retreat as thoroughly as they do everything else, and in spite of all that the papers say they have had very few casualties and have lost an extraordinarily small number of guns. Of course they fired Peronne and Bapaume so as to get rid of military stores and to destroy billeting accommodation.

March 20th, 1917.   Camp 56, CAPPY.

I went over again to see Pearson this afternoon. Thank God he is going on all right, but I couldn't stay long as a nurse came and turned me out in order to dress his wounds. But I think he is better, though he has eaten practically nothing yet and has had little real sleep.

I have never felt anyone's loss so much since Conny left and am utterly depressed. He was an awfully good boy and didn't care two pins for shells or anything else. He has been for ten months continuously with the Battalion—in every show and in all trenches. He was ready for anything and never groused. Now he goes from those who liked and admired him, unthanked, and still a temporary Second Lieutenant, or whatever he is, with nothing to look forward to except three or four months in bed and then a wretched existence in the third line. If I felt that I had done as much hard and useful work as he has I should be more than satisfied with myself.

March 21st, 1917.   Cartigny.

At last we are really busy—open warfare is in full swing—and you mustn't mind if there are longish intervals between my letters, as we are already ten or fifteen miles from our old positions. But you must not be anxious, as it is a much safer job than the old trench warfare, though we all feel very ignorant as to how to set about it.

We got orders to move up directly new bridges had been made and we spent our first night in Boscheland proper at Peronne.

Imagine our disgust and anger when we found that literally every house in the whole town was gutted! It is a pretty large town, as you know, and its evacuation was hailed with joy. But the whole place is irretrievably destroyed, though not by shellfire, mark you, because the Allies had purposely spared it. The fronts of the houses had been carefully dynamited on to the streets; fires were still burning, the whole place looted—even the chairs had their legs broken off. In the main " Place " a large notice was stuck up in German, " Don't be angry—only wonder at us! "

My Company was allotted the remainder of a huge building with gaping walls and holes, and I didn't think much of it. It was frightfully draughty and the whole place was in a filthy mess. I slept in an old medical chair (like a dentist's) which my servant found somewhere. Next morning I was sent on ahead with my Company to the next village to fill in an enormous mine crater which the Germans had left at an important cross-roads. In the next village, only a small place, we saw that the work had again been systematically carried out. Not a house was standing—and it is the same for miles round. The Germans must have used tons of high explosive, as nothing has been left except the bare walls. Even the apple trees have been cut down.

Last night I found a village in which I thought there might be some accommodation and sent back to the C.O. for leave to remain out and billet my Company here on detachment. This was granted and we all got into cellars and dug-outs. However, another Company was sent up and I found myself O.C. detachment and advanced infantry, with only cavalry patrols out in front and our line of outposts. But nobody minds the Bosche much nowadays.

This morning the rest of the Battalion moved up and I have been on my legs since 9 a.m. hunting for cellar accommodation for Oxfords, Gloucesters, R.E. and Gunners, until I was off my head and told them all to go to the devil.

From the two villages in front of us to which I sent out small patrols this morning it is reported that about five hundred civilians have been left with a day or two's rations. Meanwhile we are waiting to push on, but the Bosche has got the start of us, as we can't advance without proper roads for the guns and for supplies.

We are part of a flying column—just two regiments

of infantry—a few guns, R.E. and a little cavalry. It's going to be most energetic and I am looking forward to it all tremendously; I only hope we shan't have to stop at some carefully prepared line and start trench warfare all over again.

Will you please send me once or twice a week a parcel which should if possible contain:

> Candles (by the dozen),
> Chocolate,
> Cake,
> Soup or Bovril tablets,
> Cigarettes.
> Matches,
> Post-cards or writing-paper,

as we are now miles beyond the land of canteens and shops and may be for some time.

March 23rd, 1917. CARTIGNY.

I am glad to see that *The Times* of yesterday points out that the German withdrawal is extremely skilful and has been conducted practically without the loss of a gun or a man and that if they now fall back on to the Hindenburg Line with a shorter frontage, they will obtain a strong reserve force for dealing a blow at us elsewhere. It is curious with what complete success they have managed their retreat. It was some days before we even got in touch with their rear-guards at all. However, the next week or two will show clearly whether they mean to hold on to St. Quentin or go right back. Meanwhile our men have thoroughly got their tails up and we are all enjoying the change of going to war amid pleasant surroundings and in decent clothes.

March 26th, 1917. TINCOURT.

My Company is now well in front with some topping fellows in the Indian Cavalry, and to-night I hope to get a move on into the next village where the Bosche is at present ensconced with machine guns which the cavalry don't seem to like much.

This is the greatest fun. The village is full of civilians collected by the Bosche, and the women and children look very much pleased to see us all.

This afternoon I bicycled up with a servant to visit our outposts and found our Indian friends on the look-out. They had spotted a small Bosche patrol away on a hillside, but our machine gun made them clear off pretty quickly. I only wish the authorities would let us get on a bit, but they are dreadfully slow.

March 28th, 1917. TINCOURT.

I must now tell you about my great battle—a real battle all to myself with cavalry and armoured cars, the greatest fun in the world and a howling success.

My Company took over a village two days ago and I bicycled on to the next village, the Bosche being in another one about three-quarter miles away. I found some Indian Cavalry holding it with a few oddments of cyclists and introduced myself to a very good fellow, Captain Colin. I asked him if he would like an addition of one or two Platoons to his garrison—about forty or fifty men—and he replied that he would. Then I suggested that we should take the Bosche village in front of us at which his Hindoos were gazing rather longingly. This somewhat took his breath away, but I said that I had one hundred and fifty men who wanted to do something quick, and that if he liked to help, so much the better. Finally, he agreed that we should both send out patrols that night and should try to take the village on our own provided that I could square my C.O. I rushed back, saw the Colonel and said that I wanted if possible to take Roisel that night and had arranged that the Indian Cavalry should lend a hand. He at once sat on me hard and said that I was anticipating the official programme by two days, as the Staff had arranged a little show for the 28th (to-day) with guns and armoured cars.

However, I persuaded him at any rate to let me send out the patrols and I got him to arrange that a similar patrol should go out from the south bank of the river which runs through the village. I sat up to hear the result and was told that they had run into a lot of Bosche, that the place was strongly held and even had a few trenches in front of it. But to my joy a chit came round about 1 or 2 a.m. to say that between 10 and 10.30 two guns would fire a few rounds into the village and that it would then be attacked by two companies of infantry, one from the north and one from the south bank of the river. A squadron of cavalry was to sweep round on either flank, cut off any retreating Bosche, and generally protect our flanks. Meanwhile four armoured motor-cars had turned up simply bursting with energy.

As usual this was all sprung on me at a moment's notice. However, at 10.30 after an ineffective exhibition from one or two small guns, I sent out two Platoons with an officer. They started off across country in open warfare formation—just like a Field Day. The Indians did a buck forward on the ridge on my left, but on meeting with some rifle fire came back. An armoured car boosted off down the main road and got right to the edge of the village, where it stuck in a big crater until some of my men arrived and dug it out.

Colin then came along past my headquarters with a small troop. He told me that it was getting a bit sticky on the left because some enterprising Bosche had a machine gun; could I get hold of a tank or an armoured car?

I telephoned to the C.O. and asked him if he could send me up an armoured car at once, but he said that he didn't know how to get hold of one. Just at that moment a friendly signaller interrupted our conversation to say that there was a car outside his billet (two miles back in the next village) filling up with petrol. So I sent off a bugler on a cycle and in a few minutes a car dashed up at sixty miles an hour and up popped a merry-looking devil from the conning tower shouting out: "I say! Is there a war on near here?" I showed him the road and told him to bunk off and slay Bosche: another chap whose car had broken down yelled out: "Wait a moment for us," and hopped on also and they ripped off to the ridge. Three minutes later there was the deuce of a rattle and the Bosche disappeared.

I rang up the C.O. and explained the little outburst going on on our left about a mile and a half away from the village we were attacking and he was much amused.

At any rate by 11.30 we had got into the village. It was a very large place and absolutely blown up. Some of our men had been into it two days before and

The Times of Saturday had a headline " CAPTURE OF ROISEL." I am wondering what the Monday papers will put in, as they haven't mentioned its recapture by the Germans. At any rate we got it finally and held it for twenty-four hours before they relieved us. The men are thoroughly pleased with themselves. It was a most amusing little show and everyone was delighted.

March 30th, 1917. TINCOURT.

We are now billeted in leaky cellars and ruined barns quite close up and are preparing to " *dig trenches.*" Isn't it too ghastly? But the Staff is nothing if not cautious and the Bosche is developing a certain power of resistance.

We marched in here last night in pouring rain and on arrival found practically no accommodation—bivouac sheets and a few tents—otherwise mud and wet and filth. But within two or three hours the men had got themselves in somehow, had cleared out the filthiest-looking cellars covered with débris and had got great fires going. They are never depressed by mere appearances and are always prepared to make the best of everything. Indeed I am very much pleased with my lot. I couldn't wish for better ones now that I have got these Cavalry lads to replace the old Derbyites who came out in August.

We are having great difficulties with the commissariat, as transport is difficult and there are only about two bridges over the Somme. Two or three R.E.'s stand by them night and day with hammers and tin-tacks, and every time a wagon passes over they rush forward, put in a few extra nails and let the next one go over. I hear that a whole gunner limber—six mules—careered over the side the other day and went right in. It contained all the officers' mess stuff, and for days afterwards their servants were to be seen angling for lost tins of salmon and bottles of whisky, to the joy of the spectators.

The latest craze is a beastly thing called the " Cruciform Post," an arrangement of trenches in the form of a cross which is supposed to possess many virtues for offence and defence. But I imagine that they will be an awful bore to dig: at any rate I am going out to-night to dig one, so I shall see.

April 6th, 1917. VILLERS FAUCON.

We have had the greatest success—my Company again too. Congratulatory wires from the Commander-in-Chief, Rawlinson, and all the other Commanders. My Company captured two machine guns and about 17 or 18 prisoners and killed God knows how many Bosche; quite a bloodthirsty affair but with remarkably few casualties on our side. We are all as pleased as Punch—it's the best and biggest show we have had since we came to France.

Our objective was a high ridge with three villages together in a little knot, which the Bosche were holding in force with a great many machine guns. As it was only a mile or two in front of the Hindenburg Line it was within range of all their heavy guns. We came up into the outpost line two days ago, and my Company having done the last attack was in battalion reserve behind.

The first night was simply filthy—heavy snow and rain. Consequently when orders arrived next morning for our Battalion to find two companies for this attack at dawn on the following day, the C.O. said he would have to send me again. I was only too delighted at the opportunity, having become rather bloodthirsty of late. So at 4.45 yesterday morning you would have seen me with my Company and one other formed up in dead silence upon the snowy ground about one thousand yards from the enemy's outposts. Another battalion was attacking on our left and another on our right and there was to be *no* artillery bombardment for a change—we were to rely entirely upon surprise. At 4.45 my front wave began to move slowly forward up the hill with ten yards between each man. I had eight lines to start with, with only about fifteen men in each.

We came under rifle and machine-gun fire almost at once, but I don't think that at first the Bosche spotted that anything particular was up. When he did, rocket after rocket went up bang over our heads, brightly illuminating the whole ground. We had to lie down a bit owing to their machine guns and one or two men got hit. But my little Company Lewis guns got going against theirs and with good effect, for when we did get to their machine guns we found the six Germans composing the gun teams all stretched dead round their gun—not bad shooting for a dark and misty morning.

We again moved forward and again had to lie down for a bit. However, I yelled myself hoarse doing the old dodge of short rushes forward and then lying flat, until my rear sergeant got annoyed with me, jumped up and against all regulations started a cheer. Everyone took it up and the whole Company became a great mob yelling and cheering like the devil. The old Bosche were caught absolutely napping. They fought their machine guns to the end—or rather till all their men were killed. Then for the first time our fellows really got a chance with the bayonet. It was simply glorious. Swarms of Berks came surging up from the right and hand in hand we went through those old villages.

We got into the most frightful muddle when we reached the other side, and I found myself in command of practically a whole company of Berks as well as my own, as they had lost a good many officers. We were just about to push on beyond the village when our own guns opened fire according to a prearranged scheme on a line five hundred yards behind the village. This unfortunately just caught us, and as the very first of our shells knocked out two men quite close to me we had to bunk back. I had had only one man killed and about ten wounded up to then, which was not bad.

We then got to the farthest ridge, about five hundred to nine hundred yards in front of the village, and posted outposts. I withdrew my Company to some trenches of sorts behind a sugar factory just outside the village and prepared to spend a quiet day. I got my telephone up and spoke to the C.O., who was in a village about two and a half miles behind. He told me that everyone was very much pleased with the attack and that the General had met some of my men at the dressing station and had told them they had done excellently.

More Bosche prisoners kept turning up out of cellars and a great many were pretty badly wounded.

I kept three of them at my headquarters for a bit and tried to talk to them in French, while one of my subalterns tried his hand at German. Two of them were very fed up with the war, and when asked if they hated the English, one of them said that he had met some quite nice English in Hamburg. Another scowled and shrugged his shoulders when we mentioned old Hindenburg, but was instantly shut up by an older man.

The next day the Germans shelled the village heavily all day, but as we didn't stay inside it, they did us little harm. But they didn't neglect my rather conspicuous position near the ruined *sucrerie*, and here I had the narrowest shave I have had for some time—a blooming great Black Maria plum on top of the ruins and only about fifteen yards or so from me. I fell flat down, was covered with débris and muck and got wounded again!! Just a scratch over the left eye and the bridge of the nose. I ran like a rabbit to my Sergeant-Major, who thought I had been outed, but it was nothing at all and this time you won't see my name in the casualty list though I had to play the wounded hero last night, as my corporal stretcher-bearer insisted on putting on a huge lint bandage as my nose was inflamed. It's quite all right this morning.

In this way the enemy carried on all day. It was pretty sickening. I couldn't move about and had no food to speak of, as we were under observation from a ridge about two miles away.

At 6 o'clock I decided to move my Company back in very small parties to our billets behind, thinking that we shouldn't be seen. Unfortunately, a Berks company which was relieving me came right forward over the top in full view, absolutely giving the show away. I was just on the point of going out with my sergeant-major when a trio of enormous crumps crashed down. God knows how we weren't all knocked out. My sergeant-major, worse luck, got a bit in the chest and stomach, one of my officers, who was just behind me, was hit, and the man crouching next to me was killed outright. I was awfully shaken and really must confess to temporary insanity. After that the remainder of my men ran out and scattered, but fortunately over the reverse side of the hill on the top of which our position had been.

For ten minutes the Germans kept putting these crumps over, but in about five minutes my men had got clear away in scattered groups to the valley beyond where they were safe. I was terribly afraid that my sergeant-major had been killed and also my new officer—whom I hadn't seen. I picked up my Scotty officer and went back towards the vile spot after sending the Company back. I then heard that an awfully nice boy in the Brigade Machine Gunners who had been attached to me throughout the last two attacks, and with whom I had just had tea, was very badly hit and I met him on a stretcher. I sent him back with four men to a dressing station, but he died this morning. I am awfully sorry. Otherwise all went well.

I met my officer: my sergeant-major got carried away all right and I only had one man killed. I *was* relieved, I can tell you. The C.O. was awfully kind about it. I spoke to him on the telephone from the first village I reached on my way back.

On my return I was received with congratulations

and jubilations. The C.O. sent me up a bottle of champagne and to-day I have been busy sending in the names of N.C.O.'s for decorations—immediate awards too—which is a great honour. I have also put my Scotty officer in for an M.C.

Our captured guns are fine trophies and I have already had them stamped " Captured by ' B ' Company 1/4 Oxford and Bucks Lt. Infty." They will go to Oxford at the end of the war.

I think the Division may now be relieved, as we have secured all our objectives and have been warmly congratulated—by Corps, Headquarters, Army Headquarters and the C.-in-C.

April 12th, 1917.   Camp K, 5, Central.

The prospect as I write is scarcely cheering even to a hardened veteran like myself—in fact it is absolutely repulsive. A sodden tent in the snow with a smoking coke fire at the entrance trying to give out as little heat as possible and myself with wet feet hunched in discomfort on a ration box.

But as a set-off to these ills, a large post has arrived with your letter and *parcel*—the latter bringing just the very food which is so necessary on the eve of proceeding again to the outpost line. The poor beggars up there must have had quite enough of it in this awful weather.

I am delighted to hear to-night that two of my N.C.O.'s [1]—a sergeant and a lance-corporal—have been awarded the Military Medal. They are both good chaps and I hope the latter may get the D.C.M. as well —he is a ripping boy simply bursting with life and go.

[1] L/Sergeant A. C. H. Wiggins and L/Corporal J. Upstone.

We have just had a wire from G.H.Q., but unfortunately it is in some sort of code so that all we know is that Platinum has captured Pimple and taken thirty-three more guns and prisoners. This is undoubtedly very satisfactory, but we are left rather in the dark.

April 14th, 1917.   Outpost Line, RONNSOY.

Here we are again in the outpost line: the present-day substitute for our old friend the trenches.

My Company having had a lion's share in the recent operations is in reserve in a sequestered vale, with a few bivouac sheets and odd pieces of corrugated iron. The men have dug themselves into the hillside remarkably quickly and sensibly and will be quite comfortable to-night, though last night they had rather a chilly time.

We got no post yesterday, to my annoyance, but have since heard a certain amount of news. Apparently the Russian Government is experiencing some difficulty from a strong Socialist Party which wants an immediate peace. I hope they will be strong enough to squash this effectively. There is very little news from the Arras front for the last twenty-four hours and what there is is rather disquieting. As usual, some of our Colonials have got themselves into a mess through lack of discipline combined with an excess of zeal. I don't suppose this will appear in the papers and perhaps I had better not have mentioned it; they really ought, by this time, to know better.

My headquarters are in a little tin shanty—and I have a very comfortable German stretcher for a bed—they are, of course, much better ones than ours!

April 18th, 1917.   Outposts outside RONNSOY.

We are again in front; this time I am in the outpost line with my Company, but it is a thousand times pleasanter than the old trench life. My headquarters are in a filthy old bell tent which someone found abandoned and covered with dirt and brushwood. We hold about 2000 yards of front now instead of those narrow little sectors where the enemy knew every spot and exactly where the dug-outs were. I hope to be relieved to-morrow night and to go back to billets in a village which the Germans haven't blown up—but really it isn't much fun because they have very cunningly put mines everywhere. This morning a cellar where our Battalion headquarters had recently been for two nights blew up, killing the Colonel, the Second-in-Command, the Adjutant and Doctor of the 6th Gloucesters; also a stable went up knocking out eleven horses. It makes one prefer tents and bivouacs.

Two of our companies are doing a little attack to-night, but I shall just hang on to the outpost line.

April 19th, 1917.   Outposts outside RONNSOY.

I am thankful to say that my two days' tour is drawing to an end. I hope to get relieved to-night about 9 o'clock. Unfortunately there is a seven- or eight-mile march back to billets, which is rather a trial after two days without sleep in a muddy field. Fortunately it has been very quiet on the whole; though at 9 o'clock last night, just as I was finishing dinner, the Germans opened a heavy bombardment all along my outpost line and kept it up for about half an hour without a stop. I got a bit windy at first and thought they might be going to attack. But it was just the reverse; they evidently expected an attack from us and were dropping a curtain of fire on our front line. Curiously enough an attack *had* been arranged for exactly that hour and was only put off at 5 p.m. It looks as if they had tapped a message somewhere.

April 20th, 1917.   Outpost Line GUILLEMONT Farm.

We were relieved last night about midnight after an exciting little dust-up and I didn't get my men back to their billets till 4.30 this morning. We were all dead tired although, thank Heaven, I had my horse on the journey back. I slept till about midday to-day and then had " brunch " in bed.

Last night we got orders to do a little attack before being relieved against a small strong-point which lay between us and the great Hindenburg Line. Unfortunately this had already been attempted three or four days before and been a ghastly failure and the Bosche was very much on the " qui vive," keeping up a constant stream of " Verey lights " in front of it. My Company was holding the outpost line to the right and so were not concerned save with the possibly unpleasant effects of hostile shelling.

I thought it better to withdraw my headquarters and reserve men to a deep sunken road some way behind and I sat down about 7.30 at the end of a telephone prepared to listen to other people's bravery. Our artillery started bombarding the strong-point at 7.30, but with only about twenty-five guns in all—just enough to give the show away.

As it was still light the Germans could see our fellows (D Company) going over and appear practically to have wiped out the first wave of the attack—killing one Platoon Commander, an amusing Scotty called Dinwoodie, wounding the other, and knocking out most of the N.C.O.'s. The Company Commander then took over the other two platoons but also got held up. Finally, I heard him telephoning back to Battalion headquarters to say that he was lying out with the remnants of his Company about two hundred yards in front of the German position, and that he wanted some more men and some more gunfire in front of him. It was rather extraordinary to be able to listen to the whole thing at the end of a wire and to hear the poor devil who was getting men killed all round him and was expecting to be crumped any moment talking to his C.O., who was giving him instructions and then himself getting on to the Brigade.

I shall take jolly good care to cut myself completely off from anyone behind next time I do a show. They telephoned back first, if you please, to the Brigade and then to the Divisional General (who was out) for leave to send over another company to help the first. The G.S.O.I. said that he couldn't advise without the G.O.C.'s leave. Consequently the Company was ordered to come back and we all went home to bed, with a Company weaker by 45 men wounded, nine killed, four missing, two officers gone and all for nothing. Thank Heaven it wasn't my Company: it would have been a heart-breaking business. Personally I *will* not take instructions from the man behind once the show has been launched. It is fatal and has been proved to be so hundreds of times. The man on the spot must be given power to decide. To-night I believe the people who relieved us are attacking with three battalions! The Staff lives, but God knows if it ever learns much. Fortunately they get the right men now in command, which makes a lot of difference and they are constantly sending people home. But it's among the lower grades that we lack the qualities so much in evidence on the German side.

April 25th, 1917. HAMEL.

I am very much afraid I have missed the post, but there was some excuse, as last night at about 9.30 we got orders that the Battalion were to have their breakfasts by 4.15 a.m. and to stand by ready to move forward at once, as the Brigade in the line was doing an attack on a German position between us and the Hindenburg Line. So we all turned in at once to get a little sleep and were woke up at 3.30 this morning. I got so bored with it that I didn't dress fully and at 4.30 I went to bed again in my clothes and slept soundly till nine o'clock! It is now after ten but we are still standing by—God knows why—and there is no news of the battle except that I believe we took and lost the position—for the third time.

I am so delighted to hear at last that Pearson has gone to King Edward VII Hospital. His wounds are, he says, very much better. I was so afraid he might miss the last boat home, as I think that in future they are going to keep all stretcher cases in France because of submarines. Would you please send him round as a present from me some grapes and strawberries or any other delicacies that invalids like. Perhaps a large box of chocolates would go down well: I expect he sees plenty of illustrated papers, but if you can think of anything special, please send it to him and

I will repay. You can't think what a help he was to me all through those unpleasant weeks last August in front of Pozières and Thiepval.

April 26th, 1917.   HAMEL.

We are really having a wonderful rest! The night before last we were told to stand to at 2 a.m. because the people in front were attacking. So we got up in the early hours and shivered. Then we had to stand by in billets the whole of the day following because the attack had failed. The next night we were told to move up to support at 2.45 a.m. and had to parade and march up four or five miles to a camp occupied by someone else, where we waited, still shivering, till 9 a.m. and were then sent back to our billets and told to spend the night there.

At 5.30 p.m. we were ordered to pack up again and move up to the line, where we arrived angry and exhausted and quite unprepared to repel the German counter-attack which was so confidently expected by our panic-stricken Staff. However, in spite of the most disquieting orders and instructions to stand to at dawn and to be prepared to move at any moment, we all slept like logs till 10 a.m. this morning and feel quite ourselves again.

The weather is glorious with a very chilly wind which blows into this little tin hut where I was about ten days ago. I suppose we shall stay here to-night—at any rate I have ordered a five-course dinner! To-morrow we move into that beastly outpost line for two days. After that I really cannot imagine that we shall stay up here any longer, as the Division is absurdly weak—first from casualties and now from sickness. My Company for fighting purposes has fallen to below a hundred; but I am really very well off, some battalions having only three hundred men all told.

No word yet of my application for leave. But at least it hasn't been sent back and the Staff Captain has rung up for further particulars of my long martyrdom; so perhaps something may happen in a day or two. Be sure I shall let you know at once.

FOURTH LEAVE. 3 Weeks.

May 18th, 1917.   HERMIES Trenches.

I had a wretched journey up to the line yesterday, starting at 7 a.m. and arriving at Béthune about 6 p.m. We have been unexpectedly shifted north and are next to the Anzacs—in fact actually under Birdwood. Fortunately I got some dinner at Divisional Headquarters. I then had to wait until our Mess Cart, for which I had wired, arrived at 9.30. It took two hours and a half to reach our transport, where I spent the night as the Battalion was in the line. I joined them this morning and found everyone pretty happy as it is very quiet here.

May 22nd, 1917.   Trenches HERMIES.

Last night provided a good example of how the war is carried on. We had arranged rather a large show for Mister Bosche at the usual hour of the night and this necessitated, you will understand, a wind of a certain kind and strength. Before this little affair I had to withdraw some of my men from the front line. First the bally wind blew one way and then ten minutes later another, just hovering round the exact point of the compass which was fixed as the limit. Finally, within ten minutes of the hour it again proved fractious, the whole show was abandoned in disgust and everyone had to tramp back again.

The poor fellow in charge of the operation is waiting to go on a month's leave, but until he has got this off his mind he can't go. He is really the only person at all keen about it!

May 25th, 1917.   Reserve Trenches, DEMICOURT.

We were relieved last night about midnight, and are now in a series of foul-smelling holes in the side of a sunken road from which we cannot move by day for fear of being observed by hostile " sausages " or aeroplanes. The Hun has so sited his blooming Hindenburg Line that he can overlook our positions for nearly two or three miles behind the line. So we can't move anywhere by day. Cunning blighter!

A couple of those marvellous Anzacs managed to escape from Lille the other day and got back to our lines. They brought all sorts of information. They said that there were street cars still running in Lille, which was very gay at the moment and full of German officers and men. Personally I think they are preparing to evacuate again pretty soon.

Did I tell you that the General knocked me up the other morning? When he had got home and was safely entrenched in his office he wrote a stinker through his Brigade Major to the effect that he had found men in the forward system of trenches sleeping—apparently with their boots off! " Please take ACTION and render explanations in writing." This in due course was passed to me, so I had to devise some reply.

I first thought of just writing "Guilty, my Lord" across the report, but reflecting that this might be considered frivolous I took the offensive and stated that "I had ordered the men to remove their boots for medical reasons." But when I saw the C.O. two or three days later, he said that he thought I should have invented a better yarn than that.

June 2nd, 1917. Trenches HERMIES.

Everything is pretty quiet, though last night at about eleven the Bosche treated us to a display of fireworks—red, green and white rockets and golden rain. As far as I can make out each side thought that it was being raided by the other. It was mainly interesting to us because as we were watching the business one of our orderlies suddenly pointed out that we couldn't see the lights as a dark mass of clouds or mist had rolled in and was apparently coming towards us. Some idiot suggested gas and we all became extremely alert. The illusion was helped out by the very strong smell of powder which was coming down wind. We soon got over our anxiety, but when later I was relating this to a friend in the front line whose post I was visiting, he said, "We thought exactly the same and actually got as far as putting our helmets on!" The pack-mule which was bringing up rations to the front line for the first time that night, scampered off home with its driver as fast as he could go!

June 6th, 1917. VELU Wood.

Our new Commanding Officer has turned up, Lieut.-Colonel R. Stevens of the Oxfordshires. I met him at the Base in February, when he had just arrived from

Mesopotamia as a Captain. He is a very Senior Officer in the regiment and a very nice fellow indeed, like most regular soldiers.

I am back with my Company again, but I have been told that I am still to understudy the Second-in-Command, which means that I am allowed to command as long as all is peace, but have got to go to Battalion headquarters directly there is a battle. I suppose this will please you, but it seems ridiculous to me.

Our Divisional General, Fanshawe, has been given the K.C.B. He has commanded us since May 1915, and to him is largely due the efficiency of the Division. I am very glad indeed. Our C.O. should have been given the D.S.O. but appears to have been left out.

June 28th, 1917. Rest Camp.

I have a piece of news which I suppose will please you, though I don't know whether to be pleased myself.

My name has been submitted to attend the next course of instruction at the Army School of Instruction, starting about July 3rd: it means *five* weeks' rest and holiday from the line, right back near Amiens. But although I am certain to enjoy it I hate leaving the regiment for so long. They will, I expect, be going out of the line for a bit, but where they will be when I rejoin I cannot imagine, probably miles away.

We are spending three days here in this rest camp— a very nice and comfortable life. I was woken by my servant at about 9.30 with a cup of tea, had breakfast in bed about 10, got up about 10.30. This afternoon I shall go for a ride.

July 5th, 1917.   5th Army School, Toutencourt.

I have never worked so hard since I came to France. We parade every morning at 8.30, do four hours' work till 1, then parade again from 2 till 5. Pretty hot stuff.

There are one hundred officers on this course and we are divided into four Platoons or " Syndicates " under an Officer Instructor. To all intents and purposes I am a Tommy again. It is a curious feeling.

This morning we had a lecture on trenches and how to dig them, followed by twenty minutes' physical drill under a sergeant-major of the old type. We were then told off as a working party, had to draw picks and shovels and were allotted tasks, going through all the preliminary procedure though without actually having to dig. This afternoon we had a two-hours' lecture on Advanced Guards, which was immediately followed by an hour's lecture on Battalion Organisation.

This evening we so far relax as to attend the " What Nots," a troupe from the 7th Division, who are giving a show in the local Y.M.C.A. hut.

All to-morrow morning we shall spend on bayonet fighting and squad drill, and the afternoon on instruction in the Lewis gun.

There are a great many Australians here, and of course officers from many different regiments. We all mess together at four different tables and it is not too bad. We don't work on Sunday and Saturday is a half-day. There are buses to Amiens on both days.

The C.O. is a very strict disciplinarian—quite one

of the old school. Everything is done in the grand manner and the parade this morning was staggering; you couldn't help being smart, though I find that a rifle comes a bit awkwardly to the hand. I think I shall learn a good deal, or rather systematise and pigeonhole a lot of knowledge about which I was uncertain before.

The Instructors' remarks on trenches and trench fighting are given with all deference; they fully understand that we do know a certain amount about things. The object of the course is primarily to make officers efficient instructors in drill, bayonet fighting, engineering and field-work, in all of which subjects we get very rusty in the line.

July 17th, 1917. TOUTENCOURT.

Life is rosy tinted. Yesterday the ante-chamber of the Mess was a seething mass of officers shouting my name and handing me parcels, letters and papers with many expressions of envy, especially from the poor Australians, who only get a mail once a month and not always then. The general impression is that I must be married and I haven't the courage to tell them that it isn't so, and that the only girl I ever hear from is my own sister.

We had an hour's bayonet fighting this morning: I paired off with a tall Anzac, an awfully jolly fellow called Mulholland. The difference between these Australians and our own newly-gazetted officers is enormous. They have *all* served in the ranks first, and though most of them have lived rough lives in Australia, they are gentlemen, extraordinarily good-natured, without an ounce of brag about them and not a bit spoilt by all the advertisement they get.

There is no news of an official kind except for a piece of private information to the effect that an invention has come out which will do away with aircraft and submarines. A boy of nineteen is said to be its inventor and is reported to have refused a princely sum from the W.O. for it!

July 31st, 1917. TOUTENCOURT.

This last week has been as full of military training as ever—from learning how to fire German machine guns to lectures on staff duties and aeroplanes. A young Colonel in the R.F.C. talked to us yesterday on the work of the R.F.C. in France: he was only twenty-six years old and was very nervous at first.

Our mastery of the air over here is so complete that even we ourselves do not realise it. He was telling us of the big bag we had on July 27th. We brought down thirty-one machines and only lost three. Practically all aerial operations are carried on miles behind the German lines. Every day and night we bomb their headquarters and aerodromes as far back as Brussels and Valenciennes. But few people realise how free we are from similar attentions from Bosche airmen.

This battle in Flanders is simply " Gargantuan," days and nights of endless bombardments from the sea to Lens. Even Napoleon would have stood appalled. No one seems yet to know definitely if the infantry have gone over the top, and we all rush every morning for the Paris *Daily Mail* to see the news. We are the more interested as our regiments are for the most part concerned.

I leave on Sunday and shall have a longish journey. I can't say when or where I shall find the regiment though I know approximately their position.

THIRD BATTLE OF YPRES

August 10th, 1917.   Reserve Billets, HOUTKERQUE.

Conditions are ghastly in this region. The weather is a nightmare; continuous rain for weeks has left the ground soaked in water. Consequently the troops are without cover of any sort and nothing can be done to get on with the war. It is even worse than on the Somme last year, and that is saying a great deal.

The battle is practically confined to artillery work, scarcely a shot is fired from a rifle, but shells go backwards and forwards unceasingly, both night and day.

However, I must set your minds at rest. Yesterday after an excellent luncheon at the club at Poperinghe, I rode out on an ambulance along the main road to the front and finally came to a wood in which our Divisional Headquarters were.

One of the first people I met was dear old Alan Gibson, now Divisional Transport Officer, looking perfectly beautiful and not at all perturbed by the responsibilities of life in Flanders. I then met another friend of mine, an A.D.C. to the Artillery General, and finally I got to the headquarters office, where the D.A.A.G. told me that I was down on my Battalion list to be left behind and must go back at once about nine miles to a Divisional Reinforcement Camp. The authorities are so frightened of losing all the officers of a battalion at one swoop that about three or four are always left behind and are not allowed to be sent for save under exceptional circumstances.

Alan Gibson gave me some news of the regiment. They have only been in the line for two days, during which both the Colonel and the Adjutant were wounded. The Intelligence Officer and another new officer were killed and Maclean, one of my best Scotty friends, was badly wounded. They had about ninety casualties in all and are now in support somewhere behind. Colonel Bartlett has been sent back to us to command, and I am very much pleased as I like him awfully, and always know where I am with him.

I am afraid leave is taboo just now, but there may be some going in October, if the fighting is over. God knows how this battle is going to end; the elements are fighting for the Germans and ruining our plans. With fine weather we should have gained an enormous victory by now.

August 13th, 1917. HOUTKERQUE.

Each of the four regiments of the Brigade has left one hundred men behind as reinforcements, and as I am the senior Company Officer I am acting as Adjutant of the Brigade Company. This morning I took them—four hundred strong—for a couple of hours' route march, then put in two more hours' training and so finished the day's work. Not very energetic.

There is no news. Nothing much is happening at the moment, but the weather, thank God, is drier and the war may be renewed at any moment.

August 16th, 1917. Reserve Camp, HOUTKERQUE

We believe that the regiment went over the sandbags this morning about dawn. There was, I am told, a terrific bombardment at that hour, but no news has come back to us, and we shall probably have to wait for the London papers before we know what has happened.

The Flanders mud which saved the British Army in 1914 has saved the German this summer. This low-lying country is a very curious sight. You can see for miles, and it is quite attractive, and densely populated with little villages and farms. The people are more refined than the French peasants of the Somme country, and the women dress much better.

The day before yesterday Pickford and I rode over to a town ten miles away where it was understood that ices were obtainable. We had a perfect tea, vanilla ices well sugared and lots of cakes.

August 18th, 1917. Reserve, HOUTKERQUE.

We can get no news of yesterday's battle, except that our Brigade have, I am afraid, taken rather a severe knock. The whole attack seems to have been pretty successful except at one or two points, but we cannot get any reliable information. I believe that the Brigade has been taken out and I suppose that it will have to be reorganised. But the fog of war is too thick to allow me to make any predictions.

These big pushes are greatly to be preferred to the old trench life. Here you meet friends every moment. The roads are like Piccadilly, every regiment is represeted and there is plenty of life and movement.

Last night I went to a perfectly marvellous show given by the " troupe " of a Scottish Division—the " Balmorals." We only just got in. They had a very good orchestra and there was a most perfect girl. A sort of gasp went up when she came on—it was difficult to believe that she was a wolf in sheep's clothing.

The Tommies are making merry in the next room and rag-time is being played on a wheezy old accordion. Like most Flemish farms this is also an estaminet, and between 6 and 8 in the evening the men are allowed to make free with the *vin blanc* and beer. " Take me back to dear old Blighty " is going strong and the din is terrific.

August 18th, 1917. HOUTKERQUE.

We have been standing by since last night expecting to rejoin our Brigade at once, but no orders have yet come through.

As you will see by the papers, we gained a fair success at Langemarck; but our Brigade has taken a heavy knock. We still cannot get any definite news. But last night I got a short note from the transport Officer, who had heard from the Colonel. Apparently every officer was hit except two subalterns and I am sorry to say that a good many have been killed. The other regiments in the Brigade have also suffered heavily and the Division wired for all our Brigade reinforcements last night. But the Corps Commander apparently refuses to allow them to be used, as they are supposed to be kept absolutely intact whatever happens until all the fighting is over: whether this will be possible I don't know.

Everything is in such a chaotic state that I c

tell at all what will happen. I see that to-day's papers are very optimistic, especially over Lloyd George's " U " Boat speech.

August 24th, 1917.   Dambre Camp, Vlamertinghe.

It is difficult to keep cheerful just now with so many friends gone west. I have just met Davenport of the 2/4th. They too have taken a bad knock and all except three or four of the officers are killed or wounded—many of my friends among them. My solitary subaltern is dining in Poperinghe to-night with two of the others. I send him off at every possible occasion to enjoy himself, poor little devil. He has only just left his Public School and has had about enough of it.

A poor woman wrote to me to-night begging me to send her husband on leave: she hasn't seen him for fourteen months; but I had to write and tell her there are many who haven't been home for sixteen and eighteen months!! All I could promise was to keep him out of the trenches the next time we are in. The men have a lot to put up with and one cannot think of one's own case when one remembers theirs. Poor devils! The initial enthusiasm has disappeared and has been succeeded by a sort of dumb and disciplined resignation. On the whole they are wonderful, but at times one yearns for the old crowd, they were so awfully different.

August 25th, 1917.   Dambre Camp, Vlamertinghe.

I have been up since 3.30 a.m. this morning and took a long walk up to the line and back to see the ground. I had two subalterns with me, one of whom, being Intelligence Officer, led the way. We made this early start because we wanted to get there between 5.30 and 7.30, the only time when things are reasonably quiet on this most accursed of all fronts.

It was a gorgeous morning, but very cold before the sun rose. The desolation is indescribable, almost worse than the Somme, though of course there are fewer trenches, nothing but these famous concrete blockhouses, which have caused us such a very unpleasant surprise. They have put the Bosche one up on us, as we haven't yet devised a satisfactory method of dealing with them. They are enormously strong and almost shell-proof except for the biggest. I went right up to the farthest one which caused us all our casualties and which we failed to take. Lord knows how many of them the Bosche has got behind. It rather takes the wind out of our sails, as it's going to delay us a good deal. Surprise is a tremendous element in war, and the Germans have certainly done something clever this time.

August 27th, 1917.   Canal Bank, YPRES.

Just a line to let you know I am just off in an hour's time to do an attack—a full-dress affair. If all goes well we shall be relieved to-morrow night and come right out of the line.

Don't worry about it: when it is over I will drop you a line as soon as possible.

There is an awful lot to see to—getting things served out and making final arrangements. We have rather a difficult job and last night it rained hard, which is rotten luck.

I hope all will go well, but our numbers are low and

German Pill Box, Cheddar Villa. Third Battle of Ypres, 1917
Courtesy Imperial War Museum. (*Facing Page* 234)

both the officers and the men are very tired. However, you never know your luck.

August 29th, 1917. DAMBRE Camp, VLAMERTINGHE.

All is well and I am again preserved after the worst experience of modern warfare I have yet struck. You mustn't mind my telling you fully of my adventures. It is a relief to write them down and they may interest you.

At 2 o'clock on the afternoon of the 27th the bombardment started. We were then a good four miles behind the line in a deep cutting on a canal bank, and as the noise began we started to move up. The companies were only at half their proper strength, the men were gloomy and dispirited and I must confess that the officers were not optimistic. Conditions were against us; it had rained heavily during the night and after a fine morning it had begun again at about 2 o'clock.

From zero hour we had to go through four miles of open country to get to our starting-point, from which four hours later we were to pass through the first attack and capture a vaguely defined line somewhere in front, a difficult operation even under good conditions.

We started off across the plain, loaded up with rations, tools, bombs, flares for aeroplanes, sandbags, etc., toiling along a narrow wooden track as the mud is practically impassable.

The mist and rain did, however, in a large degree save us from the heavy shelling we should otherwise have got. The noise was tremendous. Thousands of guns of all calibres were firing at their maximum rate, an overpowering spectacle. After the first two hours we came more closely upon the scene of action and had a few casualties—lucky fellows with "blightys" who hobbled delightedly to the rear. Meanwhile we had to deploy and flounder in the mud as the track was being shelled.

About 4.30 I got up to the original British front line. I tried to reorganise my Company, get in touch with the companies on the right and left and find suitable holes to halt in, as we had two hours to wait before we attacked. Meanwhile reports came back that the advance had been held up and was making no headway.

My men and I were now in scattered groups in small trenches and shell-holes all full of water. At 7 o'clock our bombardment, which had now been going since 2 o'clock, increased again to its full intensity which was to be the signal for my lot to attack through the front Brigade to the farthest objective.

As they had unfortunately not got their first objective and as I had had special orders not to become involved in a fight for it, I remained where I was in masterly inactivity, getting shelled to blazes, as there were one or two derelict tanks near by, which always attract fire. The hideous din went on till about 10 p.m. plus the rain. We were all soaked to the skin and caked in slimy mud as we crouched in those filthy shell-holes, shivering under a cutting Flanders wind. There was no definite news except that the attack was not making progress.

At 10 p.m. things quietened down. We rearranged ourselves and tried to dig little holes and trenches to get into, but the water was everywhere.

I have never spent a more miserable night. At dawn, which broke dark and threatening, I tried to push on and relieve the Brigade in front which had had pretty heavy casualties, but they were so disorganised and the country was so exposed that we couldn't do much. The Bosche snipers got to work very soon, and from 3 a.m. till 1 p.m. I sat cramped and wet and cold in my shell-hole with a young private, my orderly, and tried to sleep but without success.

At 1 p.m. I got out and made my way back to Battalion headquarters, where I got a hot drink and some food from the Colonel. He told me that we would be relieved about midnight.

We hung on and the relief at last arrived, poor devils, to take over our shell-holes. I didn't get away till 5 a.m. I could scarcely walk for fatigue and mud, but had to struggle back four miles to a camp of bivouacs where I found the regiment.

Fortunately I had secured as my headquarters a huge and enormously strong Bosche concrete fort, one of the ones that have caused all the trouble here. I washed and changed out of my Tommy's uniform which I had been wearing for the attack, and felt absolutely refreshed. We marched on back here about 11 o'clock to our old rest camp. The Division has been relieved and we start trekking backwards to-morrow, so you can imagine how happy we feel.

I shall be very tired by this evening, but at present I am quite fresh, which is surprising after being up for two such days and nights. Thank God it's all over!

August 31st, 1917.   Camp S. JANS TER BIEZEN.

We are in a ripping camp, the weather is fine, and everything is jolly.

Yesterday I took my subaltern into Poperinghe and we spent an afternoon buying new mess kit, which sadly needed reorganising. I enjoyed showing off my Flemish, but it didn't go very far. However, we sent the Mess Cart back loaded up with fruit, eggs, crockery and all sorts of other things and then I gave him a good dinner.

To-day we have been frightfully busy absorbing drafts and getting smart again. I am going to entertain every night and shall make my Mess President do a lot of work. He is also O.C. Amusements and will have to get up concerts and football matches—anything to make the men forget the nightmare of the trenches.

September 1st, 1917.   S. JANS TER BIEZEN.

Leave is going excellently, one officer per four days: may it long continue. I sounded the C.O. on the subject of a month's leave, but he didn't exactly jump at the idea, or rather he said that he didn't think that the General would. However, I shall try. What a pity I am not engaged to be married: that would simplify matters greatly, but I doubt if it would be worth it.

I am busy to-day inspecting my men and making them clean buttons and tunics and polish their boots. The Corps Commander—General Sir Ivor Maxse—was to have inspected us to-morrow at Church Parade, which I now hear is off. However, in any case I am a firm believer in polish and smartness as an aid to discipline, as it undoubtedly is.

September 5th, 1917. Corps School, VOLKERINGHOVE.

We have all come over here for three days for a course of lectures on " The Battle " under the auspices of the Corps Training School. I am living in a tent which I share with only one other officer, Crouch, a Captain in the Bucks whom I know well. We owe our comfort to the fact that we are the two senior officers in the Brigade here. Actually I am not, but anyhow I wangled it and the others are all pigging it with one servant between six in a large marquee.

Maxse gave us an opening lecture yesterday evening. He is a personality, very bluff and outspoken and extremely amusing. Eight officers from each regiment in the Division and a few machine-gun and trench mortar officers came, about one hundred in all. We are to be immersed for three days in the battle atmosphere. We discuss future operations, have lectures on tanks, aeroplanes, artillery and other technical subjects, and try and produce ideas for dealing effectively with the latest Bosche method of defence, which certainly is a puzzler.

The authorities are again optimistic and there is no doubt that in spite of our extraordinary ill-luck in the matter of the weather we are steadily and surely wearing down the Bosche. I don't think that his advance in Russia will help him from a military point of view. The Russians can retreat to almost any extent and the gap thus created will only serve to occupy more German troops, which they will very soon need elsewhere. If we can only get another month's fine weather a great many things should happen in the west.

. . . . .

FIFTH LEAVE. A Month.

October 21st, 1917. CALAIS.

I had a very smooth crossing and bearing in mind your advice about keeping warm, I hired the Captain's cabin where there was an excellent fire. We didn't start till 5 p.m. so it was dark and misty when we arrived. The Captain's steward regaled me with stories of the air raids they had endured at Calais and said that when they arrived the other night bombs were falling all round them.

As I knew where the A.M.L.O. lived I walked straight into his office while the other officers mobbed in a queue outside his window. I secured a cab but just as I arrived at my Hotel, a siren went off and the cabby gave a shriek of "Zeppelins" and almost forgot to look at his fare. Inside no one seemed to be bothering much. The siren continued to shriek periodically, but nothing happened and dinner proceeded.

As I write another air raid is in progress. The sirens went off about ten minutes ago, and people began to rush about. Two Taubes are flying about over the town and dropping bombs—the anti-aircraft doesn't seem very brilliant here. I expect the objectives are the docks and railway stations as it is a daylight raid. I shall be quite glad to be back at the peaceful front.

October 22nd, 1917. VILLERS-AU-BOIS Huts.

After many vicissitudes I have got back to the dear old regiment and have found many friends. I arrived just in time for dinner and found three or four new officers, very decent fellows. We have had a cheery evening and all seems well.

We are in a camp some distance behind the line, and according to everyone it is very quiet and pleasant here, thanks to the large ridge which has been captured by the Canadians and which we now occupy (the Vimy Ridge).

Thank Heaven they don't go in for air raids here; it is much too civilised.

November 3rd, 1917.   Trenches AVION LENS.

The C.O. has just gone home on fourteen days' leave (it has been extended to that now) and I am Second-in-Command and am going to live at Battalion headquarters to-morrow. They are in a very deep dug-out and I expect that it will be as full of life as most German dug-outs are.

It makes an interesting change. I am responsible for all the work on our front, which is an exceptionally wide one. I was walking for two hours this morning before breakfast and only covered half the distance. On the left we are within forty yards of the Bosche, but on other parts of our front we are as much as a thousand yards away—a very long distance in trench warfare.

We are living in a dug-out which is phenomenally deep and has no less than six entrances. Scouts, signallers, orderlies and servants each have their own separate compartment, while in another are all the headquarters officers, the C.O., the Adjutant, the Scout officer, the Signal officer and the Liaison officer from the Gunners. The trenches are excellent and a suggestion of home is introduced by the names which the Canadians have given them. Our front line is Billie Burke, approached through Vesta Tilley. The support line is Doris Keane and headquarters are in Teddie Gerrard.

The Mess is full of officers all day long and most of the night; artillery officers intent on observation: R.E. officers with grievances about draining: medical officers talking sanitation at the top of their voices: signal officers discussing telephones: staff officers trying to find out where the trenches are without going to see for themselves: machine gunners who come in to apologise for firing at our men (they killed one last night and wounded another): trench mortar experts trying to get permission to fire their beastly little guns: every branch of the service is represented.

I am deadly tired, as I only slept from 2 till 5 last night and that in my boots, and from 12 to 5 the night before. But I must now write a long report on the work which it is proposed that we should do in the sector, a dull job, as we know well that with the first thaw all our labours will tumble down. No earthworks can stand that. But we are really having a very good time and are quite a happy family. The Acting C.O., Lloyd Baker, who was Staff Captain to McClintock at the beginning of the war, is a very nice fellow indeed—an old Etonian. He belongs to the Bucks Battalion and I have known him for a long while.

November 17th, 1917. SAVY.

We have been spending this morning on a detailed Kit Inspection by the Brigadier [1] which started at the

[1] Brig.-Gen. D. M. Watt commanded 145th Brigade till the end of the War.

unholy hour of 9 a.m. He walked round attended by the Platoon Commander, the Captain of the Company, the C.O., the Adjutant, myself, as Second-in-Command, and several Quartermaster-Sergeants—absolutely absurd. I am dining with him to-night at Brigade Headquarters.

The Colonel is due to return to-day or to-morrow, but whether I go back to my Company or not is still uncertain as I may be kept on at Battalion Headquarters as Third-in-Command. In principle I disagree with this, but actually I like it very much better than living with about seven or eight other officers in extreme discomfort, and I have had my share of commanding a company by now.

The war is developing along the strangest lines and God knows what the end of it will be. But I am once more persuaded that military life is full of excitement and romance. It is something to be able to spend one's youth gloriously in France, Flanders, Italy, Egypt and Palestine visiting the scenes of the victories and defeats of one's ancestors instead of living at home and being hustled round the Continent once a year *via* Cooks. Should I ever have seen Arras and Ypres, Albert and Peronne under such interesting conditions if there had been no war? I doubt it.

The next few weeks are going to be some of the most interesting in my life. We shall probably be moving far away from here in three or four days' time. I will write whenever I get a chance, but you may have to wait for a week or so after receiving this letter.

. . . . . .

November 22nd, 1917. SAVY.

We are off to Italy at ten o'clock to-night. My Company and I are on the first train with the C.O. The men are in splendid fettle and very much excited. We are well up to strength, which is a good thing—my Company is over one hundred and seventy strong.

November 24th, 1917. In the train to ITALY.

We have now been travelling for thirty-six hours and it has occurred to me that I may possibly be able to get a letter off through a British Railway Transport Officer at one of the stations along our route, though we have long since passed the zone of the British Armies and are breaking new ground with a vengeance.

We started with the possibility of a journey of three to six days and have food on the train for an even longer period. It is quite comfortable, as I have a first-class carriage with the other Captain, my old subaltern Allan.

Subalterns are in third-class carriages, three in each, and as we have our cook and two waiters on a coach next door, I have been getting regular hot meals—so far! How long the eggs, pork chops and other delicacies will last I don't know, as of course we are getting no fresh food—only bully beef, biscuits, bread and dry rations. We were to have had a regular four-hour halt daily for exercise and a hot meal, but these have been cut out and we are reduced to uncertain halts of not much more than an hour's duration. The weather is very mild, and as I have my blanket, two coats, and all washing materials with me, I can wash, shave and sleep in comfort. All we want are English newspapers in which to read about this great success at Cambrai, and of course the post, which God knows when we shall see again.

We passed through the outskirts of Paris yesterday amid scenes of moderate enthusiasm and yesterday evening stopped at Troyes for a short time.

I must wait until our next stop, as I can't write while the train is going.

Later.

Another wayside halt in the midst of a great plain, slightly wooded but otherwise entirely under cultivation. I don't know at all where we are, as we have no maps and the names of the small stations help us little. We should, I imagine, be somewhere between Troyes and Lyons.

The train moves on again and I must stop.

November 26th, 1917.   In the train to ITALY.

We have just halted at a station for breakfast, so I am scribbling this to give to the R.T.O. I sent you a card last night amid a scene of tremendous riot and enthusiasm which recalled the early days in France. When we got to Turin, it was too dark to march through the streets as had been previously arranged, but crowds of people were at the station with flags, chocolates, soap and gifts of all kinds.

The men were regaled with hot coffee from fifty different tubs and the officers were taken into a small room and given vermouth, coffee and cigars. I had a long chat with an Italian officer there who knew London slightly, and most of the ladies either spoke English well or were themselves English.

The train departed amid great cheering on both

sides which continued wildly for two miles as we went through the city. I am sorry that we didn't see more of it.

You mustn't worry if you don't hear from me regularly; you will know that it's all right. Our journey should end some time to-day.

Later.   TURIN.

We are still in the station from which I sent off my last letter to you, where we have been for about three hours, but as we never know when the train may take it into its head to move on we can't do much. The confusion is pretty bad as is only natural, and one has to keep very strict discipline in case of accidents which have already taken their toll, though not of any of our men, thank God. But a train-load of gunners which has just come in had six casualties due to a gun getting hitched on to the electric overhead wires and electrocuting them. The A.P.M. looks a bit fagged and worried, but everyone else is in the highest spirits. Food arrangements have been wonderful and my servant, Painting, turned up this morning with scrambled eggs, sausages and hot tea directly the train stopped. Then I had a wash and a shave. Under such conditions a long journey is nothing.

The train shows signs of moving on, so good-bye.

November 28th, 1917.   CEREA, ITALY.

At last we have reached our journey's end. The train stopped just before dawn this morning and we took about three hours detraining: the horses had been in for five and a half days without a rest, poor beasts, and were very tired. Then we marched four miles to a village in which we were to be billeted. My pony became awfully fresh after a bit and did her best to pitch me off.

The excitement on our arrival was tremendous. No English troops had been here before, and certainly none had been billeted. Two of my Platoons were put into the Girls' School, to the great joy of the children, as the village Padre has closed the place until further notice.

Our billets gave us the surprise of our life. The houses are spacious and beautifully swept and garnished. As for headquarters, although only the house of a well-to-do farmer, it is like a spacious " palazzo," huge rooms, rather bare but everything very solid and good to look at with tapestried pictures on the walls.

The dear old Padre, a big bluff old boy full of go and with an enormous " tum tum," seemed to take a great fancy to me and patted me on the head, to my great embarrassment. On going to my billet I discovered it was his house. He demanded to know where " Il Capitano " was. When I told him that I was the man, he roared with laughter, slapped me again most vigorously and demanded my age. I said " quaranta," which I had learnt from the dictionary and so shut him up. He then showed me into the most spotless bedroom I have seen outside England: I was delighted, as I had expected to have to sleep in a bivouac. It only shows how unwise it is to indulge in anticipations, as we are far better off here than we have been in most parts of France.

The people are extraordinarily kind, and sent us in three different kinds of wine to drink for lunch. They have also been giving the troops some awfully strong black stuff which knocks them absolutely silly. We have had to warn the men very strongly.

The Italian soldiers don't make such a good impression and they are, as you probably know, the most appalling thieves. My fellow Company Commander discovered that all his Company cooks' spare clothing had been stolen this morning: it made me laugh, but is rather sickening for them as they lost all their clean suits of khaki. But the Entente is going pretty strong; our men are so very easy to get on with. They just put an *o* on to the end of each word and think they are speaking Italian.

To-morrow morning we march on again to our proper concentration area. How long we shall take to collect together at this very slow rate and what we shall do when we have done so I don't know and couldn't very well tell you if I did.

December 6th, 1917. PAVIOLA.

We have now marched for the eighth time in nine days. It is very hard on the men, who have to carry full kit and equipment—about *ninety pounds*.

Yesterday we had a marvellous billet in a large empty hotel. My room was a big one on the first floor with a large verandah and French windows and with a bathroom leading out of it. Not bad for active service! The Colonel nearly turned me out when he saw it.

We moved on again to-day, but only three miles: I suspect that Brigade Headquarters wanted our hotel: at any rate I met Kitson, the Brigade Major, this morning, and he told me that he was moving in there to-day. But I have again got into an excellent house and, best of all, the Mess is in a warm cosy room with a big fire. Unfortunately it is the only living-room and at times rather full of people. At the moment there are only two rather pretty girls who are trying to learn English and to teach us Italian through the happy medium of French. But I have succeeded in inducing one of them to start playing the mandolin, and as the other is busy smoking a cigarette I can get on with my letter. They have been chatting away ever since dinner, saying that the English women are cold and the men very cold and all sorts of unintelligible things!

We can now hear the guns rather plainly but we are still a very long way off. It is said that things are ridiculously quiet and that the Italian women are doing their washing in the Piave between the two armies. I have no great fear of this front; nothing can well be worse than Flanders or the Somme.

December 9th, 1917.   PAVIOLA.

We are still in the same village and are very comfortable, but to-morrow we move on again.

Last night I dined with one of the other companies, who are billeted in the house of a jolly Italian doctor with a young wife and two pretty nieces. They all speak French and are very hospitable. After dinner we went into the drawing-room and two men from the regiment played English and Italian tunes on a mandolin and banjo. We had a very jolly and noisy evening.

I wonder if this will arrive anywhere near Christmas Day. I send you my love and wish you the very best of luck.

December 10th, 1917. PAVIOLA.

I have just finished paying my men for the first time since we left France and was received with cheers: God knows what they will be like on to-morrow's march after the wine they will have drunk—that is if we do march, but we have now been here since Thursday and it is now Monday. We may go at any moment, but whether east or west depends on the Germans.

The men are in splendid fettle except for a few sore feet. On the whole they are pleased with the change. As usual we are all optimistic, including, I understand, our Generals. We are all praying for snow on the mountains, and do you do the same, as it may spell disaster for the Austro-German Army if their communications are seriously affected.

December 22nd, 1917. TEZZE.

Still no post. Each night we are put off till the next, but to-morrow they say we shall really get six days' arrears.

To-morrow I have a twenty-mile trip in a car and am to reconnoitre some confounded mountains. It will be beastly cold and I shall have to start early, which is annoying on a Sunday morning.

Yesterday I sent two officers with a small limbered wagon and my pony into the big town.[1] They most unexpectedly came in for a bombardment: their first taste of war for many a long day. The Italians, poor devils, got very panic-stricken and refused to sell anything at all. They abandoned their shops and began streaming out of the town with chickens and geese tucked under their arms. A number of

[1] Bassano.

them arrived back here last night, quite convinced that the Austrians were advancing; I suppose it is only some long-range gun they have brought up.

December 24th, 1917. TEZZE.

Yesterday I spent one of the most interesting days of my life. With three or four other officers I left at about 8.30 a.m. in an Italian lorry to invade the mountains. We started from the bottom of the foothills and began climbing. At first the road ran in broad circular sweeps, among the wooded slopes, which rather reminded me of the Dordogne country, though with the big white slopes sheer above us it was far grander. Soon we came to snow; we left the foot-hills below us and the air became colder and colder.

I elected to sit outside with the driver while the others remained inside, but I was very glad I did so, as the view was glorious. On one side of us sheer rock, and on the other a steep precipice. Finally, at about three thousand feet, we reached a village with a lot of Italian troops in it and long straggling lines of tiny little mules carrying enormous loads of food and clothing to their army.

We could now hear the guns quite plainly, as we were only about three or four miles from the actual front. There was a good deal of artillery activity, for it is the most vital spot on this front and the world is waiting to see what will happen here.

We stood on literally the last mountain barrier between the Germans and the plains. If they succeed in crossing this range they will come straight down into the low country, the Italians on the Piave will be cut off and God knows what will happen. Retirement to the line of the Adige would mean giving up some of the finest towns in Italy: Vicenza, Verona and Padua. You can understand it is a critical moment.

At present the Germans are attacking almost daily, but not yet with their full force. They have only one avenue of approach and are fighting for the heights which command it. One cannot but admire their cleverness and skill. They are past masters of the military art. In France and Flanders they have succeeded in forming an impassable barrier against which in spite of our superiority in guns and men we have thrown ourselves in vain until dry rot has now set in. They have attacked Roumania, Russia and Italy in turn and already they have succeeded in creating an atmosphere very largely favourable to peace.

December 26th, 1917. TEZZE.

I couldn't write yesterday: I was much too busy.

The men have had the best Christmas since they left England: it was a huge success.

We arranged a football competition—six a side—which kept the Company occupied all the morning and afternoon and caused great excitement and enthusiasm. In order to make the thing go, the officers entered a team, but as we are only six in number we all of us had to play, including myself. It was a bitterly cold day and the Italians must have thought us quite mad. We turned out in white cotton pants supplied by one of my officers who seems to have a big supply, and the men called us the

"Lily Whites." We put up quite a good game and are challenging the Headquarters officers the day after to-morrow—the Second-in-command, Adjutant, Assistant Adjutant, Scout officer, Doctor and Transport officer. I am trying to buy red stockings and red shirts, which are my Company's colours, in order to make a real splash.

Dinners were at 1: the men were all able to sit down and the N.C.O.'s waited on them. We gave them pork and roast beef with piles of potatoes and greens. The plum puddings were followed by apples, oranges, nuts and cigarettes. Of course beer was out of the question, so we bought some red wine, dosed it up with sugar and lemon, and boiled it into a sort of mulled claret. Later we gave them cold suppers and my mess cook made them a rum punch, with some vermouth in it and lemon. But the best of all was the arrival of a three or four days' mail in the middle of dinner: it came as a God-send.

The officers had lunch about 3, and a good dinner at 8. The C.O. gave us a magnum of champagne and two bottles of port.

In the evening my Sergeant-Major sent up a message to say that the Sergeants' Mess would be very much pleased to see Captain Greenwell at any time before 9.30, so I went down there, had my health drunk and drank theirs in rum and milk, champagne, whisky, Marsala and God knows what else.

Presently we heard some carols outside, and thinking that it was some of the Company, one of the sergeants threw a bucket of water at them. It was then discovered that they were my other officers plus the officers of another company under their Captain, one of my old subalterns, who had come to visit us. They burst into the Sergeants' Mess and we kept the show going with songs until midnight and so to bed!

This morning I had the whole Company on parade for Physical Drill and Games. There were a lot of frowning faces and tired eyes, but they got through it. In the afternoon we organised a big Sports Meeting: races, tug of war, jumping, and then comic turns, of which the most amusing was the officers and sergeants blindfold drill. Both were blindfolded and the Sergeant-Major also blindfolded started drilling us: it was the most laughable performance. In two minutes everyone was all over the shop. Then we had a jockey race: each Platoon Sergeant carried his Platoon Officer and the Sergeant-Major carried me: the Quartermaster-Sergeant carried my Second-in-Command, Fox. The latter won and I was second. Apples were then suspended on strings which the men had to rush at, eat with their hands behind their backs, and then race back. The Quartermaster-Sergeant's ear was bitten, which caused amusement!

Finally, I gave away the prizes. It was really a great success and I think the men have thoroughly enjoyed themselves.

I have managed to fix up a recreation room for them where they can read and write in peace. If you have any friends who are eager to do good, please ask them to send me some Virginian cigarettes for the men, as they are very short of them. They should be bought out of bond, as they are then much cheaper.

1918

January 11th, 1918. TEZZE.

I am perfectly happy and satisfied. Another large post turned up last night bringing me your letters, which told me that you had received mine in a bunch. Your mind will be at rest now that you know what a good time we have been having.

The Italians here are all agog with excitement owing to the rumour of an Armistice on the Western Front. I suppose that it is German propaganda.

I am dining with the C.O. to-night: he got the D.S.O. yesterday I am very glad to say.

January 14th, 1918. TEZZE.

We are still having a splendid time, but it rains one day, freezes hard the second and snows the third. To-day it did all three and Church Parade was very uncomfortable.

It is now thought that we may be here for any length of time. More or less complete stagnation has set in on the mountain front, which I understand that the Austrians are holding with Slav and Czech troops who are only restrained by fear from surrendering. We are really remarkably lucky to be here, as the big fighting will be in France as before. That is where the decision will be reached, though when it is difficult to say.

January 15th, 1918. TEZZE.

Lloyd Baker, who is now second-in-Command, is going on leave to Rome soon, so I am going to apply when he returns and have asked Marochetti to write to any friends he has there or at Milan. Do you know of anyone to whom you could write?

Last night I got up a Company concert with some difficulty owing to lack of space and lighting. Finally, I found a place. We put in two oil lamps and innumerable candles, served up hot wine with sugar for the troops and got two fellows with mandolins to assist. It went off very well. I gave a dinner-party afterwards and the Italian ladies produced all their china and glass to make a good show. They are now waiting for me to play a hand of whist, the only form of cards we indulge in—and that not even for penny points.

January 19th, 1918. TEZZE.

We are still living quietly here and are having really ideal winter weather though it has been thawing to-day, which has made things muddy. My only worry is that I have a good many men down with poisoned hands and feet and boils. I simply can't make it out. Every little cut seems to fester at once, and the boils are very painful. Opinions differ: some think that it is the water; others attribute them to tinned food combined with a lack of vegetables; others to the bread, which has been very sour lately. I am having the stream where they do all their washing tested to-morrow. Otherwise the health of the troops is very good indeed, far better than in France during the winter, when as many as forty or fifty men would go sick in a day.

January 25th, 1918.   BRUSAPORCO.

I expect there has been a gap in the post during the last day or two, as we are on the trek again after our long stay at the foot of the mountains. We started marching yesterday. The roads were very bad indeed and the men had a rough time, but stuck it very well. I had a motor lorry for my baggage—an utterly unprecedented affair and very convenient. On arrival we found very poor billets. No provision had been made for the officers at all. However, my billeting sergeant had secured me a clean and comfortable room and I was the only officer in the regiment besides the Colonel to get a bed.

Our Mess is an absolutely bare room with white-washed walls and a stone floor—rather Spartan after our cosy quarters at Tezze, but that is the fortune of war. This room we share with the chickens and pullets, which roam freely and fearlessly in and out of the door.

We remain here to-day and to-morrow resume our march eastwards. We have fifteen miles to do, which is a very long way for the men, who now carry nearly 80 lbs. of kit. We shall break it with dinners *en route*, which will make it easier, but it will be very trying, expecially for the men with sore heels.

The water is a constant source of anxiety: it is very dangerous and I have constantly to chase the cooks and servants away from the wells until they have been tested.

January 28th, 1918.   PUNTA SAN VIGILIO, LAKE GARDA.

You will never guess what I am doing. I am sitting in a very comfortable little bedroom which looks over the most gorgeous view I have ever seen. I am, in fact, in a villa on Lake Garda, and to-day has been as sunny and warm as an English summer's day. There is not a single other Englishman except my servant in the house. I am living with the French Army, and I don't know how to begin to tell you about it.

We left our comfortable billets on the 24th and marched about nine miles the first day and fifteen miles two days later. The men were splendid—not a single one fell out from my Company although it was a hot day and a lot of them had raw feet. The Divisional-General gave me a slab of English chocolate for them—to their great amusement.

The night before last we got into billets; the officers were very badly off in a big living-room with about ten women and a lot of grubby children, besides the servants who had to cook there. However, I got that altered at once and moved into a quieter spot next day.

As I was getting out of bed that morning, a note arrived from the Adjutant saying that I had been selected to attend the French course for Chefs de Bataillons and Commandants de Compagnies at Lake Garda; I was to get there as best I could by January 28th. Only four British officers have been sent, one from each of the Divisions in Italy; a young Lt.-Colonel of the H.A.C., a Major, and another Captain.

I got myself and my kit by motor lorry into Padua; where I had to wait till 9 p.m. for a train to Verona.

I managed to get some dinner at a restaurant—a very bad one—in the middle of which all the lights went out on account of an air raid. After a good deal of hanging about my train arrived and there was a hideous rush for it, as a great many civilians are leaving Padua because of air raids. However, I got into a first-class carriage with three Italian officers; one of them assured me in excellent English that I couldn't get my valise into the carriage, much less on to the rack, and suggested that there would be more room in the luggage van. I told him very politely that I would see him damned first and he calmed down again.

We arrived at Verona at midnight, I got my valise into the cloak-room and after a row with the Italian police, managed to get into the vestibule of an hotel, where I spent a most uncomfortable night. It was too cold to sleep and at 6 o'clock I made my way to the station and took the train to Garda.

On arrival we were met by a young Chasseur Alpin Captain who conducted us to headquarters and from there to our billets. He presides over our Mess, which contains six other French officers—none of whom speak a word of English: it is really a most splendid opportunity for improving my accent, of which I shall take full advantage.

After lunch I walked down with some French officers to the opening lecture given by Colonel Fleury—an elderly, square, black-bearded man with a keen eye and a professor's manner and diction.

Work begins at 8 in the morning and goes on till 10. We start again at 1 and from 2.30 till 5 we do " equitation," which, I believe includes sword practice. I shall have to get up at 6 o'clock every day, but I don't think that there will be much difficulty about that. The course will go on till about February 19th.

I have been told that I am to consider myself as a guest and am not to pay for anything.

January 30th, 1918. SAN VIGILIO, GARDA.

I am having the most delightful time here imaginable: it is like a dream. The weather is perfect, glorious sunshine day after day.

Yesterday we had lectures on various subjects: *dejeuner* at 11 a.m. and a demonstration by a small body of French *poilus* afterwards. A French officer came up to me and told me that he recognised me quite well: I had met him exactly a year ago when we relieved a French Division on the Somme in front of Peronne, when he took my photograph and young Pearson's.

To-day we had a demonstration of infantry attacking with real rifle grenades, bombs and maxim guns; the scene was very realistic; there was a frightful noise, but nobody was hurt. The organisation is splendid and the French officers are excellent; very keen and not a bit depressed by the war, though they have many of them been fighting since 1914.

I have made friends with everyone and we have the greatest fun. The French and English get on splendidly together and form a very exclusive mutual admiration society. They are amused at the meaning of the expression " tirer les jambes " which I have taught them, but they are getting to know me now.

February 18th, 1918. PORCELLENGO.

I have returned to the regiment to find them in first-rate billets. The men are very fit and cheerful. One of my subalterns has started the band and it is playing now outside my window in the sunny piazza.

Please excuse this note; I am very tired and have to prepare a lecture for the officers on my course. It will be no easy task—but the order has gone forth.

February 23rd, 1918.   PORCELLENGO.

I am putting in for leave to Rome next week and I hope I shall get it. I am told that it is not worth while trying to see Florence as well, so I shall probably spend the whole week in Rome and, fortified with a dilapidated Baedeker which I have bought for two lire, I shall tour the city. Whether I shall summon up courage to call on the various Contessas and Marchesas to whom Marochetti has given me introductions I do not know. But he has also given me a letter to a Bishop at the Vatican and I shall certainly call there.

Last night I had a most successful Company concert in a large barn. The band appeared in force and two players with a mandolin and banjo respectively. All the Company were there and most of the Battalion. When I arrived about a quarter of an hour after it had begun, I was met by the Italian farmer wringing his hands and making signs of distress by which he sought to convey to me that the floor would give way. When I got upstairs and saw the huge crowd of visitors I was extremely nervous, but my Amusements Officer, who was running the show, succeeded in reassuring me. Everything went as merry as a marriage feast; it was a howling success especially as we had arranged for hot and well-sugared wine to be passed round in the interval.

What is going to be done with us I cannot imagine.

At present we gaze across a broad river at some very unenterprising Austrians and do nothing, though at night we try to ford it by tying men together with ropes. The only result is that they get soaked to the skin in icy water, which doesn't appear to me to serve any useful purpose. However, we must, I suppose, do something for our pay.

March 2nd, 1918.   Trenches, MONTELLO PIAVE.

You must forgive me for not writing for a day or two, but I have been extremely busy. We came into the line on February 28th and I went to headquarters as Second-in-Command. I went the rounds the first night and it was like a fairy tale, scarcely a shot was fired.

But yesterday I suddenly received orders to proceed " *at once* "—it is always " at once " in the Army—to a village some miles behind the lines to take charge of a Brigade School. I was furious at having to leave the regiment again, but I had to go.

I had tea with the General at Brigade Headquarters on my way back. He was grumpy and said nothing about the school at all; and when I was fixing up a few details with the Brigade Major afterwards, the latter told me that the General didn't want a Brigade School at all, but had been ordered to start one. The result was that I staggered into this village with my servant at about 11 o'clock last night, could find no one and had to start a school within twenty-four hours.

I was up at 8 a.m. this morning and have been on my feet ever since. No arrangements had been made for cooks or any of the thousand and one other necessities. However I now hear from the Brigadier

Trenches on the Montello overlooking the Piave River, February 1918
Courtesy Imperial War Museum. (*Facing Page* 262)

that I may go back to the regiment as Second-in-Command, as the Brigadier had got to send a Colonel down and make a proper show of it. So I hope to be able to rejoin them to-morrow.

[On leave in Rome.]

. . . . .

March 23rd, 1918. S. MARIA DI NON.

I am back with the regiment, but this morning we moved out of our comfortable billets getting up at 6 a.m. to do so. As the C.O. is spending the week-end at Rome for the International Sports I am Second-in-Command. I remained behind to see that everything was left clean and followed later on a bicycle. We only marched about two miles and I have got very good billets here and a nice Mess. Also I am near a mill where I have already managed to buy 20 kilos of flour for my Company, which is a good addition to the rations, as my cooks make excellent biscuit puddings with it of which the men are very fond.

The river runs about a mile away from the village and this afternoon I walked down there and discovered a beautiful secluded stretch of quite deep water. I found that it was quite warm and to-morrow I shall try to get a bathe.

This morning we got our first communiqué about the big German offensive in France. It has come at last and the rivers are again running with blood. It is certainly on the grand scale and whether we shall succeed in checking them is not at present apparent. One feels rather " out of it " here; it must have been terrible for the poor devils who had to bear the first brunt of the attack, knowing that their lives were foredoomed and simply waiting for the slaughter to begin. Pray Heaven we may be able to take the offensive soon.

March 28th, 1918. S. MARIA DI NON.

The only thing which interests us here is the big battle in France, which everyone feels to be decisive. Of course the moral effect of the enemy regaining almost at one blow all the ground in the Somme area held so desperately since July 1st, 1916, is very great; but one must not let one's sense of proportion be destroyed. In this war, as in any other, the loss of ground is in itself insignificant: on the other hand, the numbers of guns and prisoners reported captured is large, but not larger than is to be expected in such a tremendous battle, and it must be remembered that all the wounded fall into the enemy's hands in a defensive action.

But there is no doubt that the situation is extremely serious, though the Higher Command here are extremely optimistic and of course the men and officers are completely confident in our ultimate success. I myself think that we *shall* stop them, though possibly not until Amiens has been taken and they have added another slice of France to their conquered territory; but whether this will give them any real advantage I very much doubt. For nothing short of the destruction of our army can give them that, and it seems to me that that danger has now passed, though one cannot be completely certain as news is extremely scanty and I see that the London newspapers say practically nothing.

We are still in our billets behind the line and are

trying to reassure the Italians, who undoubtedly think the whole British Army is defeated, as they believe all the absurd lies which the Bosche airmen drop over their villages and circulate in the newspapers.

April 3rd, 1918.   GALZIGNANO-COLLIEUGANEI.

We have marched into a beautiful country of foot-hills for training and I am perched on top of a little hill in a most comfortable house, where I have a nice big room with a comfortable bed, a writing-table and two or three armchairs. I am in luck as usual. The house is a Curé's. I haven't met him yet, but I am told that he is charming.

We shall have a strenuous time I suppose: but we must do something: it is terrible to be doing nothing at these times.

April 7th, 1918.   GALZIGNANO.

This afternoon we did an attack with air bombs for the benefit of the Allied Staff.

Guns fired smoke shells; everyone else fired or threw smoke bombs; fifty or sixty fires were lighted and we were completely cut off from the view of the distinguished spectators as we plunged coughing and spitting into the thick clouds of smoke. They will now at least be able to judge whether smoke hides attacking troops or not, which was the main object of the experiment.

To-morrow, Saturday, I am having a Company concert in the village school attached to the church. The Colonel is coming and is stopping to dinner afterwards. He hasn't dined with me since September 1916 when old Carew Hunt was my Mess President.

April 8th, 1918.   GALZIGNANO-COLLIEUGANEI.

We had a most successful evening yesterday. The concert went off very well indeed. We had beer for the men in the interval, which always helps to make things a success. The C.O. turned up to dinner at 8, having been to the concert first.

My butler had surpassed himself. The table was decorated with flowers and we had some very good glass and china, borrowed from the Italian Padre. I had some excellent Chianti for the C.O. to drink, and the cook produced a marvellous dinner. Later we played bridge and went on playing till 1 a.m. I think the C.O. enjoyed himself. He appreciates a good dinner.

Next week we start training in earnest. We shall have rather a busy time climbing up and down these hills in full kit, but it will keep us very fit.

My Company Sergeant-Major is going back to England to-day for a commission. He will be a great loss as he was a private in the Company at Writtle, and except for two periods when he was wounded has been with us ever since then. He is young and popular, a good singer and thoroughly understands my ways. Still, it is a good thing for him.

April 12th, 1918.   GALZIGNANO.

The situation here is the same as it has always been on this front. There is no fighting at all. At the same time there is a lot of talk of an Austrian offensive, though this may well have been started by the Bosche to keep our hands full. But it may quite well come if they are successful in France. It will be a difficult job to advance either on the mountain front or on the Piave and I don't think that the Austrians have much stomach for the business.

We are very busy climbing hills every day now, and I feel as fit as I have ever done in my life. I beat three out of five of my subalterns at firing to-day at two hundred yards range. I am not so blind as they imagine.

April 19th, 1918. CASTELGOMBERTO.

We did three days' marching from the 16th to 18th, which accounts for my silence. Last night we arrived here and are pretty comfortable, though it has been raining continuously for some time, which makes the little town rather dirty.

I had hoped to have had a good rest in bed this morning after three early starts, but to-day I got orders from the C.O. to do a reconnaissance of the mountains. We started in a car at 7.30 a.m. and climbed up to over 4000 feet—a three-hour journey. It was exceedingly cold up there and there was a little snow on the ground. It was raining and very muddy, so we did not stop more than half an hour: but just had a look at a strong line of prepared positions ready for the Bosche.

Coming back we met my old friend Alan Gibson, now on Corps staff. We all had tea together at an Officers' Club at a little town at the foot of the mountains. He drove me back in his car.

April 22nd, 1918. SARCEDO.

We are in a funny sort of Mess. Two Italians are eating " polenta " in a corner; the cook is cooking at the fire while we sit round the table. But it's only for two nights and then another move.

We are in colder regions now and the weather is absolutely poisonous. We got soaked on the march yesterday, but it only made the men more cheerful. It is always the same with them; it needs really rotten circumstances to get the best out of them.

There is nothing doing here at all. The mountains are devilish high and steep with long winding roads overlooking precipices.

April 26th, 1918.　　　　　　　　　　VALLE DI SOPRA.

I have just returned from another all-day trip to the mountains and am rather tired.

We started at 9 a.m. in a little lorry and were soon shivering with cold. The roads were very slippery and every time we took a corner I thought we should shoot over the side. However, we got to the top all right and found the roads covered with half-melted snow and slush. We were able to go practically up to the line in the lorry and only did about a mile and a half on foot through the dripping pinewoods.

We just came up to look round and get in touch with the conditions. We shall be moving up in a few days now and I can only hope that the weather may improve, as it has now rained continuously for several weeks.

May 1st, 1918.　　　　　　　Trenches, S. SISTO ASIAGO.

I am sitting down in my little log hut on the top of the mountains in the most beautiful pine forest imaginable, and with a brazier of sweet-smelling pinewood and charcoal to keep me warm. All the

Asiago. November, 1918. Courtesy Imperial War Museum. (*Facing Page* 268)

officers have gone off, one to bed and three to the outpost line.

My Company is in support, and bivouacked among the pine trees and rocks. It has rained for two or three months, but May Day was fine and we are all hoping that this may mean a fine spell, though the Italians say it always rains up here except in July.

I walked all round the front line this afternoon with one of my subalterns. It is a luxurious place, built in places out of the solid rock and reveted with pinewood.

I am reading Napoleon's campaigns in Italy. I only wish that he was commanding us now. But I suppose that we shall get through somehow.

May 11th, 1918.   Trenches, S. Sisto.

It is most pleasant here, warm and sunny with a cool breeze through the trees. To-morrow we move up to the line for three or four days, which simply means shifting from one log hut to another: then we come back again. Not a very exciting life but peaceful.

Only Italian leave is open. I doubt whether there can possibly be any English leave until the operations in France have quietened down.

All the letters which I get from France are most optimistic. I hear that our men are fighting better than they have ever done before and the morale is noticeably better than during the Somme and the third battle of Ypres, due to the fact that they have been killing so many Huns, which is always heartening.

I am more and more persuaded that the internal

condition of the Central Empires may precipitate disaster at any moment. Nothing but military rule pure and simple is keeping the people down.

May 17th, 1918.　　　　　　　　　Trenches, S. SISTO.

We came out of the line into support yesterday afternoon and shall go further back in a day or two, possibly right down again into the plains.

I had rather bad luck the last night I was in. The night before we had stirred the Bosche up a bit and had sent out a fighting patrol which had done very well and had got right up to their front line and bombed it. At any rate we were expecting reprisals of some sort last night, and the General, whom I met in my trench in the afternoon, told me to keep quiet and give the enemy a rest. Well, about 10.45 p.m. they must have got a bit frightened by our patrols and they planked a barrage of big stuff right down on the front line. We didn't pay much attention to it, as it is a wonderful trench, very deep and built out of solid rock: unless they could score a direct hit everyone would be quite all right. They must have put over about two hundred shells, of which nearly all were well behind. But one landed in our trench. I saw it burst just beyond me on a little shelter where by evil luck I had three or four men. It brought the whole thing down and one man was killed outright, one of my best fellows, an old friend who had been out nearly two years with the Company. Two others were wounded, one rather severely in the head. Except for that piece of bad luck, nothing whatever occurred in the whole tour.

May 19th, 1918.   GRANEZZA.

We were relieved this afternoon and have just arrived back. I had a further piece of bad luck. Four of my boys were wounded by shrapnel just after breakfast: it was bad luck because it was simply a single shell which went wide and there were some safe trenches quite close. The men were shaving and idling about in the wood. Two are quite all right but the condition of the other two is more serious.

To-morrow we march down into the plains again. No one can quite understand why, as we have only been up here about three weeks and have had a very soft time.

May 21st, 1918.   S. MARIA.

I cannot imagine when you will get this letter as we are again trekking the countryside. Yesterday we started our march down from the mountains under a perfect sky and sun. The whole plain was wrapt in a hazy mist, and it got warmer and warmer as we descended the difficult mule track.

The journey down was almost worse than the journey up and during the last three-quarters of an hour's march along the high-road a good many men fell out completely exhausted. We bivouacked for the night and this morning got up at 5 a.m. and marched off at 6.30. By 7.30 it was very hot, but I enjoyed the perfectly marvellous scenery. The change in three weeks is amazing. The ground is hidden by the most luxurious green trees and the whole place is like a garden. It was only a very short march and we were in by 8.30. But we go on again to-night at

10.30 p.m. and march all night till 6 o'clock tomorrow morning. It will be trying for the troops, but it is out of the question to march by day, especially with full kit. Many of the troops behind are wearing drill and I actually saw a pith helmet to-day.

May 27th, 1918. BROGLIANO.

The heat is terrific here and makes one disinclined for anything. To-day we have all been equipped with khaki drill and pith helmets, which pleases the men tremendously as you may imagine. I myself have given way to shorts, which are very much nicer. Unfortunately the men have to wear long drill trousers like their old khaki ones, as shorts are not allowed in the battle area owing to the possible effects of mustard gas on the skin. Officers, however, are allowed to wear them behind the line.

Yesterday I had a very hard day. I started off at 6 a.m. with the C.O. and three or four other officers in a small motor lorry. We went up to the mountains, three and a half hours' drive, to reconnoitre and spent about two hours looking through field-glasses and telescopes at the Bosche positions on the opposite mountains. We took our lunch with us and after a long roundabout journey to visit a wounded officer got back to Brigade Headquarters in time for a lecture by the General on the fighting in France.

May 30th, 1918. BROGLIANO.

We marched again at 5 a.m. this morning and arrived here at about 10 a.m.

General Fanshawe, who commands the Division,

then inspected us and as my Company marched past he stepped forward and said, " Many congratulations on your long record with the Battalion." Very nice of him. Later on we passed the Brigadier, and as I suddenly came round the corner I saw him standing at the side of the road, looking at me with a broad grin on his face. I saluted and said " Good morning, Sir," and wondered what the devil he was laughing at. The C.O. later told me that it was because he couldn't see me on account of my helmet! We were wearing pith helmets for the first time, and mine *is* rather a big one and reminds me of my first turn in a top-hat.

We are in a " staging " camp, which means a sketchy affair of tents and bivouacs put up temporarily to accommodate regiments on the march —no furniture or even cook-houses. Dinner has to be cooked on French fires. However, we shall move on again soon I expect.

June 2nd, 1918. SERONA.

This morning we had to start marching at 5 a.m., which meant being called at 3.30. Just as Painting brought my cup of tea to my tent, we heard anti-aircraft guns going, which I haven't heard since March or February when the Germans all left Italy. Actually two Bosche or, as I hope, Austrian aeroplanes had come across. As far as I know they soon cleared off and I didn't hear any bombs.

We marched from 5.30 till 9.30—four hours. I, rather foolishly, omitted to have breakfast before starting: it was so early and I thought that it would only be a two-hour march; it was 11 o'clock before I got it, so I was pretty hungry, especially as I had walked all the way.

One of my boys has got a touch of the sun; he is quite a youngster and seems very much frightened because his temperature has gone to 101°. But I don't think it is more than sun and fever.

June 4th, 1918.   Trenches CANOVE.

We finished the last stages of our march yesterday afternoon and are now back again among the pine-woods. Of course it is very much cooler here than the plains, and we have all put away our sun helmets, though we still have to wear the khaki drill, which looks and feels slightly out of place. It is quite mild though and I don't think we shall come to much harm, except that a slight touch of fever is very prevalent and a great many men are down with temperatures. The doctor sent round five quinine pills for each officer to take after dinner last night, which, with other reasonable precautions, ought to keep us secure.

Things are very quiet and last night an Austrian deserter came in, kissing effusively the hand of one of the officers on support duty.

THE LAST AUSTRIAN OFFENSIVE

June 17th, 1918.   CARRIOLA.

I do hope you haven't been anxious about me and that you received my Field Post-card.

We have had a very strenuous time and the regiment was in the thick of it. We were actually in the front line on the 15th, as on the night of the 14th we had warning that something was afoot for the following morning and were consequently to a certain extent prepared. But we were not prepared for what really happened. We never thought the enemy would actually attack on our front and expected only a certain amount of bombardment. As a matter of fact a bombardment did start at 3 a.m. just as I was going to bed, and was the most intense I have ever known even in the worst days of the Somme or Ypres. Since we had been on the front scarcely an Austrian gun had fired and we naturally supposed they hadn't got many. But they shelled at the most intense pitch for four and a half hours without a stop and continued it for miles behind the lines, even dropping shells right back over the mountain range on to the plain.

The woods were devastated and the trees crashed down, while most of our guns were silenced pretty successfully by high concentrations of gas shells. The tear gas or lachrymatory shells filled the whole place with a reeking mist.

At about 7.30 a.m. the beggars were seen coming over at us all along the line. They very soon penetrated our flanks and began to take us in the rear. However, once we saw what was up we rallied the remainder of the regiment, cooks, pioneers, servants, orderlies and God knows what, rushed them up and counter-attacked the enemy out of our front line. Then they again came on and drove us back, as we were by that time absurdly weak and no supports had been sent up at all.

But we brought them to a stop about a thousand yards away behind our front line and they never got any further. They were simply slaughtered in thousands and the Division got almost a thousand prisoners. By noon they were completely fought out and began giving themselves up.

Our men were simply magnificent, considering that no help at all was given us and we were left to settle the business for ourselves.

After a jumpy night the enemy advanced posts began retiring at 2 a.m. By 6 a.m. we were back in all our old positions and very soon we had regained the little ground which had been lost.

The brutes had been in my Company Headquarters all day and had rifled every blessed thing—boots, field-glasses, clothes, blankets, papers. I also lost 1500 lire of public money, which disgusts me. All my washing and shaving kit was gone. The dirty devils took their own lousy shirts off and bagged mine, much to everyone's amusement.

We marched back last night along roads reeking of gas and I went to bed for the first time for two nights, taking my clothes off for the first time for eight days.

The General was extremely pleased and said that it was the best thing which the Battalion and the Division had done. Lord Cavan issued a communiqué in code as follows this morning:—" By resolute staunchness of ' State ' and determination of ' Rally ' (ourselves) to lose nothing to Austrians our line is intact. Hearty congratulations to all and my sincere thanks.—CAVAN."

The attack has been smashed all along the line though the enemy were five or six to one.

My Second-in-Command was killed and I have a big work to do, reorganising with only two officers to help me, writing letters and getting new kit for the men, not to mention myself. I have no coat, but the Adjutant has lent me one and I can write for another. Field-glasses and compass I can, I suppose, get replaced sooner or later. Our mess stuff has all gone west, and will be difficult to replace out here. A few old knives, forks, spoons, and any picnic paraphernalia you may have knocking about would come in useful.

The Italians are doing splendidly. Already 9000 prisoners have been taken. I'm afraid that you must have been very anxious, especially with the beastly newspapers talking about "fearful odds" and "desperate fighting." But once the bombardment was over everyone was quite happy and more than ready to deal with the Austrians, though once or twice things did look a little blue.

June 20th, 1918. CARRIOLA.

I have been down with fever but am feeling very much better to-day. I think the worst has passed. The doctor took my temperature this morning and found it only just above normal. Some of the others have been very bad with it, and the Second-in-Command and the Adjutant went off to hospital to-day. Both my other officers have it and nearly all the men, and everyone is looking absolutely miserable and eating nothing.

One of my officers met Summerhayes down on the plains yesterday. He asked after me and when told I was seedy said I must go down to his new hospital, as he had a splendid place which would just suit me, but I shan't have to go now, I am glad to say.

The weather is putrid, raining all day, cloudy and

cold; and this morning comes the news that our Divisional General has been recalled to England. He has commanded the Division since May 1915 and is a fine soldier. Everyone is very sorry for him and we are disgusted at the news.

June 24th, 1918. MARZIELE.

I am sorry that I haven't written for a day or two, but we have been on the move and yesterday I had a busy time being in charge of the motor lorries detailed for shifting the regiment. We are now in a little scattered camp of bivouacs and tents on the slopes of the mountains overlooking the plains, with a perfectly wonderful view when it is not obscured by thick drifting mists as it has been this morning.

We are still reduced to about nine officers, but it doesn't worry us much. I do hope you didn't have two or three days of anxiety after the first news of the attack. But I am afraid you did. I sent off a Field Card on the 15th to reassure you.

The Austrian offensive appears to have been a howling fiasco. The Italians have got their tails well up, and are doing awfully well. People are saying that with a little luck this may be turned into a big Allied victory. At any rate it is already a nasty smack in the eye for the Austrians, and I don't know how the news will be received in Vienna. Their losses have been colossal and they are having a very bad time on the Montello, as they have only got one bridge across the Piave, which is bombed and shelled night and day.

We hope in a short time to be taken down into the

plains for a change, which will be jolly again after a month up here.

I forgot to tell you that I am now quite well again after my short bout of fever. It was a most unpleasant business while it lasted, which I am glad to say, was not for long. My old maxim of " Never go to bed " has been triumphantly justified.

June 25th, 1918.　　　　　　　　　　　MARZIELE.

The news is splendid. The Italians have completely re-established their line, are across the Piave in eight places and have taken Conegliano. There is also a rumour of a revolution in Budapest. So everyone is talking of the beginning of the end. The Austrians are in a rotten state and there will be trouble when the news of their defeat becomes known.

I am longing to get down to the plains for some warmth and sunshine. It is tantalising to see in the distance these beautiful fields and rivers and to be stuck on a cold and windy hillside with nothing to do. I feel as if I were watching the Garden of Eden from an iceberg.

June 27th, 1918.　　　　　　　　　　　MARZIELE.

Yesterday a gorgeously apparelled staff officer came to the camp and turned out to be my old friend Alan Gibson. I told him I was bored to death and longing for a joy-ride and he promised to give me an outing in the car when we go down to the plains.

Life is insupportably dull: I live in a tent on the bare hillside with two officers and it is very cold and cheerless. Last night I dined with the Colonel and played bridge till midnight. He is keen but rash. I was partnered with him against the doctor and the Adjutant and just managed not to lose.

June 29th, 1918.   MARZIELE.

At last I believe we are going down to the plains, starting to-morrow morning. It will be like marching into the Promised Land after these windy chilly mountains, though it has been gloriously fine to-day and I went to sleep on the grass outside my tent this afternoon wrapped in a leading article of Garvin's on the " Hidden Hand."

Pickford, now Second-in-Command and an old friend of mine, has got the D.S.O., which he thoroughly deserves, and the C.O. has got a bar. One of my corporals has been given the D.C.M. and four others military medals: unhappily one of them has since died of wounds.

July 2nd, 1918.   BROGLIANO.

I have three unanswered letters of yours beside me and feel very guilty. We started down from the mountains at the ungodly hour of 1.30 a.m. three mornings ago, and came stumbling down infernal mule tracks under the moon until the dawn broke in its glory and helped us out just as we were getting exhausted. We got in at 7.30 after a six-hour march down the mountain sides—most frightfully tiring.

The next night we moved on again, starting at 11.30 p.m. I was very drowsy, having gadded about all the morning in the sun, and nearly fell off my horse in my sleep. However, we were revived by hot tea at 2 a.m., after which I felt splendid, especially when the sun got up about 5 a.m.

We were marching back along the same beautiful stretch of country to the very same place and billets where we had had such a good time exactly a month ago and everyone was very much pleased, as we always are at going back to the same people. We got in at 7.30 a.m. and had breakfast. Then, after a bath, I turned in at about 10, and slept on till 4. It is an ideal spot and the Italians literally fell on our necks with joy at our return; they were very tearful over the gaps. We were six officers last time but now we are only three.

The C.O. has asked me if I would like a week at Garda, but I am not going. I shall be twice as happy with the regiment.

July 7th, 1918. BROGLIANO.

I am furious: I have again been torn from the regiment by an unkind fate and put in charge of the Brigade School by the General, and this in spite of a protest from the C.O., who said that he couldn't spare an officer and that I should be wanted as Second-in-Command, as he might be going on leave. So I had to pack up last night and hand over my beloved Company.

I am allotted a factory about half a mile outside our village. This is a comfort, as I can see plenty of the regiment and get all I want from them.

The Instructors assembled yesterday and to-day the students turn up. I am very busy preparing long lists of "wants" which I shall have to take over to Brigade Headquarters.

Starting a Mess in itself without food or mess kit is a big enough problem. And to teach Lewis

Gunnery, Bombing and Musketry and Scouting I shall need a lot of material. It is a great bore, especially when I have such important work to do reorganising my Company. And worst of all my servant, Painting, has just gone on leave and has left an ex-coachman to look after me.

July 13th, 1918. BROGLIANO.

The School is going well. The men are all very keen and smart and don't seem to mind working hard. I am learning a lot myself, which is a great thing. The heat is terrific; everyone disappears from 12.30 till 5 to pant in peace.

But getting up at 4.30 a.m. to work is a bit of a strain, because somehow one doesn't seem to go to bed any earlier and I can never sleep in the middle of the day. However, I am situated on a hill overlooking the village where the regiment is and the air is fresher.

To-day I am having tea with the regiment and am going to ride over afterwards to see the final of the Bayonet Fighting Competition. My Company is representing the Regiment and everyone says that it rests between them and a Company of the Gloucesters. But the latter have got an officer just back from the Base who has been doing nothing but instruct in Bayonet Fighting for the last three months!

July 21st, 1918. Brigade School, BROGLIANO.

My Brigade School is just coming to the end of its first course, which I hope and believe has been a success. At any rate the men have enjoyed themselves.

We had a rifle shooting competition this morning to wind up with, and ever since 10 a.m. I have been busy, clothed only in a pair of shorts, writing reports. The heat is colossal and I am as brown as a berry.

The course ends to-morrow and the new one begins at 4 p.m. the same day with a further batch of students: there is not much time in which to make preparations. But things are now in working order and it ought not to be difficult to get going.

That is if the Brigadier leaves me here, which is doubtful, as I know that my regiment is asking for me as they are very short of officers.

July 26th, 1918.   Brigade School, FARA.

We were brought back here in motor-buses or rather light lorries, starting about 8 o'clock. The School Staff only came as far as the foot of the hills to a village teeming with life as it accommodates all the various " base wallahs " who don't go into the line—the Transport, Quartermaster's Department, Ordnance Stores, Veterinary Services, etc.

I went up into the mountains with the returning students as I had to see the General, and climbed up the last mile or two on foot as the Brigade was in the line. I didn't see anything of my regiment as they were in the front line, but I saw the General and got everything I wanted out of him, although he was rather snotty on the subject of officers' servants and Mess cooks. Personally I like a decent Mess staff, but the General flung the single word " Man-power " at me and told me it was no good arguing, which I knew already.

I lunched on top with a friend, and thinking myself

very lucky motored back to my new abode in time for tea. I found I was fixed up in a splendid billet, a clean cool little house, with a large cool bedroom, electric light and every convenience, and with a nice bright and cool Mess.

The Town Commandant, Bolton of the Sussex, is an old friend of 1915 days; the Area Commandant is a Colonel of the Bucks in our Brigade, whom I know well. The Chief Quartermaster and Transport Officer down here are both subalterns of my regiment, and there is an Officers' Club, so I shan't want for much.

The course begins on Monday, but the students are here already, and I am busy building cookhouses, ovens, ranges, bombing grounds, and fighting medicos and Ordnance Officers to try and get butter muslin, which I have at last succeeded in doing. It is a most necessary protection on account of the flies. We make frames with it and put them in the windows of the rooms.

I have only two officers with me now, but I shall see plenty of friends here and I expect I shall go up and see the regiment for the week-end. The General told me I might do so if I could get away.

The heat is more intense here even than it was further down in the plains, the flies are a tribute to Beelzebub, simply infernal, and there are all manner of creeping things also. I am bitten from head to foot.

I am very keen on the Commissariat Department and take it as a cardinal principle in training men, that you can't feed them too well. It's all a matter of experience and trouble because with our rations you can do wonders. Monotony in food makes me swear.

July 27th, 1918.   Brigade School, FARA.

I have been undergoing another terrible "offensive" which began yesterday, after an excellent breakfast, with a bombardment in the lower regions and was followed by violent sickness. I felt most frightfully ill and finally lay down from 10 a.m. till 7 p.m., only drinking occasional glasses of water. A friend of mine on the Divisional Staff came in and told me that he had motored down with the General, who wanted to see me: I begged him to keep him away. However, the old boy turned up and showed great concern, though I am glad to say that he didn't come upstairs. He told my officers that I was to be made to see a doctor to-morrow if I wasn't better. But you know my abhorrence of them.

I went to bed at 7 p.m., still having only taken cold water as a cure, and woke up this morning feeling much better. So I advanced my diet to one boiled egg and some dried toast, and although I still feel a bit weak I am really quite all right again now.

The General, having been in India, thinks everyone has got sunstroke if anything goes wrong with them, and when two or three men on the last course went sick with sprained ankles he made me swear that I wasn't working them in the sunshine. It is very hot here and he wants to move us up the mountains, but everyone is fighting him on that point and I don't think that he will insist. But he is a North-countryman and is very difficult to manage when once he gets an idea into his head.

August 4th, 1918.   Brigade School, FARA.

Here I am snugly ensconced in Brigade Headquarters, week-ending.

I came up yesterday by car in time for lunch and found everyone pretty cheerful, as the French had captured 119 prisoners the night before on our right and we ourselves had done quite a good little show as well. The General was in good form and told me to make myself at home, and to do as I liked, so after lunch I climbed up a beastly mountain to visit the regiment.

I went to headquarters and found the Colonel just back from leave. He wanted to know what I meant by week-ending at Brigade Headquarters and said that I had been badly brought up. He was very cheery, as ever, although they had been kept awake all night by the beastly guns, which make such a reverberating shindy in the mountains. After tea we played bridge till nearly 8 o'clock. He told me he was going to demand me back at once, as I was preventing the Second-in-Command from going on leave, and he was very short of officers. So I daresay I shall soon find myself back with the regiment.

At about 11.30 p.m. all the guns in the place opened fire and we sat up to see what the racket was. We were expecting an Austrian raid, as a Colonel of Austrians who had been captured the night before had given the show away. The Bosche guns opened about 11.30 and ours of course just after. But I don't know what happened.

I expect I shall return this afternoon. The General suggested that I should stay on till Monday, but I like to start the week's work clear.

August 6th, 1918. Brigade School, FARA.

I came down from the mountain on Sunday afternoon. There had been a heavy thunderstorm and the roads were very slippery. The driver didn't seem too sure of his Alpine corners and continually kept looking over the side as we went round the bends to see if there was enough room, which there seldom was. However, we didn't go " over the top."

I left the General in good spirits. The C.O. turned up to tea, presumably to demand my return.

August 10th, 1918. Brigade School, FARA.

The course is drawing to its end and I am busy writing " reports." How I used to laugh at mine when I was at school.

The new students come down from the mountains to-morrow. They will arrive dirty, tired and rather slovenly, as is usual after the trenches, but there will be a great change after the first twenty-four hours. The first thing I make them do is to wash their uniform. Then I give them a bath and a good feed, and they look like new men. I suppose the course will finish about the 25th. It doesn't look as if the C.O. had been successful in his application, or he may have been pulling my leg. I am rather glad, I must own, because I am learning a very great deal here, and getting a lot of valuable experience, and of course I am not insensible to the creature comforts of a large and comfortable bedroom with soft bed, electric light, a good Mess and the warmth of the plains instead of the cold of the mountains.

August 23rd, 1918. FARA.

The School is breaking up on Sunday for a fortnight. I really don't know why, unless it's to give us a rest, which is almost inconceivable. However, I shan't have a bad time if I go round visiting the various commanding officers and listening to their views and complaints.

To my delight I hear that my own Company team of bayonet fighters with their officers are coming to stay here when the course breaks up in order to use my ground for training for the big Italian competition. They beat the Gloucesters the other day.

We are doing nothing for a whole fortnight: at least no teaching, but we shall be very busy building new ranges and cookhouses. I shall probably set off for the mountains after the work has got well started and stay with the General or with the regiment. But I am hoping to go on leave to Venice on Tuesday with a friend in the Flying Corps.

August 25th, 1918. FARA.

I am delighted with life. My School broke up this morning and there arrived twenty-five of my own boys, all picked ones under one of my subalterns—in fact the winning bayonet fighting team. I said that I could easily put them up here, and the General, who is simply delighted with them, has sent them down for three days. They are going to represent the Brigade in the big show at G.H.Q. next week-end. Meanwhile I am going to give them the best time I can here. It is splendid to see their faces again, and makes me want to go back to the regiment.

My friend in the Flying Corps motored over this

morning to say that he couldn't get away on Tuesday, but would I try and get my pass altered to Wednesday: that is a most difficult matter, as it means sending the pass back to the Italian authorities who issued it and it would probably not come back in time.

I rang up Brigade and they said it wasn't worth trying, so I went off to see my Colonel, who is an adept at this sort of thing, and knows everyone everywhere. He at once suggested that I should go with him on Tuesday comfortably and that we would meet my friend on Wednesday and motor back with him, so that is what I am going to do. It ought to be great fun. On Thursday I have arranged for the C.O. to motor me up to the Battalion, where I shall stay for two or three days. On Saturday I shall try and wangle a car to take me over to see the show at G.H.Q., as it is my own Company after all which is going to perform.

[I went on leave to Venice with the C.O. as arranged but on my return to Fara fell ill with trench fever and was removed to hospital.]

September 7th, 1918. Hospital.

Except for mere weakness and thinness, only natural under the circumstances, I am myself again. The powers sanctioned an advance in diet yesterday— an egg for breakfast and tea. My joy was profound; after all it is dull at any time to eat nothing, but when one is lying in bed with nothing else to do, the monotony is almost insufferable.

To-day I shall demand to get up and to-morrow I trust that I shall be put on fuller diet and start getting back strength and vigour.

No doubt the rest will have done me good: it is curious how August affected me in exactly the same way as last year; almost the same symptoms, extreme weakness and thinness.

The day is spent reading without even the interruption of having to take medicine, for I have been given none at all, I am glad to say.

September 11th, 1918.　　　　　　　　　　　Hospital.

At last I am up and clothed again for the first time for a fortnight. But I am terribly nervous. My servant tells me that I am marked for evacuation by the next train to the Base, and it has thrown me into a cold perspiration of fear. It is the very last thing I want. I simply can't stand any more of this infernal coddling. They seem to think that because I am thin and pale I want a rest by the sea. However, the next train doesn't go for four or five days and before that I shall have persuaded the doctors to send me back to work. I am going to write to my C.O. to see if he can help. And I register a vow that never to my dying day will I allow myself to fall into the clutches of these awful doctors again. Even if there was no question of leave I should be dying to get back to the regiment, where they are very short of officers.

September 19th, 1918.　　　　　　　　　　　FARA.

Tired and weary but very happy I write to say that I left hospital this morning and got back to the little village which I left very nearly three weeks ago as a " stretcher case." The School has gone, long since, but knowing the Area Commandant intimately I went over and asked him to put me back in my own billet, which he at once did.

Of course I have no Mess, but I have my invaluable Painting and I intend to live entirely alone and really rest.

No more hospital hours for me! Breakfast in bed at 10 to-morrow, a nice chicken for lunch and " niente " all day.

September 19th, 1918. FARA.

Last night the long-expected despatch from the Adjutant arrived to say that the Brigade had promised me my leave for Sunday next the 22nd, always of course provided that it isn't stopped. So I shall start off in three days' time.

SIXTH LEAVE. 1 Month.

October 20th, 1918. Trenches, POSLEN.

I rejoined the regiment this morning with considerable joy after a peculiarly unpleasant journey from first to last. Everyone seemed very well. I find myself Second-in-Command, and probably with luck may remain so for some time, as Pickford is not returning at present.

You cannot imagine how much I enjoyed my holiday at home: it makes such a break in the life out here and braces one up tremendously. But it is delightful to see my old friends again after being away so long and I am thoroughly happy.

October 24th, 1918. Trenches, POSLEN.

Things are much the same as ever. Yesterday evening we did a raid on our front, and at about 7 o'clock, just before we were going to sit down to dinner, an officer came in and said he had brought two Austrian prisoners in from the outpost line, deserters of course. They turned out to be Czechoslovaks or something of the kind and couldn't speak any intelligible tongue. The Colonel sent them on to Brigade Headquarters with a chit " First blood to us." Rather amusing, as the raid was coming off that evening.

We played bridge till midnight and then the show began. I went down with the C.O. and Adjutant to the telephone cave to hear the news. Most of the others turned in and went to bed, being uninterested.

We had a sweepstake on the number of prisoners. I put down 48, and the highest estimate was 128. The first thing we heard on the telephone was that " twelve prisoners came in before they reached the enemy line," then thirty-six and finally one hundred. And this morning we hear that the number was two hundred and seventeen—the best raid that has been done in Italy. But it's really too absurd: the enemy made no attempt to fight and simply ran in as hard as they could, bringing their blankets with them. We now hear that the French took eight hundred!! The poor old Austrian is absolutely fed up with it all.

We hear that news of another kind is coming through soon and are looking forward to it.

October 28th, 1918.   Trenches, POSLEN.

There is very little news from here, except that three more Austrian deserters came into our lines last night, saying that they had had no food for two days. The truth of their story was borne out by the voracious way in which they devoured two loaves of bread at Brigade Headquarters.

The show on the Piave is really rather disappointing. I thought it would be: they have left things too long and have, as usual, talked too much. Now it is almost November and the snow must come very soon.

October 30th, 1918.   Trenches, POSLEN.

A great change has taken place in the military situation since my last letter to you.

On the night of the 28th/29th another raid took place on our front. I went to bed after drawing a ticket in the usual sweepstake and voting high this time. But what do you think? The raiding party arrived to find the whole area evacuated and only one miserable Bosche left. So yesterday we were very busy following up the enemy with scouts and trying to find him, which we did towards evening, right on the other side of the plateau, ensconced snugly in his winter *Stellung* on the top of the mountains, where we have left him unmolested for the present. It is quite like the old Peronne days. Whether it is the beginning of a general retreat or merely a local withdrawal from impossible positions we do not yet know. It may depend on the show on the Piave, which appears to be going much better. We have just had a wire from the Commando Supremo saying that there have been sanguinary riots in Budapest, but all these things have to be taken with a grain of salt, being clearly intended as tonic for the Italians. We are remaining comfortably where we are. Our boys are enjoying themselves immensely messing about the old Bosche haunts, which bear evidence of the nasty time we gave them during the summer.

I am kept pleasantly busy with the multitudinous

odd jobs of the Second-in-Command; work on trenches and dug-outs, Christmas cards for the troops, food, boots, stoves, pioneer work, education, the canteen, etc.

November 1st, 1918.   Trenches, POSLEN.

After going off to bed last night full of peace and contentment and with the expectation of relief, I woke up at 3 a.m. to see the Adjutant (who was sharing my dug-out) busy sitting up in bed and talking through the telephone. The ominous words " the regiment will be ready to advance at once " caught my ears. By 4 a.m. we were breakfasting ready to attack at 5.30 a.m.

Apparently the Italians intercepted an Austrian wireless message last night recalling her armies to the frontier!! Hence the early morning excitement.

I was left where I was, being Second-in-Command, and the regiment moved out about 7 o'clock. By that time the ridge of mountains had been completely taken with a certain number of prisoners and little opposition.

There has been nothing much doing all day owing to the frightful difficulties of getting up guns and supplies in these mountains; to-morrow morning I hope the Bosche may be well on his way back again.

It is a rotten business being left behind here all alone. But the regiment is only about a mile ahead and has not been used yet.

November 3rd, 1918.   ASIAGO Plateau.

Yesterday I was so busy that I simply couldn't manage even a line; to-day I have less than nothing to do.

Early yesterday morning the Bosche had gone back for miles and no one could find him. Not a sound disturbed the silence of the Plateau. The regiment was miles away up in the mountains with no food and with only their overcoats with them. I walked out to Brigade Headquarters with young Pearson,[1] and we were told we could pack up and come along as quickly as possible with all the transport.

When I got back to the Transport I received further orders to go right back and to take with me the 33⅓ per cent. who are left out to form a nucleus for reinforcements. So I had to bring them right back to a point behind our old front line and there join up with the details left behind by the other regiments of the Division. So here we are with no news and absolutely nothing to do while the regiment is capturing hundreds of guns and prisoners and getting miles away into the blue. To-morrow I shall go out in search of them if I can get a motor lorry.

They have had no casualties at all; the Bosche is simply leaving everything and surrendering *en masse*. I believe that an Austrial General came in with a white flag this morning and an armistice is expected any minute.

All I have to do is to move heaven and earth to get food and drink up to the regiment; everything is moving forward helter-skelter, but the difficulties are enormous among these mountains. Fortunately the weather is still gloriously fine, though it is intensely cold at night. I tremble to think what sort of time

[1] Lieut. H. F. Pearson, severely wounded in March 1917, rejoined the Battalion in Italy.

they are having, but I believe the Austrians have left excellent billets behind them.

I walked over the old Austrian front line yesterday and through the town of Asiago. It was in an awful state; nothing but wreckage and filth everywhere. I don't know how they stood it.

I do hope that I shan't have to stay back here for long; I only wish that I were still commanding my Company instead of being Second-in-Command, which is like being a glorified Quartermaster.

However, I am going for a joy ride to-morrow to see if I can do anything.

November 6th, 1918. CALDONAZZO.

I have really had a most amusing two days since I last wrote to you. The day before yesterday I took some sandwiches and started off about 10 a.m. with another officer determined to penetrate into Austria and see the regiment again.

We started off in a lorry and found the roads blocked with traffic for miles. Thousands of Austrian prisoners with all their belongings were being brought slowly along, depressed and absolutely exhausted. Practically a whole Army Corps was brought in on our front. The advance in the mountains had been exceedingly rapid and small handfuls of men took hundreds of prisoners who gave themselves up without offering any resistance. They seem to have been given orders to retire without firing a shot and were told that there was an armistice twenty-four hours before we were. Consequently they were very unhappy at being called prisoners of war. Generals of Division with all their staff were brought in absolutely

Austrian Prisoners helping British cooks at a Casualty Clearing Station. November 1918. Courtesy Imperial War Museum. (*Facing Page* 296)

Bridge over the Val D'Assa, 1918. Courtesy Imperial War Museum
(*Facing Page* 297)

heartbroken, poor fellows, especially as they would have fought to the end but for their orders. Everyone is very sorry for them indeed, especially as they will have to be handed over to the Italians, for whom they have the most utter contempt.

The first question asked was: "Where are the Italians? We have only seen British." "Of course," they said, "they will now all come up after you and the French have done the fighting!"

They were much impressed at the smartness, quietness and kindness of the British, and have made a very good impression on us. Their officers are charming fellows and great sportsmen, though no soldiers, and we are doing all we can for them. It is simply damnable to see the way the Italians treat them, herding officers and men all together and stripping them of everything.

One Austrian officer said he would fight the Italians till his hairs were grey and hoped to be at them again in less than twelve months. Another said it was sad to see the English allied with them. Constantly they remarked: "Ah! you English, you have twice stopped us getting to Rome."

Another chap, a waiter in London, who came down on my lorry as we had collared him for a guide, told me some most interesting stories of the 15th June, and what a bad time we gave them in the Asiago Plateau.

The opinion of the officers was that this had been a great Slav war precipitated by Russia, who, they say, was mobilised two months before it was declared. They have the greatest admiration for the Russian soldiers, who, they say, fought magnificently, though they were badly led and equipped.

They were disgusted at our propagandist methods and asked if we had had any Czechoslovaks attached to us. When we admitted it they said: "How very un-English." Another remark was: "You English will always have it on your conscience that you starved our women and children for four years." They say that the food question is terrible at home, that thousands of children die and that those who live are puny and weak.

The army had stacks of food. Potatoes, white flour and forage was captured in enormous quantities, and most fortunately, as our men have gone so far that the difficulty of feeding them is acute. Lorries are working day and night, but how they will feed the prisoners and civilians in the Trentino I do not know. The Austrian Government wired frantically to the Commando Supremo imploring them to feed the men and women in the Trentino, as all their arrangements had broken down.

I managed by flagging convoys to get to the regiment. The road was strewn for twenty miles with equipment, guns, wagons, lorries and dead horses, while prisoners in thousands were wandering down into our lines, miserable, pale and haggard, an extraordinary sight.

At last we got through the big Val d'Assa, a magnificent gorge with mountains towering on either side of it, and burst into Austrian territory—a beautiful stretch of mountainous country and pine-woods. We then topped the rise overlooking the Val Sugana, a deep valley, the most beautiful sight I have ever seen anywhere. The road down was more steep and narrow than any on our side, and the lorry had to back at each corner to get round. I thought every moment that we should buzz down to Kingdom Come, but we didn't. At last we came to a complete standstill behind a huge column of straggling Italian transport and guns. The road was just wide enough for the lorry, which at certain points could scarcely pass underneath the overhanging rock. I therefore got out and walked the last stage, and after having travelled for nine hours I finally passed one of our companies which had been left behind and was also looking for the regiment, which they hadn't seen for some days. We left them behind and pushed on to a big village in the bottom of the valley, where at last I saw one of my men who took me to Headquarters. I had tea first with my old Company, and found them very cheery. They gave me Austrian bread-and-butter and sardines.

The Colonel was rather astonished to see me: I said, " Good evening, Sir: just come over to keep in touch and find out if you want anything." Of course he had made himself quite comfortable: he had got into an Austrian Army Commander's house, and wanted all his kit up, all the Mess stuff, the riding horses, the band and God knows what. I explained that it was nearly fifty miles by road; that there was *no* transport available and that it was only with the utmost difficulty that we were getting food up. But I shall have to get him what he wants somehow.

As I didn't reach the regiment till 5 p.m. I stayed the night with them and got up at 5.30 a.m. the next morning in the dark to catch the ration lorries, which were returning empty. There were 15,000 more Austrians there waiting to be sent back, but no escorts could be found. In the end they went down the roads with about ten of our men to every hundred of them.

The regiment was in the biggest Austrian distributing centre in the mountain area. There was a complete base store there with thousands of guns, rifles, ammunition, leather saddlery, clothes, knives, etc.

I wished I could have stayed. The C.O. told me that I wasn't to come up again until I had cleared everything from behind.

No one knows what is going to happen. The Italians are mad with joy and get drunk and loose off rifles, coloured flares and lights all night. They are a most beastly nuisance, straggling all over the shop, blocking the roads and generally causing inconvenience. I had a polite row yesterday with an Italian Army Corps Commander on my way back. He tried to push his car forward just when I had managed with the greatest difficulty to shift all the Italians and their carts on to one side of the road to let my lorry through. He got frightfully annoyed and said that I had no right to be on his beastly road at all, which I believe was true.

This morning I have been busy trying to get all sorts of stuff on to a lorry which I am sending up to-day. I have got the Assistant Adjutant with me here, three subalterns, who happened to be away when the advance started, and about one hundred and twenty men; also the band, a few horses and wagons, and piles and piles of baggage. I wish I could chuck it all and get back to the regiment; it's a dog's life—no news and no post yet.

Surrender of Austrian Corps to the 48th Division, on the mountain front. (*Facing Page* 300)

Colonel Howard, G.S.O. 48th Division, taking the surrender of Town and Province at the Town Hall, Trent. (*Facing Page* 300)

November 8th, 1918. GRANEZZA.

We are very busy sorting out and collecting stores which are scattered all over the country. The regiment will be coming back soon and we shall be all together again, which will be better. If we are going to occupy parts of Austria we are in for a long business, but nobody knows what is going to happen, and it is idle to speculate.

Everything depends on what the Germans do. It is almost certain that they will now give in, and the only question is whether they will agree to an unconditional surrender. But I don't think our friends the Italians are very keen on invading Germany through Austria.

November 10th, 1918. GRANEZZA.

The regiment is coming back to-morrow and I am busy making preparations for their arrival. Then we shall move on and I hope have a rest for some time.

The rapid collapse of Austria is almost too incredible. Presumably the Germans will give in now and we expect at any moment to hear that an armistice has been signed.

Yesterday, to my great joy, I heard that a party of British prisoners of war had returned from Austria. I walked over to see them and found eight or nine of my poor boys who were missing on the 15th June and had been captured. They have been living on "sauerkraut" and water and practically nothing else. They said that the Austrians were quite kind to them, but couldn't give them any food as their own people were starving. The Austrians let them get away as soon as the retreat began and very glad they were, poor devils.

They said further that the Austrians had the most marvellous system of intelligence and knew everything. One of my men was asked the name of his Company Commander, and on replying that he didn't know as he had only joined up lately, they told him my name. It makes one feel quite important.

. . . . . .

November 14th, 1918.　　　　　　MAGLIO DI SOPRA.

Since my last letter to you the war has ended somewhat abruptly, but certainly as dramatically as one could wish. The internal condition of Germany appears to have been completely rotten; nothing else can explain the complete collapse of their army. But it is difficult to realise that it is all over. Here there has been practically no excitement, only a period of most strenuous work.

The regiment started about five days ago marching through the mountains from the Trentino, and for the last two days we have been moving to our back area, which we reached last night. The men were absolutely tired out; they have been marching for days and were in the trenches for a fortnight before the advance began. We are settling down here for a good long stay, as it does not appear likely that we shall be part of an Army of Occupation. I suppose we shall do nothing much except the usual routine.

I don't suppose that we shall get back to England for a little time yet, though I think we shall probably leave Italy soon.

Graham H. Greenwell, 1918. *(Facing Page* 312)

November 18th, 1918. MAGLIO.

I have begun seriously to consider what I am going to do now that the war is over. I should love to stay on in the Army, but really it is very difficult to decide, as we don't in the least know what sort of conditions will be offered us. But I can guess what you will think about it.

I wrote to Carew Hunt the other day and asked him to find out what was the position at Oxford. Students are " Class 43 " on the demobilisation list —the last but one, whereas " gentlemen " are in " Class 37." So it would seem better to be a mere gentleman.

November 22nd, 1918. MAGLIO.

I have never been so busy before in all my life. I have a thousand and one jobs, being responsible for education, concerts, the barber's shop, bootmakers, tailors, food and football. However, we are living very happily and my friend Maurice Edmunds turned up the other day from England, which was delightful.

There is absolutely no news except that I am pretty certain that we shall remain here over Christmas, for which I am making great preparations. Then we shall, I expect, get demobilised here and not return to England as a Division.

November 25th, 1918. MAGLIO.

This afternoon I went out for what I thought would be a short walk with the Colonel. He called in turn on every Staff Officer in the Division, all of whom were out. Finally, he unearthed the Chief Engineer sitting over a huge fire in his bedroom and made him give us an authority for a dozen stoves. He then made someone else give us a lorry and went off five or six miles in a cold raw foggy evening to draw the stoves from a dump. We got back at 6 o'clock to tea, frozen to death. But we have got our stoves, if through somewhat unofficial channels.

We are badly overcrowded but are settling down and are trying to get food for Christmas. My envoy who was sent out to buy pigs reports that they cost 20,000 lire each, nearly £70. Could you have believed it? It is an enormous price, but these Italians are bandits.

December 9th, 1918.

I have written to the Dean of Christ Church and to-night I heard from Carew Hunt, who thinks that it would be a good thing for you to do the same. The Christ Church authorities can then, he says, make special application for me and this will expedite demobilisation. I have also written to Sir William Osler asking him to help. I quite agree with you that after four years in the army I cannot do anything better than go up to Oxford. It will do me good and will give me a rest.

Another friend tells me that there will be a great many vacancies in the Home and Indian Civil Service which will have to be filled by nomination instead of by examination, and he suggests that this would suit me better. But the main thing is, I think, to get to Oxford. So please see what you can do as I am quite helpless. The feeling here is that it will take three or four months to demobilise the Division. If I could only get back in May or June I could get a summer holiday at home for the first time for four years. I need a holiday.

December 26th, 1918.   MAGLIO.

The end is drawing near more quickly than I had anticipated. Some of " Class 43 " leave to-morrow and a big batch go off on January 6th. I shall not have to wait much longer for my release.

Bridges is spending Christmas with us. He tells me that I should certainly make every effort to get to Oxford for the summer term, and this I shall try to do. My friends tell me that I shall do no work. But I am determined to get my long-neglected brain into order again. I shall read some History and try to take an honours degree in five terms. Only I must have a month or two of rest first.

Many of the friends I have made out here are also going up. I shall not feel too much out of it. But it will be very hard to leave the regiment after so many years. . . . Could you ever have guessed how much I should enjoy the war?

       .   .   .   .

I was demobilised in January 1919.

FINIS